I0754486

THE POETICAL WORKS OF JAMES GATES PERCIVAL.

WITH

A BIOGRAPHICAL SKETCH.

IN TWO VOLUMES.

VOL. I.

BOSTON:
TICKNOR AND FIELDS.
M DCCC LXIII.

UNIVERSITY PRESS, CAMBRIDGE:
ELECTROTYPED AND PRINTED BY WELCH, BIGELOW, & CO.

CONTENTS

OF THE FIRST VOLUME.

BIOGRAPHICAL SKETCH

OF

THE AUTHOR.

[The late Erasmus D. North, M.D., himself a man of genius and learning, and, from his long and intimate friendship with Dr. Percival, well qualified for the undertaking, was requested to prepare a biographical notice and critique to accompany this edition of his poems. He had collected many materials for the work, and had written out extended portions of it; but a long illness, terminating in his death, June 17, 1858, prevented its completion. His manuscripts, left in a fragmentary state, had been partially condensed by near relatives for their own satisfaction; when, at the request of the Publishers, they were, by permission, kindly placed in the hands of L. W. Fitch, Esq., a friend of Dr. North, who, by combining selections from them with some materials derived from other sources, has prepared the following sketch.

In justice to Dr. North's memory, it should be here stated, that his original plan contemplated a full and complete estimate of Percival's character, attainments, and works, together with a survey of his times in their bearing upon his intellectual growth. Large portions of this plan were elaborated by Dr. North, and still remain unused in the possession of his family.]

BIOGRAPHICAL SKETCH.

It is seldom that the outward life of the scholar is fraught with sufficient incident to admit of an extended record. Especially was this the case with the subject of the present sketch, since the refinement of his taste, the peculiar delicacy of his feelings, and his extreme native diffidence, not only withheld him from taking an active part in public affairs, but even formed a charmed circle between himself and the world, so that in the place of his daily walks he remained to the end a stranger to all but a chosen few.

James Gates Percival was born in the parish of Kensington and town of Berlin, Connecticut, the 15th of September, 1795. He was the second son of Dr. James Percival, a physician of the place, who, dying in 1807, left his three sons to their mother's care. His ancestors were among the earliest settlers of Kensington; and, if we may judge from the name, our gifted bard may have sprung, far back in history, from what the world has been pleased to designate as "gentle blood," although such descent could in reality confer no lustre on him that would not have grown dim before the splendor of his own genius, "that patent of nobility," as a certain one has said, "that flows direct from God Almighty."

The father of Percival was one of a class of physicians of that generation in Connecticut, who were men of extraordinary merit, whose professional ardor absorbed their minds, and was only equalled by their unworldly enthusiasm and disinterestedness. They also acquired what literature they could, buying and reading books, and especially acquainting themselves carefully with the progress of medical science in Europe. Young Percival was early sent to the district school in his native place; but it is recorded of him, that, having soon learned all which the school could teach, he became an unwilling attendant where his time was spent to little purpose, — greatly preferring to remain in his father's library at home. He seldom engaged in the common sports of the school, even with the boys of his own age. He shared in that distressing diffidence and sensibility to suffering, from the rudeness of the older members of the school, which Cowper has so feelingly described in his own case. An anecdote is told of him at this period, which indicates remarkable strength of mind and energy of will in one so young. He had just begun to spell, when, in compliance with the custom of the school, a book was lent to him on Saturday, to be returned on the following Monday.

He found by spelling through its first sentences that a portion of it related to astronomy. This so excited his interest that he set diligently to work, and by dint of hard study, with the aid of the family, was able to read the portion he desired on the Monday morning with fluency. This achievement created in him such a confidence in his own powers, that, as we have stated, he soon compassed the limited standard of the school. He did not, however, as might have been feared, become a mere bookworm; for with that intellectual craving, that bound him, as by a spell, amid the histories, biographies, voyages, romances, poems, &c. that enriched his father's library, — with this intellectual craving there was also united that warm adoration of the heart which called him forth to commune with Nature amid the unwritten revelations of her beauty and her grandeur. And Nature presented herself to his opening imagination under peculiarly favorable circumstances. The precincts of Kensington are remarkable for the rich and varied beauty of their scenery, — the geological formation presenting the waving swells of the sandstone, interrupted and crowned by picturesque precipices of trap, with "scattered groves and wooded hills." But he has himself best described it: —

" And then a pastoral scene from my own land, —
  Groves darkly green, white farms, and pastures gay
With flowers, — brooks stealing over sand
  Or smooth-worn pebbles, murmuring light away, —
Blue rye-fields, yielding to the gentle hand
  Of the cool west-wind, — scented fields of hay,

Falling in purple bloom, — free hearts that feel
Their being doubled in their country's weal."

Among the influences which should be mentioned as having moulded the youth of Percival, is the simplicity of character and manners which was a marked feature of his native town. Fifty years ago, Connecticut had no towns larger than what would now be styled villages. The people were not rich, neither were they poor, or wholly illiterate. Practically democratic, they prided themselves in the peculiar designation which their small State had acquired, as "the land of steady habits," and were mostly independent, content, and happy, being to a great extent free from the evils which are engendered by a highly commercial state of society. Percival compared this to the pastoral state, and was highly delighted when, in later years, being employed as a geologist in New Brunswick, he discovered the same style of life and manners in a district which had been settled by a company of Loyalist emigrants from New England.

At the age of fourteen Percival wrote a poem of considerable extent; this was a burlesque on the times, in which the "Embargo," among other topics, was not forgotten. Two years later he entered Yale College, but ill-health caused an interruption of his studies, so that he did not graduate until at the end of five years. Of his college course, little is known. He has related of himself that he obtained the respect of the Freshman class by writing satirical verses against some of his classmates who had commenced persecuting him. During his Sophomore year he submitted to the Society of Brothers in Unity a remarkable poem, which caused considerable comment at the time. Of this poem, the outline of what was afterwards published as the Prometheus, Mr. Edward Everett said, "Not a few of these verses have all the dark sententiousness of Byron, clothed in an uncommonly easy versification." While in college he was eminent for his mathematical abilities; in proof of which we may mention that, on a certain occasion, he solved, at the last moment, while the bell was ringing for recitation, the celebrated Catholic proposition in Spherics, in Webber's Mathematics, a feat which none of his classmates succeeded in performing. He deliberately avoided attempting to obtain the valedictory, — the highest honor, — and determined to take the second. Being no speaker, however, he received only an English oration. This stimulated his pride, and "accordingly," he said, "I took much pains to prepare myself; I practised myself in distinctness; I *articulated* my words." The result showed his ability; for President Dwight remarked to him, "Why, Percival, I wish I had known you were able to speak so well, I would have given you the *Valedictory*." His tragedy of Zamor,* afterwards published in his first volume, formed part of the Commencement exercises at his graduation.

* A production which the author rejected from his works on account of its immaturity.

One of his classmates, in a familiar letter to the Editor of this edition, thus speaks of him: —

"ALBANY, January 24, 1859.

"I regret that it is but little that I can tell you of my classmate Percival. He joined my class at the beginning of Sophomore year, having, I think, been a member of the class that preceded ours, and been absent from college part of the year, — perhaps on account of ill-health. He was not in my division, so that I was not accustomed to hear him recite until Senior year (when we both came under the instruction of Dr. Dwight), but he always had the reputation of being a good scholar in everything. He was of about the middle size, of light complexion, of an agreeable face, that did not easily change its expression, and as shy as the most modest little girl you ever saw. He seemed to be essentially of a solitary turn. You would rarely see him walking with anybody, and when he walked at all, it was usually in some retired place. I think he had few acquaintances in college, though I never knew that he had any enemies; and the fact that his intercourse was so circumscribed, was doubtless to be attributed to constitutional reserve, and not to the consciousness of his own superiority. Everybody looked upon him as a good-natured, sensitive, thoughtful, odd, gifted fellow. He wrote a good deal of poetry in college, and some of it, I think, he gave me; but nobody then, I believe, dreamed of the eminence to which he was destined.

He was a great reader, and I used to be surprised at the extent of his information on a great variety of subjects. I remember once having occasion to prepare a college exercise on the subject of the Crusades; and happening to mention to Percival that I needed to increase my knowledge of the subject a good deal before writing upon it, he at once put into my hands an elaborate essay on the Crusades, which showed a familiarity with the history of that whole period that amazed me. I am not sure that I ever saw him more than once after we left college, and that was after he had acquired his celebrity, both as a genius and a hermit. One of our common friends, to whom I mentioned my intention of calling upon him, advised me not to do so, as he thought the effort to see him would be unavailing; it proved otherwise, however, and he not only received me, but was more genial and cordial than he used to be in the days of our comparative intimacy. His library, which he showed me, was very large and valuable, but the place looked solitary and dismal, and as if it were never invaded by a broom. He was emphatically a man by himself, not merely in the sense of living alone, but in the sense of being an anomalous specimen of humanity. If you can succeed in reproducing him as he exists in my mind's eye, you will have done something that will at once amuse and amaze the world."

On leaving college, he was engaged as an instructor in one or two private families in Philadelphia. The year after his graduation was unusually prolific in the labors of his pen, as during this year he composed nearly one half of the volume afterwards published in 1820. In his choice of a profession he was led in part by the example of his father, and in great part also by his love for nature and natural science. It was quite in accordance with his prevailing tastes, then, that he should do as he did; namely, choose the study of medicine, inasmuch as this study not only suggests many topics in reference to man's being and history, but leads directly into wide fields of physical and natural research. He entered the office of Dr. Eli Ives, who is still living at New Haven as Emeritus Professor of the Materia Medica in the Medical Department of Yale College. This gentleman had already distinguished himself by his enterprise and ardor as a native botanist, having been one of the first Americans to import the works of Linnæus and others, and having acquired at an early period a remarkable reputation for his knowledge of such of our plants as are valuable in medicine. Percival caught the spirit of the office, being peculiarly predisposed and qualified by nature for that class of studies. An attempt being made about this time to establish a botanical garden in connection with the Medical College, Dr. Ives offered to him the place of Curator, which he gladly accepted; but he soon resigned it, and indeed the enterprise itself failed to succeed. Previously, however, the Professor had endeavored to help out the slender pecuniary resources of his pupil, by procuring a class of boys for him to teach.

In 1820 Percival made his first decided appearance as an author, by publishing a volume, containing the first part of the "Prometheus," a poem in the Spenserian stanza, and a few minor pieces. This was well received by the public. In this same year he was admitted to the practice of medicine, upon which he made two unsuccessful trials to establish himself in that practice, the first in his native place, and the last at Charleston, S. C. Here he engaged in literature, issuing the first number of "Clio" in 1822. This publication, a neat pamphlet of about a hundred pages, was made up mostly of verse, to which a few essays in prose were added. A second part soon followed, composed entirely of verse.

Meanwhile he appears to have abandoned the practice of his profession, perhaps from an uncontrollable antipathy to some of its harsher and less genial requirements. This is apparent from the following extract from a letter written by him in 1823. "I have little to say," he writes, "of my prospects. I have undertaken to edit a newspaper, because I could find no better means of supplying my immediate necessities. . . . . . I do not like my profession. I cannot be reconciled to the practice, and if I was, I cannot obtain that practice."

In 1822, he delivered an oration before the Phi Beta Kappa Society of Yale College, on "Some of the Moral and Political Truths derivable from the Study of History," — in which special applications were made to the existing state of things in our own country, with cautionary suggestions for the coming time.

In February or March, 1824, he received, through the influence of John C. Calhoun, the appointment of Assistant Surgeon in the United States Army, and immediately thereupon was detailed to West Point, as Professor of Chemistry in the Military Academy at that place. But in July of the same year he resigned his office, not, as has been somewhere stated, in consequence of ill-health, but because he had been deceived in his anticipations. It had been represented to him that the duties were light, thus affording him sufficient leisure to pursue his favorite studies. Instead of this, however, he found that his whole time was taken up with daily, and almost hourly, exercises as a lecturer and teacher. During this year he superintended an edition of his select writings, which was published in New York City in one octavo volume, and soon after reproduced in two duodecimo volumes in London. After his resignation at West Point, he was appointed a surgeon in connection with the recruiting service in Boston. While a resident of Boston, he was a frequent contributor to "The United States Literary Gazette"; and he also edited several works for the press, among which was a republication and emendation of Vicesimus Knox's Elegant Extracts.

About the year 1827 he removed to New Haven, Connecticut, which place henceforward he made his permanent residence and home. In the same year he published the third part of "Clio," and also commenced, for a Boston publisher, a revised translation of Malte Brun's great work on Geography, from the original French, with notes. This was not fully completed until 1833. It forms six large octavo volumes. In 1827–28 he was engaged in revising and correcting the manuscript, and in superintending the printing, of Noah Webster's Dictionary, the first quarto edition, in two volumes. For his exertions in aiding the publication of this great work, so honorable to the genius and perseverance of Webster, Percival deserves no little credit. The great lexicographer frequently acknowledged his obligations to the learning of the poet, and to his extensive knowledge of ancient and modern languages. There was probably no one in our country so competent to the task as he, or who would more devotedly, and with such self-denial and disinterestedness, have given his time and talents to the work. In reference to these labors, namely, those upon the Geography and the Dictionary, Percival wrote as follows, in a letter bearing date May 9, 1831, to Professor Ticknor of Boston: — "The employments in which I have been last engaged have been difficult and laborious, but concealed. That with the Dictionary gave me no opportunity of exhibiting myself to advantage. The good I did, whether positive or negative, in preventing evil, all went to another's advantage, but was lost to me" (i. e. so far as reputation went, and thereby the power of obtaining future employment). "The

Geography is of a similar character. No one can form a conception of the most difficult part of my task, without closely comparing my edition with the English edition and the original, a labor which probably not one of my readers will undertake."

In the early part of this same year (1831) Percival received from General Duff Green of the Washington Telegraph a proposition to enter into an editorial partnership, as follows, viz.: to take the sole editorship of "The United States Army and Navy Journal," a magazine to be established in the city of Washington on the plan of "The United Service Journal" of England, and to which there had already been obtained a large number of subscribers; and in connection with this, also to render him (Green) occasional assistance in the literary and miscellaneous departments of the Telegraph. But owing partly to his political sentiments, partly to the uncertainty of the compensation and of its continuance, and in great part, moreover, to his indisposition to change his residence or pursuits, so long as he could gain an adequate livelihood where he was, he did not accept this proposition. He stated this offer and his own situation and feelings in a letter to Professor Ticknor, whose advice he solicited. In the same letter he expressed his preference for "an independent literary employment, as author or editor (not of periodicals, but of new editions of books), to any such employment as this just proposed at Washington."

In 1834 he had explored, on his own account,

the ranges of trap-rock in the State of Connecticut, and being one of the best geologists in our country, Governor Edwards appointed him, in 1835, in conjunction with Professor Charles U. Shepard, to make a mineralogical and geological survey of the State. His Report was published in 1842. This work, of nearly five hundred pages, contains the results of a very minute survey of the rock formations of the State, and abounds in minute and carefully systematized details.

Mr. Richard S. Willis, of the Musical World, in a genial and appreciative sketch of Percival, written in 1854 or 1855, gives, evidently as he received it from the poet himself, the following more particular account of this survey and its results: —

"The Connecticut Legislature (composed, like most of our State Legislatures, very much of practical working-men, farmers, and others from the country) wished to know the geological resources of the State. An appropriation was made. Percival was appointed. His is not a mind for a superficial investigation of things. Unfortunately, the Legislature expected only a superficial view, — at least, a very brief, practical report of the available State resources. This might have been all that was necessary; but practical men, and men devoted to the high interests of science, take a very different view of things. Percival formed his plan for this survey. It was a remarkable one. Those who have seen a Virginia fence can have a tolerably clear idea of his plan. For in the manner that such a fence traverses a field, he proposed to traverse the State, — with this difference, however, that whereas a Virginia fence does not return and take the other angle, Percival's plan did. In fact, beginning at a corner of the State, he was to trace over its entire expanse, a double Virginia fence, of which the following array of ×'s may convey some faint idea: —

"By this plan, he subsequently told me, there was scarcely a spot in the State, which he had not either passed over, or been within a reasonable distance of.

"Percival, at the start, bought him a horse to help him trace this Virginia fence. But he soon found this impracticable, inasmuch as drawing direct lines over a State is not exactly a horse-back road. So he betook himself wholly to pedestrianism. He had, throughout, the strangest adventures. The country farmers hunted the strange-looking man off their places, as a vagabond. Who could suspect that under that rusty, old glazed cap there was such an imposing head? or, that such faded garments could cover an intellectual giant and a remarkable man? But his experience very soon taught him one truth, — that it was useless at night to ask for hospitality at the large mansions of the rich. In the humble cottages of the poor he was always sure of a welcome.

"Time wore on, and the period had expired when the Report was to be made. It was far from being ready. Another appropriation was unwillingly made. A second period expired, and still the Report was not ready. The Legislature then grew impatient, and, as too often is the case under such circumstances, ungenerous imputations were thrown out, derogatory to the character of the poet.

"To a man of Percival's intellectual pride, this must have been exceedingly galling. One could not be surprised if it stung him to the quick; or, that he recoiled at it, as though stung by an adder.

"A long difficulty ensued. Percival had accumulated enormous materials. The collected specimens nearly filled a room. A full report, voluminous as it might have been, would have proved an invaluable and remarkable work of a great geologist. But, finally, a condensed, and to Percival, doubtless, unsatisfactory report was made.

"This experience must have injured Percival, and driven him to the extreme of seclusion again, and — of poverty."

Within a period of three or four years, from 1841 onwards, he was an occasional contributor of metrical versions of German, Slavonic, and other lyrics, (accompanied with critical and explanatory essays,) to the New Haven papers. About the same time he addressed a short poem of eight stanzas in the Danish language to the celebrated Ole Bull, who was then making a brief professional visit at New Haven. And here it may not be out of place to mention, that Percival, at various periods of his life, wrote poetical compositions in foreign languages, some of which were regarded by Professor Ticknor, who was favored with a perusal of them, as very remarkable. But few of these, however, have appeared in print.

With "The Dream of a Day," published in 1843, Percival's larger literary activities, so far as the public were concerned, appear to have ended. For the next ten years he lived in comparative obscurity, although never in indolence. Some time within this period, his extreme poverty, joined to his gradually increasing indebtedness, drove him to lay aside his customary reserve in respect to his pecuniary matters, and to apply to the generosity of his friends in New Haven for a loan, so that he might save his valuable library from a legal attachment and sale. This application was most liberally responded to, with no expectation on the part of most of a repayment; a sufficient sum (of from one to two thousand dollars) was raised, and his library was saved. In justice alike to the memory of Percival, and to the good faith of Dr. J. L. Jenckes, his legatee, it should be stated that this loan has been entirely repaid, principal and interest. Within this period, also, he labored in the department of lexicography again, translating for Professor E. A. Andrews letters A and B of Freund's Latin Lexicon, and, with his usual diligence and faithfulness, verifying examples and establishing authorities.

In 1853 he accepted an offer made to him by the

American Mining Company, to survey their lead-mining region in Wisconsin. "The succeeding year," Dr. J. L. Jenckes writes, "he was appointed, by Governor Barstow, State Geologist, through the influence of prominent citizens of the lead-mining region, who petitioned the Governor to that effect. He was actively engaged in the survey of the State until within a short period before his death. His first Report was published in February, 1855. His second, which he had nearly completed, will probably be issued next month." (This letter is dated in 1856.) "He visited every County, with the exception of Douglas County, which borders on Lake Superior. I have heard him estimate the distance he had travelled in his buggy, which was, I think, nearly or quite six thousand miles. . . . . . Occasionally he met with parties of the Chippewa and Winnebago tribes. His intercourse with them, as he stated, was unusually interesting. Alone in the forest with his red friends, — who were always friendly to him, — he succeeded in learning something of their language and history.

"Notwithstanding his labors while at the West were arduous and almost incessant, subjecting him alike to the inclemencies of the weather, and, in sparsely settled portions of the country, to great privation, yet he considered these three years in Wisconsin as the happiest period of his life. It would have rejoiced his friends, could they have seen him at this time. Translated from the isolation of a lonely room to the happy influence of a home, free from the immediate pressure of pecuniary want, surrounded by little children and a circle of appreciating friends, few would have recognized in this active, energetic, and social man the reserved Percival of former years. His affection for children, especially for those he fancied, was frequently shown by a kind attention to their wants, and a great solicitude for their welfare. He would often take them in his buggy, and ride two or three miles for their diversion, evidently enjoying it himself as much as did his little companions. His sincerity and childlike simplicity caused their attachment to be mutual.

"Music was his favorite recreation. For this art he had an exquisite taste, and he would frequently spend hours at a time in playing on the accordion or piano.

"During the first two or three months of his last illness, he often sought the soothing influence of music." Dr. Jenckes goes on to speak more at length of this illness, which appears to have been a general decline of the vital powers, brought on by exposure and hard work. He says: "I found it difficult to form a satisfactory diagnosis. There were no indications of organic disease. General physical debility and emaciation gradually increased until the end. He often remarked to me, 'Since living in the West, I have overtasked my physical strength, and I feel that I am worn out.' He expressed from the first a firm conviction that he should not recover, and this conviction no efforts on the part of his friends availed to remove. When asked if, in the event of his death, he wished to be carried to New Haven, he replied, 'No, I wish to be buried here; and let my remains be undisturbed.' He appeared to exercise a tranquil and serene faith in view of the future. We occasionally saw him on his knees, engaged in prayer. . . . . .

"In the presence of several gentlemen of this place, he made arrangements with regard to his temporal affairs. During his illness he received every care and attention from his friends here. . . . . . I would add, that no other man, I presume, would have been regarded by the people of this State with more respect and admiration for his scientific attainments than Dr. Percival. . . . . . We regarded him almost in the light of a sinless being."

His death elicited various public demonstrations of respect and regret in the State of Wisconsin; among which we may mention the proceedings of the State Historical Society at their monthly meeting next subsequent, a record of which now lies before us. His loss was deeply felt, moreover, by the mining interest of the State, by the Germans especially, to whom he had endeared himself by addressing to them numerous patriotic songs in their own language.

For many years Percival had contemplated building for himself, for a permanent residence, a house after his own mind, where he could execute, in quiet, several of his long-cherished plans. This was finally, from his own earnings, with the aid of the contributions of his friends, commenced in November, 1854, and completed in February, 1855. It contained but two rooms, the larger of which was destined for his choice library. But he was not permitted to occupy it, even for a single night. Nor was his library, or any portion of it, ever deposited there.

In November, 1854, on revisiting New Haven, he arranged and packed his library, and stored it in the attic of the State Hospital, a large and substantial structure of solid masonry. In April, 1855, he returned to resume his labors in Wisconsin, and there worked on with his usual resolute energy and faithfulness until overtaken by death.

In figure Percival was somewhat tall, and thin, almost to emaciation; his forehead was high, his nose prominent, his lips thin and mobile, his face oval, and his complexion pale, inclining to sallow. But his eye betokened, even to a casual observer, the presence of rare genius. It was flashing and deep-glowing, like the diamond. Its color was blue-gray, its vision far-searching, yet microscopically minute. Nothing seemed to escape its observation. It was the eye equally of the naturalist and the poet.

The deep and brooding melancholy, which so eminently characterized Percival through life, sprang undoubtedly from some sufficient cause. Current report has ascribed it to an early disappointment in love. But we have his own authority for denying any such fact. He undoubtedly loved;

but loved some far-off ideal object alone. This sadness of disposition is, however, amply explained, when we consider his delicate and sensitive organization, its unfitness for the struggles of the world, and the consequent pain that he must have felt in view of the rooted selfishness of humanity.

His mind, nevertheless, appears to have been ever active, whether in compassing new subjects of attainment, or in discovering new analogies in the vast and varied field of knowledge already attained, thus catching sublime glimpses of that grand unity, towards which, under the guidance of a Divine hand, all noble human endeavors in religion and philosophy, science and art, are continually tending. This remark seems fully justified, if we take a survey of the subjects which occupied his attention.

After leaving college, he read the Greek and Latin classics, to an extent sufficient to excite great admiration: in addition to this, he commenced an ardent pursuit of all the branches of Natural History; composing voluminous extracts, not of their general views and doctrines merely, but carefully copying the specific descriptions of all birds and beasts known at that period from Cuvier, Linnæus, Wilson, and others; making much progress, also, in a work which should briefly characterize all the plants then known. He mastered the science of chemistry, as it then existed; and became a minute and practical mineralogist and geologist, exploring fields, hills, and forests, with the athletic energy of the true naturalist.

The mathematics and the mathematical sciences he had prosecuted with pleasure while a boy in college; but it is not known that he devoted any special attention to them in after life. It is certain, however, that he found them neither difficult nor uncongenial.

Geography had been his favorite study in boyhood, and was pursued in youth and early manhood, with that reference to everything necessary to a complete picture of a particular region of the earth which Humboldt and Malte-Brun were the first to exemplify, and which qualified him, after a few years, to correct the errors which occurred in almost every line of the English translation of Malte-Brun's voluminous work. Moreover, geography for him was incomplete without a knowlege of the language and literature, in addition to a picturesque conception, of the country. Hence one of his earliest works in prose was an exhibition of the languages of the globe, condensed and arranged from Adelung and Vater. Here his poetic impulses were in sympathy with his ardent love of accurate scientific knowledge. Hence he was one of the first in our country to revel in that latest and only scientific mode of studying languages which has received the name of *linguistic science.* Bopp, Grimm, and others of the profound Germans, were imported by him, and had long been his familiar companions, before either their names or their discoveries had been heard of by most of our ablest professors of language.

Linguistic science became to him a key to infinitely more than a dry and barren knowledge of words; it not only classified the wondrously varied tribes of men according to their mutual relations of descent and consanguinity, but it became the foundation of the philosophy which unlocked for him, as a student of mankind, the inmost recesses of the human heart. As a scholar, he could thus appreciate the degree of culture of various nations, as shown in their literature, and as a poet could enter into a warm and intimate sympathy with them as brethren of the human family.

He excelled especially in the study of the European languages. Into this study he was led by his poetic impulses; the interest with which he regarded the early efforts in literature of the less advanced peoples being derived from other causes than their intrinsic merit. In addition to the French, Italian, and Spanish of his earlier years, he delighted in constantly adding to his stores of German, ancient as well as modern, expressing in it his choicest thoughts and feelings. Not content with gratifying his romantic tastes through the study of the Gaelic and Welsh, and his curiosity and sympathy with the stern and heroic by mastering the Norse, Danish, and Swedish, he was indefatigable in his devotion to the Slavonic tongues, with the poetry of which, more particularly, he was unwearied in making himself familiar. The more uncouth the appearance and the sound, the greater was his zest in overcoming the sense of strangeness by the most minute linguistic study, and by persevering till he felt at ease, and, as it were, among friends with whom he could sympathize. The Russians were found to be unexpectedly interesting, from the tenderness of sentiment among their peasantry; the vigor and spirit of the Polish did not disappoint him; the Hungarian Magyars were peculiar as well as wild; and in the Servians he took extreme delight. As a linguistic student it was a matter of course that he should labor at the Sanskrit. It is known that he once made, by request, to a Society, an elaborate report on the grammar of the Basque; but it is not known that he also examined many other languages which he did not read.

To conclude this enumeration, during many of his later years, music was a cherished study with him. Its scientific theory, and the philosophy of its origin, nature, and effects, gratified his love of knowledge, as did also its manifestations among different nations, cultivated and barbarous. He diligently collected the peculiar airs of all ages and nations, and made the same use of them, as interpeters of national sentiment, that he did of popular and national poetry. He experienced in the highest degree a constitutional delight in the varieties of metre in the movements of national airs, and in simple and natural melodies in music. It was one of his favorite plans to imitate, in English, all known metres in all accessible languages, from the Sanskrit downwards.

Willis, in the article from which we have already quoted, has so delightfully portrayed the musical side of Percival's character, that we cannot forbear transferring the sketch entire.

"But one subject, perhaps, remained for more satisfactory investigation, — music. Even here, he was well read, as far as possible. Everything that had been written upon the subject, in encyclopædias and otherwise, he had perused. But where is the book that treats of music intelligibly to persons who have not a practical knowledge of the subject? Therefore Percival had still something to learn about music.

"At this time, by reason of the already-mentioned serenades and other tuneful demonstrations, music was assuming unwonted prominence within college walls and under city elms. Percival caught the enthusiasm, and for a time his master-mind seemed to be filled with music, — musicalized. He had a collection of old German annuals, which contained a certain number of songs with music. These songs he translated into charming English rhyme, and, turning the music over to me, it was soon arranged in parts for our club. We met and sang the music to Percival's translations. Delightful hours these! Percival was always with us; and though he did not sing, we knew his soul was making melody with ours.

"Crowded out of the college buildings (for the swarming students in this institution [Yale] had overrun its edifices, like certain historical rats the bishop's castle on the Rhine), my own 'den' was on the first floor of a private residence in the vicinity, — first floor, namely, by Hibernian reckoning, counting from the sky downward. And, indeed, it does not seem unbefitting that the starting-point of our enumeration should ever be in the skies. I owe it entirely to music, that to this first floor Percival was in the habit of climbing, far away from the cellar of things, as found in the lower world, to engage in delightful converse on matters musical. My ear soon learned to catch his soft, springy step on the stairs, as he leaped up two or three at a time in the ascent. Books were immediately thrown aside, and our sitting commenced, which sometimes lasted for hours; for his mind, if once started on the track of a subject, was entirely oblivious to the lapse of time. This was the case, whether within walls, or on the corner of a street on a cold, windy night; and the listener who could at any time tear himself away from such instructive and fascinating communication with this wonderful mind (mysteriously vested in a long cloak, that fluttered in the wind), though it lasted not unfrequently for hours, must have been more self-denying than I could ever find myself. Frequent 'flunks' in morning recitations I willingly submitted to, from the greater knowledge acquired during long study hours from this wise, living book.

"But not I alone was betrayed by the morning; for Percival once incidentally related, that, having seated himself at a desk one evening to commence a poem for a coming Society celebration, he was suddenly aroused by what seemed to him a large conflagration, illumining his apartment. He started to the window, and found it was the morning breaking in the east. He had written all night, — and his poem was finished at a single heat.

"But this singular man was now fast becoming a practical musician, — yea, more, positively a composer, — still more, even the inventor of a musical theory. He could find, at that time, no intelligible musical system, and therefore he invented a singularly ingenious one of his own. He also undertook to learn an instrument, — the accordion; this he ordinarily brought with him under his cloak. He had, as yet, an appreciation only of the bare melody; harmony confused his ear. The chords were therefore shut off from the instrument, and the soft breathing of the accordion, in some plaintive air which he had himself composed, was all that was heard. But his voice, even in conversation, soft as the sighing of the west wind, in music was almost inaudible. Not master of the art of writing music, he ordinarily brought his compositions jotted down in illegible hieroglyphics of his own, and wished to have them reduced to shape. But the melodies were in such strange, wild measures (like much of his poetry), the numbers were so irregular, that it was almost impossible to do this. Still, in many instances the attempt was successful.

"I recollect that on one occasion our club was to sing at a little gathering of friends, and Percival, quite to our astonishment, had consented to accompany us, — for he had shunned all general society for years. Still more were we astonished when he expressed his willingness, while there, to sing a song of his own. He had brought his accordion. In a retired corner of the room sat his gaunt, thin figure, bent over the instrument. To me he had never looked half so weird-like; that noble Shakspeareian head of his, the sharply-cut, spiritual features, his eyes so full of the wild fire of genius, the thin, curling locks, all gave him the appearance of a minstrel come down from another age.

"We had already quieted the room for the expected song. Standing near him, I soon knew, by the motion of his lips, that he was singing. But no one heard him; for I myself could distinguish only the soft breathing of a melody of his, that was familiar to me. After a while the company, supposing that he was not quite ready to begin, commenced talking again.

"The bard sung on, and the song was finished; but few, beside myself, at all suspected that he had been singing, most supposing, at last, that, for some reason, he had given up his intention. But his own soul had floated off upon his melody, and he had that sufficient reward which many a bard has, — the silent rapture of song. But I believe, and hope, Percival was convinced that we shared the pleasure with him.

"It will not be thought strange that I looked upon it as a great triumph of music, — that it was vindicating its eminently socializing and humanizing character, in thus drawing back to a regretting and appreciating world a spirit which had so long been unhappily alienated from it. Percival was approaching society again."

That these studies were not superficial, appears from the fact that, in opposition to the loose and very imperfect manner in which Latin and Greek were studied at that time, even in our best colleges, Percival taught himself to read the ancient classics in the same manner that he afterwards read the modern; and to a habit, early acquired, of reading them aloud, with a full exhibition of the harmony of their versifications, may probably be ascribed much of the simplicity, purity, and energy of his diction.

In short, his attainments were truly extraordinary. Even in 1823, the North American said of him: "There is almost an encyclopædia familiarity in him with subjects in many departments of modern science. We regard his powers and resources as inexhaustible." Professor Chauncey A. Goodrich, of Yale College, in the Preface to the revised edition of Webster's Dictionary, after acknowledging the various authorities to which he had been indebted, in the revision, in single departments, adds the following tribute to Percival's universal attainments, — a tribute as courteous as it was nobly earned: —

"But it is obviously impossible for any one mind to embrace with accuracy all the various departments of knowledge which are now brought within the compass of a dictionary. Hence arise most of the errors and inconsistencies which abound in works of this kind. To avoid these as far as possible, especially in matters of science, the editor at first made an arrangement with Dr. James G. Percival, who had rendered important assistance to Dr. Webster, in the edition of 1828, to take the entire charge of revising the scientific articles embraced in this work. This revision, however, owing to causes beyond the control of either party, was extended to but little more than two letters of the alphabet." Said Professor Ticknor of him, in a letter addressed to Percival's present biographer, in 1858 : "I received the news [of his death] with the deepest regret. I felt that a very bright light had been extinguished. Indeed, he was a most wonderful person, not only from his uncommon poetical gifts, but from the vast variety and accuracy of his knowledge in departments as remote as they well can be from poetry, and hardly less wide asunder from each other."

Of his poetry, Mr. Edward Everett in the North American, in 1821, writes thus, in a review of his first published work: "This little volume contains the marks of an inspiration more lofty and genuine than any similar collection of fugitive pieces from a native bard. . . . . This Prometheus, like most of the other pieces, breathes a melancholy spirit too deep not to be real. We should sincerely regret that powers so fine as Mr. Percival evidently possesses, should want that self-consciousness which they ought to inspire, or should fail to doubt of that public favor they so truly deserve. . . . . He shares with few the gifts which make him a classical American poet." The North American, in the article of 1823, before alluded to (a notice of an earlier number of "Clio"), said of him: "He possesses the rare and divine art of imparting to language those mysterious and unearthly influences, which come to us from the strings of an Æolian harp. . . . . As you walk through the garden of his poetry, you enjoy something more than the pleasure of gazing on individual specimens, or inhaling successive sweets, or surveying gay beds or fairly ordered parterres; for the air itself is occupied with a spirit of mingled fragrance."

The following glimpse of the man in his rigid adherence to truth and accuracy, as well in poetry as in science, we cull from the already twice-quoted article by Willis:—

With the simplicity and earnestness and confidingness of a child to those whom he momentarily trusts, Percival has the proud and lofty and inaccessible *hauteur* of an intellectual prince to the world at large.

"But it is impossible, from the very heart, not to respect the man. He once indignantly spoke of the trivial, gossiping, story-telling manner certain professors have of lecturing on scientific subjects. 'All truth is sacred,' said he, 'sacred as the Bible; and it should invariably be treated as sacred, and with dignified seriousness.'"

The views which Percival himself entertained of poetry are best described in his own language, in a letter to Professor Ticknor. After speaking of the folly of literary labors as a matter of ambition, if a proper income cannot be secured thereby, he continues as follows: "There is one employment, however, which I would wish to place above interest or ambition, — which I would wish to regard as holy, — Poetry. True poetry should be a holy thing, like true philosophy and true religion; the product only of our highest intellectual and moral nature (*ein reines vernünftiges Gefühl*). I have expressed this figuratively in a formula, which I may give as my *Credo*. Philosophy, Religion, and Poetry sit enthroned as a spiritual trinity in the shrine of our highest nature. The perfect vision of all-embracing truth, the vital feeling of all-blessing good, and the living conception of all-gracing beauty, they form united the Divinity of Pure Reason. With such feelings, I can no longer look to poetry as a source of emolument; I cannot consent to use it for such a purpose; I can only regard it as the vestal fire in the *Adytum*: I must meet the world with weapons of more earthly temper." In the preface to the "Dream of a Day," published in 1843, he gives the qualifications of the poet.*

As a boy, he is remembered by Mr. Brace, his early teacher, as fair and pleasant, shy and retiring, his voice low and soft, his manner gentle and winning; and even his dress, by its neatness and beauty, seemed to symbolize the pure and beautiful soul

* See Vol. II. pp. 204, 205.

within. Nor did he ever lose this purity and almost angelic sweetness of disposition. His feelings were gentle and tender, impressible and nervously sensitive; and he was ever faithful to his trust, and conscientiously thorough in the execution of the various tasks which were committed to him.

His eccentricities, and the self-imposed isolation for which he has been censured, find abundant justification, both in his nature and the circumstances in which he was placed. His apology is best stated by himself, in a letter dated 1823: "I sometimes feel bitter towards a public that leaves authors of real merit unrewarded. If I deserve all the North American says of me, I deserve something. But I forget that the public will not buy what does not please it, and it will not be pleased with what is not of its own order. 'Like loves like,' all the world over, in England as well as here; and if I cannot come down to the public, I must sit above them, cold and hungry. . . . . . I have said enough of my circumstances. They are low and sad enough, and they have made my spirits low. I could tell a tale of embarrassments, joined to a bad constitution, injured health, and a neglected orphanage, which would do much to excuse the wrong that is in me."

But he nevertheless worked on, sustained by the fire and energy of genius. In 1832 he appears to have been under the cloud still. At that time he wrote to Professor Ticknor, requesting his influence to procure him employment. His wants were modest and few. After stating that his entire income for the two previous years was but $65 a year, he continues: "With such employments," (editing books, etc.) — "which I cannot but think I have amply deserved by my talents, my attainments, and the fidelity, accuracy, and industry with which I have accomplished what I have undertaken, — with such employments, my way will be smooth before me. Under such circumstances, I feel myself compelled to plead for employment, and with a compensation suited for me, and as is fit for a literary man who deserves encouragement. I have no wish for anything more. Only give me light and room (*ποίησον δ' αἴθρην*), and I am sure I can exert myself still with as much effort and diligence as any, and I doubt not with sufficient effect."

In conversation few showed more ability or less dogmatism than Percival. His range of topics comprised every department in science, morals, history, art, and literature. If opinions opposite to his own were advanced, he would listen calmly to the arguments by which they were sustained, replying in a ready and ingenious manner, but maintaining his own opinions with great firmness. Mere assertions he rarely ventured upon. His only fault in conversation, if fault it should be called, was that irrepressible communicativeness, so apt to result from long-continued and solitary study. The material of his conversation was rich and interesting knowledge, thought, and sentiment, — not idle words. Those who had the good fortune to obtain ready access to him, were amply rewarded for their patience as listeners. His mind could easily be led to poetry and criticism, when his remarks would be delightfully genial and suggestive; but he seldom selected these topics himself. Indeed, his conversation generally followed the lead of others.

This is not the place to enter upon a criticism of his poetry. And in fact, without reference to the circumstances of his life, all criticism, however just in itself, will fail in justice to him. He composed with surprising rapidity. Numbers of his poems were thrown off in moments of sparkling and salient feeling, and finished, as it were, on the instant. The Wreck, a poem of about forty pages, was written in three or four days. He trusted to the inspiration of the moment, and was impatient of revision. In reference to this habit, he would often remark: "After all, art is but a perfected nature." Nor indeed had his lot ever permitted him to cultivate industriously and with thoughtful care the "life poetic." It was never in his power to husband his hours for a watchful improvement of the fluxes and refluxes of his inner being, and thus to train his imagination to its highest discipline, and systematically to accumulate his resources. His want of all security for the future, and the painful drudgery and economy by which only he could live, allowed him but very few moments of leisure in which to surrender himself wholly to poetic impulses. There were times when he was unable, through poverty, to buy enough suitable food to sustain his bodily strength in a fit condition to admit of study even, to say nothing of the higher demands of creation.

The reader should also bear in mind that he rarely retouched what he had once written. This is especially true of his earlier effusions, the Prometheus among the number. It should be remembered, also, that the latter poem was written at the period when Byron's "men of one virtue and a thousand crimes" received the adoring worship of what was believed to be taste and sensibility; though Byron, unlike Percival, knew vice and moral deformity as a man, and could give to their delineations a reality which partook of the actual, though not of that truer and enduring real which can only be exhibited by the purer kinds of poetic imagination in their all-penetrating and creative power. In Percival's later poetical productions, the Classic Melodies* especially, there are marks, however, not only of a broader humanity, but also of that thorough artistic elaboration, which secures the same keen delight to the reader that the poet himself experienced in the moments of his inspiration, as he gave to "airy nothing a local habitation and a name." But at whatever period of his poetic life we regard him, he was a truly remarkable man. In his fusion of smooth and sweeping flow with strength, Saxon energy, and unaffected manliness, we hold him the

---

* See an elaborate and scholarly article on Percival's "Classic Melodies" in the New Englander, Vol. II. p. 81, from the pen of Dr. Erasmus D. North. — Ed.

equal to any of his English predecessors since the Elizabethan age.

It might be shown that it is not necessary that a poet of acknowledged genius should produce some sustained and continuous poem, and that, for the most delightful and unquestionably one of the highest uses of poetry, a volume of condensed and choice effusions is beyond doubt better than any other. It gives that rest from weariness and care, that translation to a higher sphere of mind, which causes a warmer glow of gratitude to a favorite poet, than to any other who benefits the world by his genius; and what was said of Percival many years ago will ever remain true: "All his productions breathe that spirit of genuine inspiration which can alone in characters of light

> Stamp on the immortal page
> The visions of the soul."

Percival died at Hazel Green, Wisconsin, on the morning of the 2d of May, 1856; and on the 4th of the month he was buried, with the solemn rites of the Protestant Episcopal Church.

INDEX OF FIRST LINES.

POEMS.

POEMS.

POETRY.

I consider Poetry in a twofold view, as a spirit and a manifestation. Perhaps the poetic spirit has never been more justly defined, than by Byron in his Prophecy of Dante, — a creation

> "From overfeeling good or ill, an aim
> At an external life beyond our fate."

This spirit may be manifested by language, metrical or prose, by declamation, by musical sounds, by expression, by gesture, by motion, and by imitating forms, colors, and shades; so that literature, oratory, music, physiognomy, acting, and the arts of painting and sculpture, may all have their poetry; but that peculiar spirit, which alone gives the great life and charm to all the efforts of genius, is as distinct from the measure and rhyme of poetical composition, as from the scientific principles of drawing and perspective.

THE world is full of Poetry; — the air
Is living with its spirit; and the waves
Dance to the music of its melodies,
And sparkle in its brightness. Earth is veiled,
And mantled with its beauty; and the walls
That close the universe with crystal in,
Are eloquent with voices, that proclaim
The unseen glories of immensity,
In harmonies, too perfect, and too high,
For aught but beings of celestial mould,
And speak to man in one eternal hymn,
Unfading beauty, and unyielding power.

The year leads round the seasons, in a choir
For ever charming, and for ever new,
Blending the grand, the beautiful, the gay,

The mournful, and the tender, in one strain,
Which steals into the heart, like sounds that rise
Far off, in moonlight evenings, on the shore
Of the wide ocean resting after storms;
Or tones that wind around the vaulted roof,
And pointed arches, and retiring aisles
Of some old, lonely minster, where the hand,
Skilful, and moved with passionate love of art,
Plays o'er the higher keys, and bears aloft
The peal of bursting thunder, and then calls,
By mellow touches, from the softer tubes,
Voices of melting tenderness, that blend
With pure and gentle musings, till the soul,
Commingling with the melody, is borne,
Rapt, and dissolved in ecstasy, to Heaven.

'T is not the chime and flow of words, that move
In measured file, and metrical array;
'T is not the union of returning sounds,
Nor all the pleasing artifice of rhyme,
And quantity, and accent, that can give
This all-pervading spirit to the ear,
Or blend it with the movings of the soul.
'T is a mysterious feeling, which combines
Man with the world around him, in a chain
Woven of flowers, and dipped in sweetness, till
He taste the high communion of his thoughts,
With all existences, in earth and heaven,
That meet him in the charm of grace and power.
'T is not the noisy babbler, who displays,
In studied phrase, and ornate epithet,
And rounded period, poor and vapid thoughts,
Which peep from out the cumbrous ornaments
That overload their littleness. Its words
Are few, but deep and solemn; and they break
Fresh from the fount of feeling, and are full
Of all that passion, which, on Carmel, fired
The holy prophet, when his lips were coals,
His language winged with terror, as when bolts

Leap from the brooding tempest, armed with wrath,
Commissioned to affright us and destroy.

Passion, when deep, is still, — the glaring eye
That reads its enemy with glance of fire,
The lip that curls and writhes in bitterness,
The brow contracted, till its wrinkles hide
The keen, fixed orbs that burn and flash below,
The hand firm clenched and quivering, and the foot
Planted in attitude to spring, and dart
Its vengeance, are the language it employs.
So the poetic feeling needs no words
To give it utterance; but it swells, and glows,
And revels in the ecstasies of soul,
And sits at banquet with celestial forms,
The beings of its own creation, fair,
And lovely, as e'er haunted wood and wave,
When earth was peopled, in its solitudes,
With nymph and naiad, — mighty as the gods,
Whose palace was Olympus, and the clouds
That hung, in gold and flame, around its brow;
Who bore, upon their features, all that grand
And awful dignity of front, which bows
The eye that gazes on the marble Jove,
Who hurls, in wrath, his thunder, and the god,
The image of a beauty so divine,
So masculine, so artless, that we seem
To share in his intensity of joy,
When, sure as fate, the bounding arrow sped,
And darted to the scaly monster's heart.

This spirit is the breath of Nature, blown
Over the sleeping forms of clay, who else
Doze on through life in blank stupidity,
Till by its blast, as by a touch of fire,
They rouse to lofty purpose, and send out,
In deeds of energy, the rage within.
Its seat is deeper in the savage breast,
Than in the man of cities; in the child,

Than in maturer bosoms. Art may prune
Its rank and wild luxuriance, and may train
Its strong outbreakings, and its vehement gusts,
To soft refinement, and amenity;
But all its energy has vanished, all
Its maddening and commanding spirit gone,
And all its tender touches, and its tones
Of soul-dissolving pathos, lost and hid
Among the measured notes, that move as dead
And heartless as the puppets in a show.

Well I remember, in my boyish days,
How deep the feeling when my eye looked forth
On Nature, in her loveliness, and storms.
How my heart gladdened, as the light of spring
Came from the sun, with zephyrs, and with showers,
Waking the earth to beauty, and the woods
To music, and the atmosphere to blow,
Sweetly and calmly, with its breath of balm.
O, how I gazed upon the dazzling blue
Of summer's Heaven of glory, and the waves,
That rolled, in bending gold, o'er hill and plain;
And on the tempest, when it issued forth,
In folds of blackness, from the northern sky,
And stood above the mountains, silent, dark,
Frowning, and terrible; then sent abroad
The lightning, as its herald, and the peal,
That rolled in deep, deep volleys, round the hills,
The warning of its coming, and the sound,
That ushered in its elemental war!
And, oh! I stood, in breathless longing fixed,
Trembling, and yet not fearful, as the clouds
Heaved their dark billows on the roaring winds,
That sent, from mountain top, and bending wood,
A long hoarse murmur, like the rush of waves,
That burst, in foam and fury, on the shore.

Nor less the swelling of my heart, when high
Rose the blue arch of autumn, cloudless, pure

As Nature, at her dawning, when she sprang
Fresh from the hand that wrought her; where the
eye
Caught not a speck upon the soft serene,
To stain its deep cerulean, but the cloud,
That floated, like a lonely spirit, there,
White as the snow of Zemla, or the foam
That on the mid-sea tosses, cinctured round,
In easy undulations, with a belt
Woven of bright Apollo's golden hair.
Nor, when that arch, in winter's clearest night,
Mantled in ebon darkness, strewed with stars
Its canopy, that seemed to swell, and swell
The higher, as I gazed upon it, till,
Sphere after sphere, evolving, on the height
Of Heaven, the everlasting throne shone through,
In glory's full effulgence, and a wave,
Intensely bright, rolled, like a fountain, forth
Beneath its sapphire pedestal, and streamed
Down the long galaxy, a flood of snow,
Bathing the heavens in light, the spring that gushed,
In overflowing richness, from the breast
Of all-maternal Nature. These I saw,
And felt to madness; but my full heart gave
No utterance to the ineffable within.
Words were too weak; they were unknown; but still
The feeling was most poignant: it has gone;
And all the deepest flow of sounds, that e'er
Poured, in a torrent fulness, from the tongue
Rich with the wealth of ancient bards, and stored
With all the patriarchs of British song
Hallowed and rendered glorious, cannot tell
Those feelings, which have died, to live no more.

THE DESERTED WIFE.

He comes not; — I have watched the moon go down,
But yet he comes not. Once it was not so.
He thinks not how these bitter tears do flow,
The while he holds his riot in that town.
Yet he will come, and chide, and I shall weep;
And he will wake my infant from its sleep,
To blend its feeble wailing with my tears.
O, how I love a mother's watch to keep,
Over those sleeping eyes, that smile, which cheers
My heart, though sunk in sorrow, fixed and deep!
I had a husband once, who loved me, — now,
He ever wears a frown upon his brow,
And feeds his passion on a wanton's lip,
As bees, from laurel flowers, a poison sip;
But yet I cannot hate. — O, there were hours
When I could hang for ever on his eye,
And Time, who stole with silent swiftness by,
Strewed, as he hurried on, his path with flowers.
I loved him then, — he loved me too. My heart
Still finds its fondness kindle, if he smile;
The memory of our loves will ne'er depart;
And though he often sting me with a dart,
Venomed and barbed, and waste upon the vile
Caresses which his babe and mine should share,
Though he should spurn me, I will calmly bear
His madness, — and should sickness come, and lay
Its paralyzing hand upon him, then
I would with kindness all my wrongs repay,
Until the penitent should weep, and say
How injured, and how faithful, I had been.

CONSUMPTION.

There is a sweetness in woman's decay,
When the light of beauty is fading away,
When the bright enchantment of youth is gone,
And the tint that glowed, and the eye that shone,
And darted around its glance of power,
And the lip that vied with the sweetest flower
That ever in Pæstum's * garden blew,
Or ever was steeped in fragrant dew, —
When all that was bright and fair is fled,
But the loveliness lingering round the dead.

O, there is a sweetness in beauty's close,
Like the perfume scenting the withered rose;
For a nameless charm around her plays,
And her eyes are kindled with hallowed rays,
And a veil of spotless purity
Has mantled her cheek with its heavenly dye,
Like a cloud whereon the queen of night
Has poured her softest tint of light;
And there is a blending of white and blue,
Where the purple blood is melting through
The snow of her pale and tender cheek;
And there are tones, that sweetly speak
Of a spirit, who longs for a purer day,
And is ready to wing her flight away.

In the flush of youth and the spring of feeling,
When life, like a sunny stream, is stealing
Its silent steps through a flowery path,
And all the endearments, that pleasure hath,
Are poured from her full, o'erflowing horn,
When the rose of enjoyment conceals no thorn,
In her lightness of heart, to the cheery song
The maiden may trip in the dance along,

---

* "Biferique rosaria Pæsti." — Virg.

And think of the passing moment, that lies,
Like a fairy dream, in her dazzled eyes,
And yield to the present, that charms around
With all that is lovely in sight and sound,
Where a thousand pleasing phantoms flit,
With the voice of mirth, and the burst of wit,
And the music that steals to the bosom's core,
And the heart in its fulness flowing o'er
With a few big drops, that are soon repressed,
For short is the stay of grief in her breast:
In this enlivened and gladsome hour,
The spirit may burn with a brighter power;
But dearer the calm and quiet day,
When the Heaven-sick soul is stealing away.

And when her sun is low declining,
And life wears out with no repining,
And the whisper, that tells of early death,
Is soft as the west-wind's balmy breath,
When it comes at the hour of still repose,
To sleep in the breast of the wooing rose;
And the lip, that swelled with a living glow,
Is pale as a curl of new-fallen snow;
And her cheek, like the Parian stone, is fair,
But the hectic spot that flushes there,
When the tide of life, from its secret dwelling,
In a sudden gush, is deeply swelling,
And giving a tinge to her icy lips,
Like the crimson rose's brightest tips,
As richly red, and as transient too,
As the clouds, in autumn's sky of blue,
That seem like a host of glory met
To honor the sun at his golden set:
O, then, when the spirit is taking wing,
How fondly her thoughts to her dear one cling,
As if she would blend her soul with his
In a deep and long imprinted kiss;
So fondly the panting camel flies,
Where the glassy vapor cheats his eyes,

And the dove from the falcon seeks her nest,
And the infant shrinks to its mother's breast.
And though her dying voice be mute,
Or faint as the tones of an unstrung lute,
And though the glow from her cheek be fled,
And her pale lips cold as the marble dead,
Her eye still beams unwonted fires
With a woman's love and a saint's desires,
And her last fond, lingering look is given
To the love she leaves, and then to Heaven,
As if she would bear that love away
To a purer world and a brighter day.

THE CORAL GROVE.

Deep in the wave is a coral grove,
Where the purple mullet and gold-fish rove,
Where the sea-flower spreads its leaves of blue,
That never are wet with falling dew,
But in bright and changeful beauty shine,
Far down in the green and glassy brine.
The floor is of sand like the mountain drift,
And the pearl-shells spangle the flinty snow;
From coral rocks the sea plants lift
Their boughs, where the tides and billows flow;
The water is calm and still below,
For the winds and waves are absent there,
And the sands are bright as the stars that glow
In the motionless fields of upper air:
There with its waving blade of green,
The sea-flag streams through the silent water,
And the crimson leaf of the dulse is seen
To blush, like a banner bathed in slaughter:
There with a light and easy motion,
The fan-coral sweeps through the clear, deep sea;
And the yellow and scarlet tufts of ocean
Are bending like corn on the upland lea:

And life, in rare and beautiful forms,
Is sporting amid those bowers of stone,
And is safe, when the wrathful spirit of storms,
Has made the top of the wave his own:
And when the ship from his fury flies,
Where the myriad voices of ocean roar,
When the wind-god frowns in the murky skies,
And demons are waiting the wreck on shore;
Then far below, in the peaceful sea,
The purple mullet and gold-fish rove,
Where the waters murmur tranquilly,
Through the bending twigs of the coral grove.

I HAD found out a sweet green spot,
Where a lily was blooming fair;
The din of the city disturbed it not,
But the spirit, that shades the quiet cot
With its wings of love, was there.

I found that lily's bloom,
When the day was dark and chill;
It smiled, like a star, in the misty gloom,
And it sent abroad a soft perfume,
Which is floating around me still.

I sat by the lily's bell,
And I watched it many a day;
The leaves, that rose in a flowing swell,
Grew faint and dim, then drooped and fell,
And the flower had flown away.

I looked where the leaves were laid,
In withering paleness, by;
And, as gloomy thoughts stole on me, said,
There is many a sweet and blooming maid,
Who will soon as dimly die.

THE BROKEN HEART.

He has gone to the land where the dead are still,
And mute the song of gladness;
He drank at the cup of grief his fill,
And his life was a dream of madness;
The victim of fancy's torturing spell,
From hope to darkness driven,
His agony was the rack of Hell,
His joy the thrill of Heaven.

He has gone to the land where the dead are cold,
And thought will sting him — never;
The tomb its darkest veil has rolled
O'er all his faults for ever;
O, there was a light that shone within
The gloom that hung around him;
His heart was formed to woo and win,
But love had never crowned him.

He has gone to the land where the dead may rest
In a soft, unbroken slumber,
Where the pulse, that swelled his anguished breast,
Shall never his tortures number;
Ah! little the reckless witlings know,
How keenly throbbed and smarted
That bosom, which burned with a brightest glow,
Till crushed and broken-hearted.

He longed to love, and a frown was all
The cold and thoughtless gave him;
He sprang to Ambition's trumpet-call,
But back they rudely drave him:
He glowed with a spirit pure and high,
They called the feeling madness:
And he wept for woe with a melting eye,
'T was weak and moody sadness.

He sought, with an ardor full and keen,
To rise to a noble station,
But repulsed by the proud, the cold, the mean,
He sunk in desperation;
They called him away to Pleasure's bowers,
But gave him a poisoned chalice,
And from her alluring wreath of flowers
They glanced the grin of malice.

He felt that the charm of life was gone,
That his hopes were chilled and blasted,
That being wearily lingered on
In sadness, while it lasted;
He turned to the picture fancy drew,
Which he thought would darken never;
It fled; — to the damp, cold grave he flew
And he sleeps with the dead for ever.

TO SENECA LAKE.

On thy fair bosom, silver lake!
The wild swan spreads his snowy sail,
And round his breast the ripples break,
As down he bears before the gale.

On thy fair bosom, waveless stream!
The dipping paddle echoes far,
And flashes in the moonlight gleam,
And bright reflects the polar star.

The waves along thy pebbly shore,
As blows the north-wind, heave their foam,
And curl around the dashing oar,
As late the boatman hies him home.

How sweet, at set of sun, to view
Thy golden mirror spreading wide,
And see the mist of mantling blue
Float round the distant mountain's side.

At midnight hour, as shines the moon,
  A sheet of silver spreads below,
And swift she cuts, at highest noon,
  Light clouds, like wreaths of purest snow.

On thy fair bosom, silver lake!
  O, I could ever sweep the oar,
When early birds at morning wake,
  And evening tells us toil is o'er.

O, HAD I the wings of a swallow, I 'd fly
Where the roses are blossoming all the year long,
Where the landscape is always a feast to the eye,
And the bills of the warblers are ever in song;
O, then I would fly from the cold and the snow,
And hie to the land of the orange and vine,
And carol the winter away in the glow,
That rolls o'er the ever green bowers of the line.

Indeed, I should gloomily steal o'er the deep,
Like the storm-loving petrel, that skims there, alone;
I would take me a dear little martin to keep
A sociable flight to the tropical zone:
How cheerily, wing by wing, over the sea
We would fly from the dark clouds of winter away,
And for ever our song and our twitter should be,
"To the land where the year is eternally gay."

We would nestle awhile in the jessamine bowers,
And take up our lodge in the crown of the palm,
And live, like the bee, on its fruits and its flowers,
That always are flowing with honey and balm;
And there we would stay, till the winter is o'er,
And April is checkered with sunshine and rain,—
O, then we would flit from that far-distant shore
Over island and wave to our country again.

How light we would skim, where the billows are rolled
Through clusters that bend with the cane and the lime;
And break on the beaches in surges of gold,
When morning comes forth in her loveliest prime:
We would touch for a while, as we traversed the ocean,
At the islands that echoed to Waller and Moore,
And winnow our wings with an easier motion
Through the breath of the cedar that blows from the shore.

And when we had rested our wings, and had fed
On the sweetness that comes from the junipêr groves,
By the spirit of home and of infancy led,
We would hurry again to the land of our loves;
And when from the breast of the ocean would spring,
Far off in the distance, that dear native shore,
In the joy of our hearts we would cheerily sing,
"No land is so lovely when winter is o'er."

RETROSPECTION.

There are moments in life which are never forgot,
Which brighten and brighten as time steals away;
They give a new charm to the happiest lot,
And they shine on the gloom of the loneliest day:
These moments are hallowed by smiles and by tears;
The first look of love, and the last parting given;
As the sun, in the dawn of his glory, appears,
And the cloud weeps and glows with the rainbow in heaven.

There are hours, there are minutes, which memory
brings,
Like blossoms of Eden, to twine round the heart;
And as time rushes by on the might of his wings,
They may darken awhile, but they never depart:
O, these hallowed remembrances cannot decay,
But they come on the soul with a magical thrill;
And in days that are darkest, they kindly will stay,
And the heart, in its last throb, will beat with them
still.

They come, like the dawn in its loveliness, now,
The same look of beauty, that shot to my soul;
The snows of the mountain are bleached on her
brow,
And her eyes, in the blue of the firmament, roll:
The roses are dim by her cheek's living bloom,
And her coral lips part, like the opening of flowers;
She moves through the air in a cloud of perfume,
Like the wind from the blossoms of jessamine
bowers.

From her eye's melting azure there sparkles a flame,
That kindled my young blood to ecstasy's glow;
She speaks, — and the tones of her voice are the
same
As would once, like the wind-harp, in melody flow:
That touch, as her hand meets and mingles with
mine,
Shoots along to my heart with electrical thrill;
'T was a moment for earth too supremely divine,
And while life lasts, its sweetness shall cling to me
still.

We met, — and we drank from the crystalline well
That flows from the fountain of science above;
On the beauties of thought we would silently dwell,
Till we looked — though we never were talking of
love;

We parted, — the tear glistened bright in her eye,
And her melting hand shook, as I dropped it for
ever;
O, that moment will always be hovering by!
Life may frown, — but its light shall abandon me —
never.

CALM AT SEA.

The night is clear,
The sky is fair,
The wave is resting on the ocean;
And far and near
The silent air
Just lifts the flag with faintest motion.

There is no gale
To fill the sail,
No wind to heave the curling billow;
The streamers droop,
And trembling stoop,
Like boughs, that crown the weeping willow.

From off the shore
Is heard the roar
Of waves in softest motion rolling;
The twinkling stars,
And whispering airs,
Are all to peace the heart controlling.

The moon is bright,
Her ring of light,
In silver, pales the blue of heaven,
Or tints with gold,
Where lightly rolled,
Like fleecy snow, the rack is driven.

How calm and clear
The silent air!
How smooth and still the glassy ocean!
While stars above
Seem lamps of love,
To light the temple of devotion.

THE QUEEN OF FLOWERS.

I AM the light, fantastic queen of flowers;
I call the wind-rose from its bed of snow,
I pour upon the springing turf soft showers,
I paint the buds of jasmine, when they blow,
I give the violet leaf its tender blue,
I dip its cup in night's unsullied tears,
So that it shines with richer glances through,
Like beauty heightened by a maiden's fears;
Around the elm's green arch I freely twine
The wooing tendrils of the clasping vine,
And when the vernal air is fresh with dew,
And the new sward with drops bedighted o'er,
I lend the buttercup its golden hue,
That glitters like a leaf of molten ore;
I dress the lily in its veil of lawn
Whiter than foam upon the crested wave,
Pure as the spirit parted from its grave,
When every stain that earth had left is gone,
Shining beneath the mellow sun of May,
Like pearls fresh-gathered from their glossy shells,
Or tints that on the pigeon's plumage play,
When filled with love his tender bosom swells;
I throw Aurora o'er the cup of gold
The tulip lifts to catch the tears of heaven,
Gay as the cloud whose ever-changing fold
Heralds the dawn, and proudly curtains even;
I take the rainbow, as it glides away
To mingle with the pure, unshaded sky,

And, melting in one drop its bright array,
I pour it in the crown-imperial's eye;
I weave the silken fringe, that, as a vest,
Mantles the fleur-de-lis in glossy down,
I scatter gold spots on its open breast,
And lift in slender points of blue its crown:
I am the light, fantastic queen of flowers,
My bed is in the bosom of a rose,
And there I sweetly dream the moonlight hours,
While vermeil curtains round my pillow close.

THE SPIRIT OF THE AIR.

I AM the spirit of the viewless air,
Upon the rolling clouds I plant my throne,
I move serenely, when the fleet winds bear
My palace in its flight, from zone to zone;
High on the mountain top I sit alone,
Shrouding behind a veil of night my form,
And when the trumpet of assault has blown,
Career upon the pinions of the storm;
By me the gales of morning sweetly blow,
Waving, along the bank, the bending flowers;
'T is at my touch the clouds dissolving flow,
When flitting o'er the sky, in silent showers;
I send the breeze to play among the bowers,
And curl the light-green ripples on the lake;
I call the sea-wind in the sultry hours,
And all his train of gentle airs awake;
I lead the zephyr on the dewy lawn
To gather up the pearls that speck it o'er,
And when the coolness of the night has gone,
I send it where the willows crown the shore;
I sit within the circle of the moon,
When the fair planet smiles, and brightly throws
Around the radiance of her clearest noon,
Till every cloud that passes by her glows,
When folds of fleecy vapor hang the sky,
Borne on the night-wind through the silent air,

And as they float, the stars seem rushing by,
And the moon glides away in glory there;
I lead the wild-fowl, when his untried wing
Boldly ascends the vernal arch of blue,
Before him on his airy path I fling
A magic light, that safely guides him through;
When lost in distant haze, I send his cry
Floating in mellow tones along the wind,
Then like a speck of light he hurries by,
And hills, and woods, and lakes are left behind:
When clouds are gathering, or when whirlwinds
blow,
When heaven is dark with storms, or brightly fair,
Where'er the viewless waves of ether flow,
Calm, or in tempest rolling, I am there.

LIBERTY TO ATHENS.

THE flag of freedom floats once more
Around the lofty Parthenon;
It waves, as waved the palm of yore,
In days departed long and gone;
As bright a glory, from the skies,
Pours down its light around those towers,
And once again the Greeks arise,
As in their country's noblest hours;
Their swords are girt in virtue's cause,
Minerva's sacred hill is free; —
O, may she keep her equal laws,
While man shall live, and time shall be!

The pride of all her shrines went down;
The Goth, the Frank, the Turk, had reft
The laurel from her civic crown;
Her helm by many a sword was cleft:
She lay among her ruins low, —
Where grew the palm, the cypress rose,
And, crushed and bruised by many a blow,
She cowered beneath her savage foes;

But now again she springs from earth,
Her loud, awakening trumpet speaks;
She rises in a brighter birth,
And sounds redemption to the Greeks.

It is the classic jubilee ;—
Their servile years have rolled away;
The clouds that hovered o'er them flee,
They hail the dawn of freedom's day;
From Heaven the golden light descends,
The times of old are on the wing,
And Glory there her pinion bends,
And Beauty wakes a fairer spring;—
The hills of Greece, her rocks, her waves,
Are all in triumph's pomp arrayed;
A light that points their tyrants' graves
Plays round each bold Athenian's blade.

The Parthenon, the sacred shrine
Where Wisdom held her pure abode:
The hill of Mars, where light divine
Proclaimed the true, but unknown God;
Where Justice held unyielding sway,
And trampled all corruption down,
And onward took her lofty way
To reach at Truth's unfading crown:
The rock, where Liberty was full,
Where Eloquence her torrents rolled,
And loud, against the despot's rule,
A knell the patriot's fury tolled:
The stage, whereon the drama spake,
In tones that seemed the words of Heaven,
Which made the wretch in terror shake,
As by avenging furies driven:
The groves and gardens, where the fire
Of wisdom, as a fountain, burned,
And every eye, that dared aspire
To truth, has long in worship turned:
The halls and porticoes, where trod
The moral sage, severe, unstained,

And where the intellectual God
In all the light of science reigned:
The schools, where rose in symmetry
The simple, but majestic pile,
Where marble threw its roughness by,
To glow, to frown, to weep, to smile,
Where colors made the canvas live,
Where Music rolled her flood along,
And all the charms that art can give
Were blent with beauty, love, and song:
The port, from whose capacious womb
Her navies took their conquering road,
The heralds of an awful doom
To all, who would not kiss her rod:
On these a dawn of glory springs,
These trophies of her brightest fame;
Away the long-chained city flings
Her weeds, her shackles, and her shame;
Again her ancient souls awake,
Harmodius bares anew his sword;
Her sons in wrath their fetters break,
And Freedom is their only lord.

THE GREEK EMIGRANT'S SONG.

Now launch the boat upon the wave, —
The wind is blowing off the shore, —
I will not live, a cowering slave,
In these polluted islands, more:
Beyond the wild, dark-heaving sea,
There is a better home for me!

The wind is blowing off the shore,
And out to sea the streamers fly, —
My music is the dashing roar,
My canopy the stainless sky, —
It bends above so fair a blue,
That Heaven seems opening on my view.

I will not live a cowering slave,
Though all the charms of life may shine
Around me, and the land, the wave,
And sky be drawn in tints divine; —
Give lowering skies and rocks to me,
If there my spirit can be free!

Sweeter than spicy gales, that blow
From orange-groves with wooing breath,
The winds may from these islands flow, —
But 't is an atmosphere of death;
The lotus, which transformed the brave
And haughty to a willing slave.

Softer than Minder's winding stream,
The wave may ripple on this coast;
And brighter than the morning beam,
In golden swell, be round it tost; —
Give me a rude and stormy shore,
So power can never threat me more!

Brighter than all the tales they tell
Of Eastern pomp and pageantry,
Our sunset skies in glory swell,
Hung round with glowing tapestry; —
The horrors of a wintry storm
Swell brighter o'er a freeman's form!

The spring may here with autumn twine,
And both combined may rule the year,
And fresh-blown flowers and racy wine
In frosted clusters still be near; —
Dearer the wild and snowy hills,
Where hale and ruddy Freedom smiles!

Beyond the wild, dark-heaving sea,
And ocean's stormy vastness o'er,
There is a better home for me,
A welcomer and dearer shore;
There hands, and hearts, and souls, are twined,
And free the man, and free the mind.

ODE TO FREEDOM.

SPIRIT of the days of old!
Ere the generous heart grew cold;
When the pulse of life was strong,
And the breath of vengeance long;
When, with jealous sense, the heart
Felt the least indignant smart;
When, alive at every pore,
Honor no injustice bore,
But, like lions on their prey,
Sprang and washed the stain away;
When the patriot's blood was shed
At the shrine where valor bled;
When the bard, with kindling song,
Roused them to avenge their wrong;
When the thought of insult, deep
In the heart, could never sleep,
But, though cherished many a day,
Still at last it burst its way,
Rolling with impetuous tide,
Till the foeman crouched or died.

Spirit of the days of yore!
When the lofty hero bore,
On his brow, and on his crest,
Signs of thought, that could not rest;
When the eager, active soul
Spurned, and broke through all control,
Nature was his only rule,
Feeling taught his only school;
When his vigorous frame was nursed,
By no arts that poison cursed;
When his heart was firm to will,
And his hand was strong to kill;
When he sternly struggled through
All that he resolved to do;
When he recked not if his path
Smiled in peace, or frowned in wrath;

When he started at the call
Country gave, and left his all,
Onward trod to front the foe,
Nerved to deal the deadly blow;
When the fight, to him, was play;
When he cared not if his way
Led to victory, or the grave,—
Either fate becomes the brave:
Days of strength gigantic! fled,
Valor sleeps, and fame is dead.

Spirit of the bold and free!
Mountain breath of liberty;
Parent of a hardy breed,
Fiery as the Arab steed;
Master of the mighty charm;
Knitter of the brawny arm,
Of the knee that cannot kneel,
Heart of oak, and nerve of steel;
Ruler of the craggy wild;
On a throne of granite piled,
Like a giant altar, thou
Biddest all who love thee bow,
Bend the neck, and fold the knee,
To no conqueror but thee;
In that hold thou bidst them wait,
Till some proud, ambitious state,
Marching in the pomp of war,
Spread its flaunting banner far,
And, with high and threatening breath,
Call to slavery, or death;
Then thou bidst them gird the brand,
Plant the foot, and raise the hand,
Draw the panting nostril wide,
And, with stern and stately stride,
Forward, like the eagle's wing,
On the proud invader spring,
And, in one resistless rush,
All his power and splendor crush.

Spirit of the great and good!
Such as, in Athenæ, stood,
Stern in justice, on the rock,
Moveless at the people's shock,
And when civil tempest raged,
And intestine war was waged,
With serene, but awful sway,
Rolled the maddening tide away:
Such as met at Pylæ's wall,
Ere that glorious Freedom's fall, —
When the life of Greece was young,
Like the sun from ocean sprung,
And the warm and lifted soul
Marching onward to its goal:
Such as at those holy gates,
Bulwark of the banded states,
With the hireling Persian strove,
In the high and ardent love
Souls that cannot stoop to shame
Bear to Freedom's sacred name:
Such as with the Saxon flew,
Ever to their country true,
From the rock, the wood, the fen,
From the cavern and the den,
Eager to the field of fight,
Like a cloud that comes by night,
Tore away, at once, the chain
Fastened by the robber Dane,
Drove him headlong from that shore,
And embalmed his host in gore;
Then secured their country's cause
With a bond of equal laws,
And bequeathed the sacred trust,
When their bones should fall in dust,
To that island race, who bear
Light, and warmth, and glory, where
Ocean's unchained billows roll
From the mid-day to the pole;
And to that more daring shoot,
Bent with flowers and promised fruit,

Who have dared, beyond the sea,
To assert their liberty,
Who, upon the forted hill,
Braved a tyrant father's will,
Down the bloody gauntlet threw,
Grasped and snapped the links in two;
And unshackled ventured forth,
Noblest of the sons of earth.

Spirit of the stirring blood,
Rolling in an even flood
Through the hale and ruddy cheek;
Scorner of the pale and weak,
Who in festering cities crawl,
Victims of a sordid thrall,
And for ever draw their breath,
Lingering on the brink of death:
But to thee the giant limb,
Strong to leap, to run, to swim,
Strong to guide the plough or brand,
Guard, or free, or till their land;
But to thee the godlike frame,
Such as puts our dwarfs to shame,
Firm, erect, and fair, as first
Adam from his Maker burst,
And exulting leaped to see
His angelic symmetry;
But to thee the eagle eye,
Lifted to its parent sky,
Drinking in the living stream,
And again, with ardent beam,
Sending all its fires abroad,
Like the language of a god;
But to thee the mighty brow,
Fixed to dare, unused to bow,
Now in placid kindness bright,
Like a rock in evening's light,
Then with anger's wrinkled frown,
Gathered eyebrows lowering down,

Awful as the storm whose fold
Round a columned Alp is rolled;
But to thee the mind of fire
Toil can never damp or tire,
Glancing, like a sunbeam, through
Nature with a spirit's view,
And from out its choicest store,
In its fulness flowing o'er,
Sending, like a bolt, the flow
Of thought upon the crowd below.

Healthful Spirit! at this hour
There are haunts where thou hast power, —
Haunts where thou shalt ever be,
As thou ever hast been, free;
Where the stream of life is led
Stainless in its virgin bed,
And its magic fire is still
Blazing on its holy hill.
There are mountains, there are storms,
Where thou feed'st thy hives and swarms,
Whence thou send'st them, to restore
Virtue, where it dwells no more;
Safe in those embattled rocks
Life its native vigor locks,
And its kindling energy
Lives, and moves, and feels in thee;
In those bulwarks is our trust,
For the boundless power is just,
Nor wilt thou from earth arise,
Linked with justice, to the skies,
But below, with mercy, dwell,
Till the world shall hear its knell.

LOVE OF STUDY.

There are many youths, and some men, who most earnestly devote themselves to solitary studies, from the mere love of the pursuit. I have here attempted to give some of the causes of a devotion which appears so unaccountable to the stirring world.

AND wherefore does the student trim his lamp,
And watch his lonely taper, when the stars
Are holding their high festival in heaven,
And worshipping around the midnight throne?
And wherefore does he spend so patiently,
In deep and voiceless thought, the blooming hours
Of youth and joyance, when the blood is warm,
And the heart full of buoyancy and fire?

The sun is on the waters, and the air
Breathes with a stirring energy; the plants
Expand their leaves, and swell their buds, and blow,
Wooing the eye, and stealing on the soul
With perfume and with beauty. Life awakes;
Its wings are waving, and its fins at play
Glancing from out the streamlets, and the voice
Of love and joy is warbled in the grove;
And children sport upon the springing turf,
With shouts of innocent glee, and youth is fired
With a diviner passion, and the eye
Speaks deeper meaning, and the cheek is filled,
At every tender motion of the heart,
With purer flushings; for the boundless power
That rules all living creatures now has sway;
In man refined to holiness, a flame
That purifies the heart it feeds upon:
And yet the searching spirit will not blend
With this rejoicing, these attractive charms
Of the glad season; but, at wisdom's shrine,
Will draw pure draughts from her unfathomed well,
And nurse the never-dying lamp, that burns
Brighter and brighter on, as ages roll.

He has his pleasures, — he has his reward:
For there is in the company of books,
The living souls of the departed sage,
And bard, and hero, — there is in the roll
Of eloquence and history, which speak
The deeds of early and of better days, —
In these, and in the visions that arise
Sublime in midnight musings, and array
Conceptions of the mighty and the good,
There is an elevating influence,
That snatches us awhile from earth, and lifts
The spirit, in its strong aspirings, where
Superior beings fill the court of heaven.
And thus his fancy wanders, and has talk
With high imaginings, and pictures out
Communion with the worthies of old time:
And then he listens, in his passionate dreams,
To voices in the silent gloom of night,
As of the blind Meonian, when he struck
Wonder from out his harp-strings, and rolled on
From rhapsody to rhapsody, deep sounds,
That imitate the ocean's boundless roar;
Or tones of horror, which the drama spake,
Reverberated through the hollow mask,
Like sounds which rend the sepulchres of kings,
And tell of deeds of darkness, which the grave
Would burst its marble portals to reveal;
Or his, who latest in the holy cause
Of freedom lifted to the heavens his voice,
Commanding, and beseeching, and, with all
The fervor of his spirit poured abroad,
Urging the sluggish souls of self-made slaves
To emulate their fathers, and be free;
Or those which in the still and solemn shades
Of Academus, from the wooing tongue
Of Plato, charmed the youth, the man, the sage,
Discoursing of the perfect and the pure,
The beautiful and holy, till the sound
That played around his eloquent lips became

The honey of persuasion, and was heard
As oracles amid Dodona's groves.
With eye upturned, watching the many stars,
And ear in deep attention fixed, he sits,
Communing with himself, and with the world,
The universe around him, and with all
The beings of his memory and his hopes;
Till past becomes reality, and joys,
That beckon in the future, nearer draw,
And ask fruition. — O, there is a pure,
A hallowed feeling in these midnight dreams;
They have the light of heaven around them, breathe
The odor of its sanctity, and are
Those moments taken from the sands of life,
Where guilt makes no intrusion, but they bloom
Like islands flowering on Arabia's wild.
And there is pleasure in the utterance
Of pleasant images in pleasant words,
Melting like melody into the ear,
And stealing on in one continual flow,
Unruffled and unbroken. It is joy
Ineffable to dwell upon the lines
That register our feelings, and portray,
In colors always fresh and ever new,
Emotions that were sanctified, and loved,
As something far too tender, and too pure,
For forms so frail and fading. I have sat,
In days when sensibility was young,
And the heart beat responsive to the sight,
The touch, and music of the lovely one, —
Yes, I have sat entranced, enraptured, till
The spirit would have utterance, and words
Flowed full of hope, and love, and melody,
The gushings of an overburdened heart
Drunk with enchantment, bursting freely forth,
Like fountains in the early days of spring.

HEAVEN.

The following effusion may serve to explain one of the mysteries of mythology, — the location of heaven above us.

I HAD been sitting at a feast of souls,
A banquet of pure spirits, where the thought
Spoke on the eloquent tongue, and in the eye's
Gay sparkle, and the ever-changing play
Of feature, like the twinkling glance of waves
Beneath the summer moonlight. I walked forth;
It was a night in autumn, and the moon
Was visible through clouds of opal, laced
With gold and carmine, — such a silent night
As fairies love to dance and revel in,
When winds are hushed, and leaves are still, and waves
Are sleeping on the waters, and the hum
And stir of life reposing. There was spread
Before my sight a smooth and glossy bay,
Mirrored in silver brightness, and the chime
Of rippling waters on its pebbles broke
Alone the quietude that filled the air:
But when the tremulous heaving of the deep,
Far off, along its sandy barriers, rose
And faintly echoed, as the fitful gust
Ruffled the placid surface glassed below;
Or at the call of night-birds, where they flew
And sported in the sedges, low and sweet,
Like swallows twittering, or the cooing voice
Of ring-doves, when they brood their callow young.
I looked abroad on sea and mountain, wild
And cultured field, and garden, and they lay,
Amid the stillness of the elements,
Silent, and motionless, and beautiful,
For mist and moonlight softened down their forms,
And covered them with dim transparency,
Like beauty melting through her Coan veil;
A wind rose from the ocean, as it rolled

Blue in the boundless distance, and it swept
The curtained clouds athwart the moon, and gave
The undimmed azure of the sky to light
And full expansion. There my eyes were turned,
And there they found the magic influence
Which bound them, like enchantment, in a trance
Of most exalted feeling, and the soul
Was lifted from the body, and became
A portion of the purity and light
And loveliness of that cerulean dome:
And it imagined on the mountain top,
Now silvered with the milder beam of night,
On the blue arch, and on the rolling moon,
Careering through the host of stars, who seemed
To worship at her coming, and put out
The brightness of their twinkling when she moved
Serenely and majestically by, —
On these, and on the snowy clouds, that hung
Their curtains round the border of the sky,
Like folds of silken tapestry, it laid
A world of tenderness and purity,
The quiet habitation of the heart,
The resting-place of those impassioned souls
Who draw their inspiration at the founts
Of nature, flowing from that theatre
Whose scene is ever shifting with the play
Of seasons, as the year steals swiftly on,
And bears us, with its silent foot, away
To dissolution; ardent souls, who love
The rude rock, and the frowning precipice,
The winding valley, where it lies in green
Along the bubbling riv'let, and the plain,
Parted in field and meadow, redolent
Of roses in the flowery days of spring,
And in the nights of autumn, of the breath
Of frosted clusters, hung along the vines
In blue and gushing festoons, in whose rind
The drink of souls, the nectar of the gods,
Ripens beneath the warm, unclouded sky.

I looked upon this loveliness, until
A dream came o'er me, and the firmament
Was animate, and spirits filled the air,
Floating on snowy wings, and rustled by,
Fanning the wind to coolness; and they came
On messages of kindness, and they sought
The pillow of o'er-wearied toil, and shook
The dews of Lethe from their dripping plumes
Around his temples, till his mind forgot
Its sad realities, and happy dreams
Rose fair and sweet around him, and restored
Awhile the spotless hours of infancy,
When life is one enchantment! Then I seemed
Rapt in a trance of ecstasy, and forms
Stood thronging round supremely beautiful,
Whose looks were full of tenderness, whose words
Were glances, and whose melodies were smiles;
Who uttered forth the feelings of the soul
In that expressive dialect whose tones
No tongue can syllable, the unseen chain
Which links those hearts that beat in unison.
It was that perfect meeting whither tend
Our spirits in their better hours, and find
The balm of wounded bosoms, where they dream
The eye of mercy ever smiles, and peace
For ever broods: — they call the vision Heaven.

And thus hath man imagined he can find
The region of his angels, and his gods,
And blessed spirits, somewhere in the sky;
Or in the moon, to which the Indian turns,
And dreams it is a cool and quiet land,
Where insect cannot sting, nor tiger prowl;
Or on the cone of mountains, where the snow,
Purest of all material things, is laid
Upon a cloudy pillow, wreathed around
The midway height, and parting from this world
Olympus and the Swerga's holy bowers.

A PICTURE.

THERE is a fountain of the purest wave: —
It ever floweth full and freshly on,
Laughing beneath the fairest light of heaven,
And chiming, like the tender voice of birds,
Within a dewy thicket, when the morn
Comes forth in beauty, and the winds awake
To sip the moisture in the lily's bell.

The spring is hidden in a silent cave,
The shrine of darkness and of loneliness,
And then it stealeth out to meet the sun,
And shine beneath his brightness, and reveal
The crystal of its purity, and play,
In dove-like undulations, with the airs
That gently come and kiss it, with a breath
Perfumed among the roses, till they lend
A sweetness to the waters, like the rills
That spout from marble wells in Asian bowers.

And where it cometh forth to meet the light,
The rock is tapestried in mossy green,
For ever freshening with the sprinkled dews,
And always young in verdure, as when Spring
Throws her new mantle o'er the turf, until
The eye reposes on it, as a balm
That, with its tender soothings, wins the heart
To thoughts of purity and gentleness;
For there is in the sight of fairy forms,
And mellow tinctures, and dissolving shades, —
And in the sound of rustling leaves, and waves,
That murmur into slumber, and of birds
Saluting, with their cheery notes, the dawn,
And pouring out the loneliness of heart
A rifled mother feels, when o'er her nest
She sits and sees her young ones stolen away, —
And in the scent of gardens, and young vines,

And violet beds along the meadow brooks,
There is a sweet attraction, which doth blend
The spirit with the life of outward things,
And it partaketh then in all the joy
Of Nature, when she riseth from her sleep,
And throweth out her vigor to the winds,
And boundeth in her ecstasy, as fawns
Leap in the very wantonness of heart,
When life is all exuberance and fire.

It floweth on embanked in freshest turf,
Bending its margin low to meet the clear,
Cool element, and slake its thirst therein,
And bathe its roots, like silken threads, that play,
Waving and streaming with the current's fall.
Its flow is over pebbles and bright sands,
Which, from the curling waters flashing out,
Inlay the channel with mosaic, where
The white flint shines like pearl, the agate glows
With playful tints, dove-like or pavonine,
Catching new splendor from the wave; the while
Smooth-rounded stones, deep blue and ebony,
And slaty flakes of red and russet-brown,
Lie darker in their brightness, as when gems
Sparkle from out the chilly night of caves.

Above it elms and poplars, — trees that love
The bank of meadow brooks: those with their limbs
Light-arching in a platted canopy;
These rising in a pyramid of boughs,
And glancing with their many twinkling leaves,
Bright in their varnished verdure, when they drink
The pure light in their stillness; when at play,
Checkered with freshest green and snowy down.
Beside them willows droop to kiss the wave,
That calmly crinkles by them, and they dip
Their waving twigs, so that their silken leaves
Ruffle the water to a circling curl,
Widening and lessening to the turfy shore.

From out its bosom islets lift their turfs
Of alder and of sedges, where the wind
Plays through the pointed blades, and murmuring lulls
The dreamer, who reposes on the brink,
And gazes on the ever-changing play
Of bubble and of ripple, of light plumes
Moving like pigmy vessels, as the breath
Of summer fills their fan-like sail, and throws
A sudden dimple o'er the mirrored stream.
Flowers too are on its borders; flags in blue
Carpet the hollow, roses on the knoll
Open their clustered crimson, cardinals
Lift, on the shady margin, spikes of fire,
And one,* whose feathered stem, and starry bloom
Of glossy yellow, wafted in the flow,
Floats, like a sleeping Naiad, on the wave.

MENTAL BEAUTY.

"Bellezze . . . .
Piu ch'n guisa mortal soavi e liete."—PETRARCA.

BEAUTY has gone, but yet her mind is still
As beautiful as ever; still the play
Of light around her lips has every charm
Of childhood in its freshness: Love has there
Stamped his unfading impress, and the hues
Of fancy shine around her, as the sun
Gilds at his setting some decaying tower,
With feathered moss and ivy overgrown.
I knew her in the dawning of her charms,
When the new rose first opened, and its sweets
No wind had wasted. She was of those forms
Apelles might have painted for the queen

* Ranunculus fluitans.

Of loveliness and love, — light as the fays
Dancing on glimmering dew-drops, when the moon
Rides in her silver softness, and the world
Is calm and brightly beautiful below.
She was all mildness, and the melting tone
Of her sweet voice thrilled me, and seemed to flow
Into my soul, a stream of melody,
Delicious in its mellowness; it spake
A heart at ease; — and then the quiet smile
Sat playing on her lips, that, pouting, spread
Their vermeil freshness forth, as if to ask
The kiss of him she smiled on. In her eye
Gentleness had its dwelling, and light Mirth
Glanced out in sudden flashes, and keen Wit
Shot arrows which delighted, while they stung.
She was a young Medusa, ere she knew
The evil of a world that watched to blast
Her loveliness, and make it terrible;
Striking a dead, cold horror on the heart
Of him who saw the fairest of all things,
A lovely woman, made the common prey
Of lawless passion, — but it touched not HER:
No mist breathed o'er her brightness; but the pure
Full light of virtue rested there, and shed
New lustre on the light that ever came
Through her transparent features, and revealed
Each movement of the soul that swelled within:
And they were all of Heaven, — such high desires
As angels had been proud of, — pure as light
In its primeval fountain, ere it flowed
To mingle with the elements, and lose
Its perfect clearness. She was as a flower
New opened in a valley, where no foot
Had trodden, and no living thing had left
Print of the world's pollution: there she blew
Fragrant and lovely, and a parent's hand
Shielded her from the winds that blast, or bring
Poison upon their wings, and taint the heart
Left open to their influence. Shielded there

She ripened all her treasures, and became
Full-blown and rich in her maturity,—
The dwelling of a spirit not of earth,
But ever mingling with the pure and high
Conceptions of a soul that spreads its wings
To fly where Mind, when boldest, dared to soar.
And though the form has withered, and the bloom
Has faded, she is lovely; for the sounds
That issue from her lips, and flow around
In liquid eloquence, are oracles
Of more than ancient wisdom, or they speak
Portions of that full hymn of Poesy,
Which ever rises when a mind on fire
Blends with the majesty of outward things;
And with the glories of a boundless heaven,
And a rich earth, and ever-rolling sea
Communing, swells to that ineffable
Fruition, which in hope will never end.

MENTAL HARMONY.

"Animæ dimidium meæ." — HORAT.

WE have had pleasant hours, but they are gone;
And we shall never meet again, to spend
Glad moments in the kindly intercourse
Of blended thought and feeling; they are gone,
Those festivals of fancy and of hope,
Those May-days of the spirit, when the voice
Of nature had a sweetness wholly new
And most delightful to me, and the form
And fashion of all creatures took a tint
From the fair light within me; when we gave
Days to such higher thoughts as lend to life
A swifter pinion, that the flow of hours
Be as the falling of a quiet stream,
Whose current has no sound or sign to tell

It hath an onward motion, and the sun
Go to his setting, and we know it not,
Time steals on such a silent wing away.

There is a holy feeling in the trance
Of thought; it is a calm and quiet sense
Of purer being; we have known such hours,
And they shall be remembered. Who would lose
The memory of our blessings, and the light
The recollection of departed days
Of a serener pleasure, and a deep
And happy friendship, tranquillized and raised
To more exalted union, such as bound
Two intellects in elder time, who loved
To meet in fond endearment, and to lend
In mutual talk their fullest thoughts, — the light
Such recollection pours into the heart,
Till we are circled with a hallowed sphere
Of bright emotions, — who would lose, one day,
Remembrances so gracious, for the wild,
Mad tempest of ambition, or the gay
And glittering dance of pleasure, or the pomp
The rich man piles around him? I could walk,
At the pale hour of twilight, on the path
The willow-tree o'ershadows, by the brink
Of a small run of water, and be wrapped
In a deep loneliness, and yet find more
That has in it an ecstasy, in thoughts
Cast back upon the quick hours we have known
In our long, woodland wanderings, and the sights
That we have mutely gazed on, spread o'er hill,
And plain, and sheeted ocean, than in all
Hope ever promised to my ardent youth
In the bright path of honor, or the way
That winds through roses, sweetly leading on
Its eager victim to the Bower of Love.

Nature hath lent us, with a bounteous hand,
Wherewith to make us happy, and if we

Take not the kindly offer, 't is the fault
Of our perverted hearts, which cannot find
Beauty is what is open unto all.
I have resolved within me, that the still
And pure possession of my own free thoughts
Surpasses earthly treasures, and is life
Heightened to a superior essence; hence
The wild woods are my chosen haunt, and there
I read a fairer tome, a richer page,
Than pen of man has traced with characters
Of reason or of fancy. I become,
In the society of untaught things,
Drawn from my duller and my grosser sense,
And lifted in my longings, and I learn
How little there is great in the pursuit
Of riches or of honor, how the mind,
Let in the channel of heroic thought
To flow in freedom onward, and pervade
The purer regions of philosophy,
And tasteful and impassioned poesy, —
How mind alone is the true worth of man,
And that which raises him above the sense
Of meaner creatures, and permits a hope
Of unembodied being, in a high
And holy dwelling, lifted far above
The reach of tempest, with essential light
Encircled, and with fairest wings of love
O'ershadowed, the reward and resting-place
Of such as hold their journey patiently,
And pause and faint not on their weary way.

The recollection of one upward hour
Hath more in it to tranquillize and cheer
The darkness of despondency, than years
Of gayety and pleasure. Then, alone
We wander not in solitude, but find
Friends in all things around us, for the heart
Sinks not, and in its sinking bends the mind
From its true lofty region, where it lives

Rejoicing in bright energy; and so
All things are open to the searching eye
Of an unclouded intellect, and bring
Their several treasures to it, and unfold
Their fabric to its scrutiny. All life,
And all inferior orders, in the waste
Of being spread before us, are to him
Who lives in meditation, and the search
Of wisdom and of beauty, open books,
Wherein he reads the Godhead, and the ways
He works through his creation, and the links
That fasten us to all things, with a sense
Of fellowship and feeling, so that we
Look not upon a cloud, or falling leaf,
Or flower new blown, or *human face divine*,
But we have caught new life, and wider thrown
The door of reason open, and have stored
In memory's secret chamber, for dark years
Of age and weariness, the food of thought,
And thus extended mind, and made it young,
When the thin hair turns gray, and feeling dies.

But this communion with inferior things
Still leaves a void behind it, and we seek
The kindred thoughts of other men, and bend
Attentive o'er their written souls, wherein
We see their better moments, when they cast
The slough of earth aside, and tried a flight
On an ascending pinion, and renewed
Their purer being, as the insect bursts
The walls that bound it in its second state,—
It might be a gilded prison-house,
But yet it was a prison: when its wing
Unfolded, and it knew the bliss of air,
And free and rapid motion, it had life,
And floated as a spirit floats away,
And wandered gayly on from flower to flower,
And was so light and so ethereal, man
Selected it the symbol of the soul,

And its free flight through ether, on a wing
That, moving through eternity, will ever
Be active and unwearied, and as bright
In its unruffled plumage, after years
Have gathered into ages, and have gone
Beyond the eldest memory of time.

But yet the pen of Genius cannot cheer
And heighten, like the spirit-speaking eye;
And so we seek the living, and we find
That there are spirits that commune with ours,
As if they were our kindred, and were formed
In the same mould; and when we meet with them,
We cling with childlike fondness, as if life
Had not a charm without them, and the sky
With its ethereal beauty, and the earth
Flowering or fading, and the fairest flow
Of pure and tranquil waters, and the words
Of the departed with their might of thought,
Could be to us no solace, and have power
To lend no high conception, nor subdue
The spirit unto meekness; so we lean
On an accordant bosom, and we love
The beating of a heart that beats as ours,
The speaking of an eye that tells us thoughts
Which harmonize with what we feel, and all
The light of beauty, passion, tenderness,
And purity, and love of great, and fair,
And fitly fashioned things, until we deem
A sole existence is a wilderness,
That yieldeth only terror, and a curse.

We two have met a little while, and known
How time may glide unnoticed, in the flow
Of thoughts that have a sympathy; we part,
But this shall be a token thou hast been
A friend to him who traced these hurried lines,
And gave them as a tribute to a friend,
And a remembrance of the few kind hours

Which lightened on the darkness of my path,
And gave a pleasantness to some bright days,
Bright in the light thou gavest them, and warmed
Feelings, that sank in chilliness, and waked
My fancy from its slumber, and thus drew
One volume from its treasures, into day.

RUINS.

"Tempus edax rerum, tuque, invidiosa vetustas,
Omnia destruitis." — OVID.

EARTH is a waste of ruins; so I deemed,
When the broad sun was sinking in the sea
Of sand, that rolled around Palmyra. Night
Shared with the dying day a lonely sky,
The canopy of regions void of life,
And still as one interminable tomb.
The shadows gathered on the desert, dark
And darker, till alone one purple arch
Marked the far place of setting. All above
Was purely azure, for no moon in heaven
Walked in her brightness, and with snowy light
Softened the deep intensity, that gave
Such awe unto the blue serenity
Of the high throne of gods, the dwelling-place
Of suns and stars, which are to us as gods,
The fountains of existence and the seat
Of all we dream of glory. Dim and vast
The ruins stood around me, — temples, fanes,
Where the bright sun was worshipped, — where they gave
Homage to him who frowns in storms, and rolls
The desert like an ocean, — where they bowed
Unto the queen of beauty, she in heaven
Who gives the night its loveliness, and smiles
Serenely on the drifted waste, and lends

A silver softness to the ridgy wave
Where the dark Arab sojourns, and with tales
Of love and beauty wears the tranquil night
In poetry away, her light the while
Falling upon him, as a spirit falls,
Dove-like or curling down in flame, a star
Sparkling amid his flowing locks, or dews
That melt in gold, and steal into the heart,
Making it one enthusiastic glow,
As if the God were present, and his voice
Spake on the eloquent lips that pour abroad
A gush of inspiration, — bright as waves
Swelling around Aurora's car, intense
With passion as the fire that ever flows
In fountains on the Caspian shore, and full
As the wide-rolling majesty of Nile.

Over these temples of an age of wild
And dark belief, and yet magnificent
In all that strikes the senses, — beautiful
In the fair forms they knelt to, and the domes
And pillars which upreared them, — full of life
In their poetic festivals, when youth
Gave loose to all its energy, in dance,
And song, and every charm the fancy weaves
In the soft twine of cultured speech, attuned
In perfect concord to the full-toned lyre:
When nations gathered to behold the pomp
That issued from the hallowed shrine in choirs
Of youths, who bounded to the minstrelsy
Of tender voices, and all instruments
Of ancient harmony, in solemn trains
Bearing the votive offerings, flowing horns
Of plenty wreathed with flowers, and gushing o'er
With the ripe clusters of the purple vine,
The violet of the fig, the scarlet flush
Of granates peeping from the parted rind,
The citron shining through its glossy leaves
In burnished gold, the carmine veiled in down,

Like mountain snow, on which the living stream
Flowed from Astarte's minion, all that hang
In Eastern gardens blended, — while the sheaf
Nods with its loaded ears, and brimming bowls
Foam with the kindling element, the joy
Of banquet, and the nectar that inspires
Man with the glories of a heightened power
To feel the touch of beauty, and combine
The scattered forms of elegance, till high
Rises a magic vision, blending all
That we have seen of glory, such as drew
Assembled Greece to worship, when the form,
Who gathered all its loveliness, arose
Dewy and blushing from the parent foam,
Than which her tint was fairer, and with hand
That seemed of living marble parted back
Her raven locks, and upward looked to Heaven,
Smiling to see all Nature bright and calm; —
Over these temples, whose long colonnades
Are parted by the hand of time, and fall
Pillar by pillar, block by block, and strew
The ground in shapeless ruin, night descends
Unmingled, and the many stars shoot through
The gaps of broken walls, and glance between
The shafts of tottering columns, marking out
Obscurely, on the dark blue sky, the form
Of Desolation, who hath made these piles
Her home, and, sitting with her folded wings,
Wraps in her dusty robe the skeletons
Of a once countless multitude, whose toil
Reared palaces and theatres, and brought
All the fair forms of Grecian art to give
Glory unto an island girt with sands
As barren as the ocean, where the grave
And stately Doric marked the solemn fane
Where wisdom dwelt, and on the fairer shrine
Of beauty sprang the light Ionian wreathed
With a soft volute, whose simplicity
Becomes the deity of loveliness,

Who with her snowy mantle, and her zone
Woven with all attractions, and her locks
Flowing as Nature bade them flow, compels
The sterner Powers to hang upon her smiles.
And there the grand Corinthian lifted high
Its flowery capital, to crown the porch
Where sat the sovereign of their hierarchy,
The monarch armed with terror, whose curled locks
Shaded a brow of thought and firm resolve,
Whose eye, deep sunk, shot out its central fires,
To blast and wither all who dared confront
The gaze of highest power; so sat their kings
Enshrined in palaces, and when they came
Thundering on their triumphal cars, all bright
With diadem of gold, and purple robe
Flashing with gems, before their rushing train
Moving in serried columns fenced in steel,
The herd of slaves obsequious sought the dust,
And gazed not as the mystic pomp rolled by.
Such were thy monarchs, Tadmor! now thy streets
Are silent, and thy walls o'erthrown, no voice
Speaks through the long, dim night of years, to tell
These were once peopled dwellings; I could dream
Some sorcerer in his moonlight wanderings reared
These wonders in an hour of sport, to mock
The stranger with the show of life, and send
Thought through the mist of ages, in the search
Of nations who are now no more, who lived
Erst in the pride of empire, ruled and swayed
Millions in their supremacy, and toiled
To pile these monuments of wealth and skill,
That here the wandering tribe might pitch its tents
Securer in their empty courts, and we,
Who have the sense of greatness, low might kneel
To ancient mind, and gather from the torn
And scattered fragments visions of the power,
And splendor, and sublimity of old,
Mocking the grandest canopy of heaven,
And imaging the pomp of Gods below.

THE VILLAGE GIRL.

> "Nature is fine in love; and where 't is fine,
> It sends some precious instance of itself
> After the thing it loves." — *Hamlet.*

I KNEW a pleasant village, in a lone
And silent valley, on the southern side
Of a long line of mountains, whence a brook
Came gently down, and in its winding flow
Stole through a pansied meadow, where a bank
Of beeches lifted up its tufted slope
To the warm sun of April, as it shone
Tenderly from a hemisphere of blue,
Purer because the earth sent rarer forth
Its dimming exhalations, on whose boughs
Yet hung the leaves of winter, with a low
And plaintive rustling telling to the winds
A sweet Æolian tale, and shining out
In glossy twinkling, as they lightly turned
Their surface to the light, and then veered back
With a quick-glancing motion; in a bend
Of that close thicket, where the mountain gust
Came not, but all was tranquil, and the turf
Was deeper greened, and the new opened flowers
Spread bolder out their tender leaves, and sent
Soft odors on the mellow air, that played
Silently in that hollow, where the quail
Sat often in the clear warm noon, and turned
Her red eye to the silver light, and shook
The dropped leaves in her playfulness; one day,
When all was purely fair, and the chill winds
Were hushed aloft, and as I upwards gazed,
The frosted fir, the pendent pine, and all
The sable groves of cedar, stood as still
As when a wood of lances wait the breath
Of the shrill horn and braying clarion,
To sink upon the line of fight, and rush
Forward to meet in conflict, — such a day,

When the young sod first quickens, and the pale
Blue eyes of weeping violets part their lids
To drink the first warm rays, I chanced to bend
My wandering foot along the grassy brink
Of the calm-flowing brooklet, pleased to take
With a quick eye its many turns, and dwell
On the clear dashing of its waterfalls,
And the soft gliding of its molten gold,
Where the sun met it curving o'er a root
That grew across its channel, or the curls,
That like a pigeon's plumage waving played
Over the sandy shallow, or the still
And tranquil mirror where it rested deep
And dark beneath a willow, — as I stood
Looking aside upon the velvet vest
Of the fresh-springing meadow, and above
Where the bent birches hung their tufted flowers,
New purpling like a silken shred, and faint
The scarlet maple buds put out, and fair
The downy willow catkins specked with gold
Their flaxen locks, when life awoke within
The leaf-buds of the forest, then I caught
In that still nook a pale and lovely girl,
With a fair hand fondling a petted lamb,
That bounded light around her, and with long
And oft-repeated fondness licked her hand,
And then renewed its gambols, though it took
Short turns, because a cord of braided blue,
The color of a dove-wing, or the sky
When a full moon shines over it, drew back
Her minion to a narrow circle, for
She thus had bound it in a silken chain,
As if it were a loved one, who would fly
To other lands, and leave her here to sing
Her sad notes to the evening wind, and tell
Her hours in weeping loneliness, and look
Where the far path came o'er the hill to catch
Her long departed lover, till the night
Hid the low vale in darkness, and her eye

Turned from the fruitless quest, and then she wept
Tenderly, and her sweet voice took a tone
In which despair was uttered, till it sunk
Trembling and fainting, as the night-wind falls
Softer along the harp-strings, till a sound
Just whispers through the air, and all is still.

There was a look of calmness in her thin
And delicate features, wasted to a shade,
Like a pure spirit musing on the dark
And sad afflictions of this life below,
And dwelling for a moment on the grief
And sickness of the better few, who trust,
In their most hopeless hours, they yet shall find
A sunshine after darkness, and a calm
After the tempest ceaseth, when the eye
Of love shall rest for ever on the friends
They late have seen departing on their long
And unreturning journey, whose cold lids
They closed with pious care, whose stiffened limbs
They laid in decent order, and composed
Their pale lips to a sweet and dying smile,
And shrouded all in whitest lawn, than which
No flaky snow falls purer, and no curl
Catches a softer tincture from the moon,
To throw a thin veil o'er the stars, and dim
Their brightness to a faint and mellow ray,
Like a lone taper through a curtain, when
Sleep broods above the hamlet, and the sound
Of life is hushed, and this alone reveals
To him who walks in darkness that two hearts
Are pouring out their fulness, or a voice,
In the low, consecrated tone of prayer,
Is talking with the Universal Soul,
And blending with the perfect purity
And majesty of Godhead, or an eye
Is watching o'er the page of lofty thought,
And catching inspiration at the shrine
Of intellect and fancy, till the heart,

Big with its high conceptions, overflows,
And then his lips pour out the eloquence
Of kindled spirit, and a purer stream
Of language, musical, and grand, and full
Of the quick life of mind, is sent abroad,
Than ever meets the anxious ear, when crowds
Drink in the rhetoric of master souls.

Her looks were purely Grecian, such as charm
Taste in an ancient statue, or a gem,
Or fair intaglio, where a perfect white,
Shaped to a nymph-like beauty, sparkles in
A ground of azure; — it was such a face
As had enamored Raphael, or inspired
The pencil of Correggio to the birth
Of a blue-eyed Madonna, or a calm
And pensive spirit looking up to heaven,
Poised on a seraph's wing high in the dome
Of an Italian temple, where the God
Of charity is worshipped, and the form
Of Him who died on Calvary adored.
Her brow was softly arched, and it was pure
And pale as marble, and the dew of death
Seemed resting there, and gave a fearful tint
To its else perfect loveliness, and told
Thoughts were at work beneath it, which might still
Erelong the life within her, but are loved,
Although we know them fatal, as we cling
To the Circean bowl, and dying grasp
At its alluring poison, which conveys
A madness to the brain which hath a touch
Of inspiration in its reveries,
And spreads around the spirit light and calm,
Till earth seems beautiful and life is heaven.

Her hair was of a sunny brown, and fine
As lines of light that stream across a cloud,
Ere the sun rises, or the scarlet tuft,
That floats beneath the green wave, where on rocks

The sea-plume clings, and throws its feeling threads,
Like flowing silk, around it. It was full,
And dropped in light profusion down her neck,
And o'er her bosom; and it parted lay
In native ringlets round her brow, and shone
Deeper beside the snow it rested on,
And that came fairer through the curling shade
That waved above it, as the sighing wind
Sent a sweet-breathing air to shake the leaves,
And crisp the sheeted water. As she hung
Her head in deepest sorrow, some few tears
Stole out and pearled her cheek, but these she brushed
With a light touch aside, and then renewed
A song, half sad, half playful, such as comes
From a crazed brain, that says, it knows not why,
A thousand things which are at first as gay
As wild mirth in a revel, and then fall
To a faint tone, in which despair alone
Can have a concord, and at last a sob
Closes it, and her glistening tears o'erflow.

She lifted up her head, and mutely gazed
Awhile upon the world above, and then
Her ashy lips were moving, but no sound
Came through their parting paleness; still it shone
With a faint hectic flush, like the last tint
The sun casts on a wreath of mists, and then
A most intense cerulean veils it o'er,
So that the sky seems tintless. As she looked
Far in the silent atmosphere, methought
Her blue eye had a fixedness, and saw
A form distinctly featured, and she rose
Half from her seat of turf, and threw her arms,
As if to meet it in a fond embrace,
And a sweet smile broke on her lips, and tears
Stood glistening on her eyelids, such quick joy
Stirred in her heart, and one faint word alone
Escaped, it was LEONI: — then she dropped

Suddenly on her grassy seat, — her head
Drooped languidly, and her long flowing locks
Showered their full ringlets o'er her, big round tears
Dropped thick and freshly through them, and her sobs
Shook her, they were so deep; she pressed her brow
And wrung her hands, and then she cast them down
Clasped on the sod beside her, shook her head,
And with a sweet low voice sighed out, "*No more.*"

She plucked the flowers that grew around, and kissed
Their purple and their yellow leaves, and long
Inhaled their perfume; then she opened wide
Her lips to the wild laugh that tells despair,
And it rang terribly around, and oft
She uttered it still louder, and her eye
Kindled and flashed intensely, and the spot
Of death stood glowing like a ring of fire
On the blue paleness of her cheek, and full
The dark veins throbbed upon her brow, and shot
Their branches o'er her temples, and she waved
Her hand, that seemed a spirit's, where the light
Shone with a purple glimmer through, and then
She outward turned her palm, and often pushed
Some hateful object from her, and a dark
Mysterious look of madness glazed her eye,
And her pearl teeth were set, and her frame shook
With an internal shuddering; then with slow
And broken sounds she muttered, "*False and foul.*"

Suddenly she sank down, and, bending low,
Hid her face in her mantle; one weak groan
Stole from her, like a dying wind at eve
Through a sere vine in autumn: then her lamb
Drew to her side, and looked with wistful eye
On her wild sorrow; as her dim eye caught
The innocent eye that gazed so fondly, calm
She lifted up her forehead, and composed

Her scattered tresses, and held out her hand
To the compassionate creature, who was now
The only one she trusted in; — she smiled,
As mourners smile, and, hanging o'er, she spake
Few words of tenderness: "Thou wilt not leave,
Fair face of gentleness, thou wilt not leave,
Though the world leave me." Then she gathered flowers
And grass-blades, and she wove them in a wreath,
And bound it round her minion's neck, and claspe
Its soft limbs to her bosom, with a kiss
Of sorrow and of love: her soul seemed calm,
And shone serenely through her clear blue eyes,
Which had in them a meek divinity,
All patience and all hope, that as she gazed
Upward to the pure vault and the bright sun,
Methought her spirit parted, and took wing,
And angels came to welcome it, and bear
The weary stranger to a resting-place,
And lay her on a pillow which no thorn
Hath ever entered. Such a sacred calm
Was printed in her look, that she became
Sainted to all my feelings, and I stood
To see her spurn the earth, and soar away
To the pure air above the highest cone,
That still looked white behind me; but she soon
Rose gently from her seat, and threw her hair
With a quick motion backward, closely drew
Her russet cloak, and twined her braided line
Around her marble fingers, then looked down,
And said, "We must go homeward, sweet one, night
Is coming in the far sky," and ere I
Could trace her, through the silent wood withdrew.

A TALE.

She had been touched with grief, and on her cheek
Sorrow had left its impress in the pale
Soft tint of fading loveliness. She bore
Meekly the burden of her woes, and told
To none the secret of heart. It preyed
For ever on her life, and blanched away
The roses which had bloomed so wooingly
And freshly on her laughing lips. Her smile
Grew fainter, and it only spread a line
Of a most tender carmine, where the snow
Scarce had a stain to mark it from the pure
And perfect whiteness of her cheek and brow, —
So pure, she seemed a living monument
Of Parian marble; and the flaxen curls
That waved around her forehead, and the arch
Darker and brighter bent above that eye,
Which through long lashes spoke in looks of fire,
And was the only eloquence she used, —
These, and at times a gushing to her cheek,
Like the first flush of morning, or the faint,
Fast-dying purple, when the twilight steals
Into the depth of darkness, — these were all
That told she yet was living, and was not
An image of the Graces, or the shade
Of a departed maiden, which at night
Visits the silent walks she loved, and hangs
Over the grave she watered, till she took
Her last repose beside it.
She had been
The gayest and the loveliest, and had moved
Through the light dance, and in the bending crowd
Of young admirers, like an infant queen
Proud of her innocent beauty. There was one
Who looked, but spake not; and when others took
Her hand to lead her through the merry hall
In steps all grace and harmony, he stole

Aside, and wept in anguish. He was made
Not for the place of mirth, but for the still
And peaceful shade of feeling, and of thoughts
Which have their home in higher souls, and are
Lone and unfriended and unknown below.
His was a social nature; yet not made
To blend with crowds, but find in one alone,
One fairy minister of soft delights,
And pure as they are tender, that deep joy
Which none has ever uttered. Long he sought
To win her to those calm retreats, and give
To her a spirit kindred to his own,
And lead her to the one and only love,
The harmony of thought and wish and life,
The union of all feelings, whence the deep,
Exhaustless fountain of their blended hearts
Flows ever deeper, and has ever more
Of music in its flow, and more of light
And beauty in its fulness. Thus he dwelt
On her fresh loveliness, until his life
Was linked unto her image, and her form
Mingled with every thought, and every spot,
Where the new spring looked beautiful, was filled
With her pervading presence; but he dared
Speak only to the mountain-winds her name,
And only in a whisper.
She had marked
The silent youth, and with a beauty's eye
Knew well she was beloved, and though her light
And bounding spirit still was wild and gay,
And sporting in the revel, yet her hours
Of solitude were visited by him,
Who looked with such deep passion. She too loved,
And saw more in his melancholy eye,
And in the delicate form, and the still look,
And that high front of intellect, which crowned
Features that were all tenderness and love,
Like the fair shrine of poesy, where thoughts
Dwelt high and solemn, such as from their seat

Of glory visit none but the great few
Whose language is immortal, — there she saw
More that had charms to win her, than in all
The light, unmeaning swarm, who fawned, and
 danced,
And played their tricks in envious rivalry,
Happy to draw from her one scornful smile.

She loved him with a true and early love,
And with her tenderness there was a sense
Of awe, when on those magic eyes she gazed,
Which seemed to look on spirits, not on men.
Still, in her innocent cheerfulness, she sought
To lead him from his solitary haunts,
And throw bright smiles upon that shaded brow,
And light that eye to rapture from its deep
And mute abstraction. So she laughed and sung,
And called him to the dance; but, with a gush
Of feeling irresistible, he stole
Aside and wept. Again he sought her ear,
And told her his fond tale. First she looked cold,
And o'er her forehead curled a playful frown;
Then suddenly, and with a few light words,
She scornfully turned from him, and enjoyed
The moment of her triumph; — it was short,
For with a firm, fixed look, in which were seen
More thoughts of grief than anger, he drew back,
And casting one proud farewell glance, that told
There was no after hope, he turned away,
And soon was gone, an exile, none knew where.

He wandered to another land, and found
New friends, who sought to cheer him; but a weight
Hung on his heart, and would not be removed;
The feeling of regret and injury,
The love that will not perish, and the pride
That quenches love, but does not make it hate;
The fondness that will steal at times, and melt
The heart to tears, and then the sudden pang

Of long-remembered scorn, which freezes fast
The fountain in its flow, and leaves the cold
Dim glare of one whose only hope is death.

He was in happy regions, and the sky
Above him was most beautiful; its blue
Was higher and intenser, and it took
The spirit on a journey into heaven,
And made it more than mortal: cool, soft gales
Stole from a peaceful ocean, whose bright waves
Rolled gently on to music, and they blew
Through woven trellises of all-sweet flowers,
And sported round long wreaths of festooned vines
Hung with the gayest blossoms, and o'er beds
That breathed in mellowest airs of balm and myrrh.
Music was in those bowers, and Beauty there
Crowded in mystic dances, and their nights
Were consecrated to the skilful sounds
Of a most witching harmony, to choirs
Such as once moved in Athens to the voice
Of flutes and timbrels. Many an eye was bent
Full on the noble stranger, and they sought
To win his smile; but yet he would not smile,
For all his better thoughts were far away,
And when he looked upon the lovely ones
Around him, it recalled with keener sense
Her who to him was lovelier, whom he loved,
But would not in his bitterness forgive.

When it was told her that the youth had fled,
d fled in anger, then her look was changed,
id never more her steps were in the dance,
vor were the cheerful sounds of her sweet voice
Heard in the crowd of revellers. Alone
She wept the folly which had thrown away
The only treasure she had truly loved,
And left her in the fairest of her days,
The very spring-time of her loveliness,
Only to think of what had been, and grieve.

NIGHT WATCHING.

She sat beside her lover, and her hand
Rested upon his clay-cold forehead. Death
Was calmly stealing o'er him, and his life
Went out by silent flickerings, when his eye
Woke up from its dim lethargy, and cast
Bright looks of fondness on her. He was weak,
Too weak to utter all his heart. His eye
Was now his only language, and it spake
How much he felt her kindness, and the love
That sat, when all had fled, beside him. Night
Was far upon its watches, and the voice
Of Nature had no sound. The pure blue sky
Was fair and lovely, and the many stars
Looked down in tranquil beauty on an earth
That smiled in sweetest summer. She looked out
Through the raised window, and the sheeted bay
Lay in a quiet sleep below, and shone
With the pale beam of midnight; — all was still,
And the white sail, that o'er the distant stream
Moved with so slow a pace, it seemed at rest,
Fixed in the glassy water, and with care
Shunned the dark den of pestilence, and stole
Fearfully from the tainted gale that breathed
Softly along the crisping wave, — that sail
Hung loosely on its yard, and, as it flapped,
Caught moving undulations from the light,
That silently came down, and gave the hills,
And spires, and walls, and roofs, a tint so pale,
Death seemed on all the landscape, — but so still,
Who would have thought that anything but peace
And beauty had a dwelling there! The world
Had gone, and life was not within those walls,
Only a few, who lingered faintly on,
Waiting the moment of departure; or
Sat tending at their pillows, with a love
So strong it mastered fear, — and they were few,

And she was one, — and in a lonely house,
Far from all sight and sound of living thing,
She watched the couch of him she loved, and drew
Contagion from the lips that were to her
Still beautiful as roses, though so pale
They seemed like a thin snow-curl. All was still,
And even so deeply hushed, the low, faint breath
That trembling gasped away came through the night
As a loud sound of awe. She passed her hand
Over those quivering lips, that ever grew
Paler and colder, as the only sign
To tell her life still lingered; — it went out!
And her heart sank within her, when the last
Weak sigh of life was over, and the room
Seemed like a vaulted sepulchre, so lone
She dared not look around: and the light wind,
That played among the leaves and flowers that grew
Still freshly at her window, and waved back
The curtain with a rustling sound, to her,
In her intense abstraction, seemed the voice
Of a departed spirit. Then she heard,
At least in fancy heard, a whisper breathe
Close at her ear, and tell her all was done,
And her fond loves were ended. She had watched
Until her love grew manly, and she checked
The tears that came to flow, and nerved her heart
To the last solemn duty. With a hand
That trembled not, she closed the fallen lid,
And pressed the lips, and gave them one long kiss; —
Then decently spread over all a shroud;
And sitting with a look of lingering love
Intense in tearless passion, rose at length,
And, pressing both her hands upon her brow,
Gave loose to all her gushing grief in showers,
Which, as a fountain sealed till it had swelled
To its last fulness, now gave way and flowed
In a deep stream of sorrow. She grew calm,
And, parting back the curtains, looked abroad

Upon the moonlight loveliness, all sunk
In one unbroken silence, save the moan
From the lone room of death, or the dull sound
Of the slow-moving hearse. The homes of men
Were now all desolate, and darkness there,
And solitude and silence took their seat
In the deserted streets, as if the wing
Of a destroying angel had gone by,
And blasted all existence, and had changed
The gay, the busy, and the crowded mart
To one cold, speechless city of the dead!

PLEASURES OF CHILDHOOD.

There is a middle place between the strong
And vigorous intellect a Newton had,
And the wild ravings of insanity;
Where fancy sparkles with unwearied light,
Where memory's scope is boundless, and the fire
Of passion kindles to a wasting flame,
But will is weak, and judgment void of power.
Such was the place I held; the brighter part
Shone out, and caught the wonder of the great
In tender childhood, while the weaker half
Had all the feebleness of infancy.
A thousand wildering reveries led astray
My better reason, and my unguarded soul
Danced like a feather on the turbid sea
Of its own wild and freakish fantasies.
At times the historic page would catch my eye,
And rivet down my thoughts on ancient times,
And mix them with the demigods of old.
Again I girt my loins to cross the waste
Of burning Afric, and amid the wilds
Of Abyssinia seek the modest springs
Whence bubble out the waters of the Nile,
The infancy of greatness; — how I loved

To ascend the pyramids, and in their womb
Gaze on the royal cenotaph, to sit
Beneath thy ruined palaces and fanes,
Balbec, or princely Tadmor, though the one
Lurk like a hermit in the lonely vales
Of Lebanon, and the waste wilderness
Embrace the other! — scouring with the wind,
I swept the desert on the Arab steed,
Or with the panting camel flew away.
There is an ecstasy in solitude,
Amid the broken images of power,
The serpent, owl, and jackal make their home,
Or in the heart of ocean, or the sands
Of Araby, or on the boundless plains
Of central Asia, whence the savage Hun
And Mogol in devouring torrents rushed.
Armed with the rifle, tomahawk, and bow,
How oft I wandered through the solemn woods
And tangled morasses of Florida,
Or where the wave of Mississippi pours
Its yet unsullied current o'er the steep
Of Antony, and winds among the hills
Of velvet verdure silently and slow!
The philosophic page was my delight,
To trace the workings of a hand unseen,
In earth, in air, and ocean, and the world
Of wonders, which the canopy of night
Discloses twinkling on its ebon arch.
These were my pleasures, and the varied forms
Of animal and plant, the bird, who cuts
With gliding wing the liquid air, the fly,
That flutters o'er its parent pool a day,
The polished shells that pave the snowy bed
Of ocean, with their many hues in soft
Accordance blended, like the ancient floor
Wrought in mosaic, or the sprig and flower,
That smile in vale and meadow bathed in dew.
These were at times my pleasures, but at times
The childish part prevailed. Along the stream,

That flowed in summer's mildness o'er its bed
Of rounded pebbles, with its scanty wave
Encircling many an islet, and its banks
In bays and havens scooping, I would stray,
And, dreaming, rear an empire on its shores.
There cities rose, and palaces and towers
Caught the first light of morning; there the fleet
Lent all its snowy canvas to the wind,
And bore with awful front against the foe;
There armies marshalled their array, and joined
In mimic slaughter; there the conquered fled,—
I followed their retreat, until secure
They found a refuge in their country's walls;
The triumphs of the conqueror were mine,
The bounds of empire widened, and the wealth
Torn from the helpless hands of humbled foes:
There many a childish hour was spent, the world,
That moved and fretted round me, had no power
To draw me from my musings, but the dream
Enthralled me till it seemed reality;
And when I woke, I wondered that a brook
Was babbling by, and a few rods of soil,
Covered with scant herbs, the arena where
Cities and empires, fleets and armies, rose.

VOYAGE OF LIFE.

I LAUNCHED my bark upon a waveless sea;—
The morning glowed, the sun just risen shone
In dazzling light along the glassy plain,
That seemed a golden mirror, or, as oft
A transient zephyr ruffled it, a flood
Of molten amber. How the purple sail,
And blue and crimson streamer wooed the wind.
At times the bellying bosom of the sheet
Received the rising gale, and onward bore
The white and glittering prow, as through the wave

It ploughed and heaved around the crested foam,
Like snow-wreaths resting on a ground of gold.
Again the rising zephyr died away,
The boundless air was still, the canvas flapped
And trembled on the yard, the streamers drooped,
And fluttering waved around the masthead, sea
And air were motionless: the crystal flood
Opened its awful depths beneath, — so clear,
The bark seemed hanging in the midway space
Between the sky above and earth below:
So still the elements, the briny drop,
That trickled from the prow to meet the wave,
Was heard distinctly, and the rippling shoal
Of blue-finned mackerel, or the whispering flight
Of the air-loving dweller of the deep,
Fell on my ear and woke me from my dream.
So passed the bark of life o'er childhood's sea,
But youth came on, and blustering winds arose;
Dark tempests gathered round, the howling blast
Roared through the cordage, every sail was rent,
The loosened helm gave way, and like the steed
Maddened with luxury, that flies the rein
And hurries on to ruin, so the bark
Ran wild before the tempest; now it rose
The billowy mountain, in the yawning gulf
Now headlong plunged; the shriek was then unheard
Amid the vaster tumult; then the night
Of storms enwrapped me, by the bursting foam,
The sparkling fire of ocean, or the flash,
The harbinger of thunder, or the pale
And baleful meteor of sickly green,
That on the bowsprit led the way to death,
Alone illumined. What a deafening roar
From bursting billows, how the breaker's voice,
Conflicting with the sea-beat crag, arose
And bellowed through the gloom; the sea-dog there,
Mounted above his danger, howled and bayed;
The dying whale, dashed on the splintery rock,
Groaned out his giant soul; the cormorant

Flapped his black wings around my head; the loon,
Perched on the topmast, sent his baleful scream,
Like the mad moanings of a tortured man.
So raged the storm around me, till a light,
Dimly discovered through the darkness, showed
Where help might yet be found; a secret hand
Then seemed to grasp the rudder, o'er the waves
The bark right onward held its steady course;
The tempest seemed to mitigate its rage,
The thunders ceased, the clouds spread out their veil
In thinner folds, and through a transient break
Sent a faint gleam of sunshine; from behind,
A gentle wind blew steady; in the west
The golden sky shone out, a larger curve
Of brightness every instant opened, till
The sun unveiled his face, and far away
The tempest hurried o'er the mountain waves:
It darkling flew, till on its bosom rose
The many-colored bow; serenity
Then filled the air, the white gull o'er me flew,
And the blue halcyon came and on the wave
Alighted, hid its head beneath its wing,
And slept as on a pillow; still the sea
Lifted its broad green back, and seemed to rock
Its fury to repose; I neared the land,
Blue hills first smiled, then sandy shores, like snow
Bleached on the heavenward mountain, caught my eye,
The lighthouse next, that with its warning fire
Calls from the deep the wanderer to his home.
The sun in cloudless majesty, as king
Of nature, kindled ocean with his rays,
And made the land more lovely; on I sailed,
The haven spread its arms to call me in,
And clasp me in its bosom; there I steered,
And casting anchor, where no storm can rage,
Nor tempest rock me, on the peaceful breast
Of love eternal moored my bark for ever.

A PICTURE.

SCENE. — The Valley of the Catskill River north of the Catskill Mountains.

THE glories of a clouded moonlit night, —
An union of wild mountains, and dark storms
Gathering around their summits, or in forms
Majestic moving far away in light,
Like pillared snow or spectres wreathed in flame.
Meanwhile, around the distant peaks a flow
Of moonlight settles, seeming from below,
Above the mountain's rude, gigantic frame,
An island of the heart, a home of bright,
Unsullied souls, who, clad in purest white,
Their bosoms stainless as their mantles, play
Around the gilded rocks, and snowy lawns,
And azure groves, in choirs like bounding fawns
Around the throne of some imperial fay.
Again the dark clouds brood below; their fold
A moment shrouds the mountain in dun shade,
Like midnight blackness from a crater rolled,
And flashing, as the glimmering of a blade
Amid the wreaths of war-smoke, lightnings quiver,
And crackling bolts the oak's bent branches shiver,
And rumbling echoes from the hollow glens
Roar like the voice of lions in their dens,
Awing the silent desert, — then the cloud,
Careering on the whirlwind, lifts its shroud
From off yon soaring pinnacle, and sweet,
Soft moonlight there is sleeping, like the ray
Whose flashes on a checkered fountain play
Light as the twinkling glance of fairies' feet,
Or brood in burnished brightness on the stream,
Or kiss the tufted bank of dewy flowers,
As if consoling, in his boyish dream,
Her shepherd through her own still magic hours.
Such is the brightness on those rocky towers;

And rising in an arch of double height,
Soaring away beyond that cone, the sky
Smiles to the harmonizing touch of light,
Like the blue iris of a joyous eye.
The moon is there in glory, and the stars
Shrink from her fuller splendor, and grow dim
Behind the veil of her effulgence. Airs,
As if from Eden breathing, blow; clouds swim,
Foam-like and fleecy, round the landscape's brim;
And, heaving like a storm-swoln billow's crest,
Rolls the wild tempest in the darkened west,
Its flashes twinkling through the gloom, its peals
Bellowing amid the purple glens; the rain,
Scudding along the forest, bears the bow
Wreathed round the flying storm-cloud, as it steals
Stiller and stiller through the night; the stain
Of braided colors, in a softer glow,
Bends o'er the foaming river its tall arch,
As if the spirits of the air might march
From mountain on to mountain, and look down,
In triumph, from the pictured circle's crown,
On hamlets wrapped in slumber, meadows green
And gemmed with rain-drops, woods whose leaves are bowed
With the dissolving richness of the cloud,
And brown brooks flashing down the hills, and pouring
Their tribute to the master stream, which wheels
Through the rude valley, foaming, tumbling, roaring,
And on the lonely wanderer, who steals
Abroad in silence to that echoing shore,
And, gazing on the mad wave, and the sky,
Which arches o'er the universe on high,
And on the flying cohorts of the storm
Hiding their frowns behind a seraph's form,
With soul subdued, and awed, enchanted eye
Can only bow before them and adore.

SPIRIT OF FREEDOM.

Spirit of Freedom! who thy home hast made
In wilds and wastes, where wealth has never trod,
Nor bowed her coward head before her god,
The sordid deity of fraudful trade;
Where power has never reared his iron brow,
And glared his glance of terror, nor has blown
The maddening trump of battle, nor has flown
His bloodthirst eagles; where no flatterers bow,
And kiss the foot that spurns them; where no throne,
Bright with the spoils from nations wrested, towers,
The idol of a slavish mob, who herd
Where largess feeds their sloth with golden showers,
And thousands hang upon one tyrant's word.

Spirit of Freedom! thou, who dwell'st alone,
Unblenched, unyielding, on the storm-beat shore,
And find'st a stirring music in its roar,
And look'st abroad on earth and sea, thy own, —
Far from the city's noxious hold, thy foot,
Fleet as the wild deer, bounds, as if its breath
Were but the rankest, foulest steam of death,
Its soil were but the dunghill, where the root
Of every poisonous weed and baleful tree
Grew vigorously and deeply, till their shade
Had choked and killed each wholesome plant, and laid
In rottenness the flower of Liberty.

Thou fliest to the desert, and its sands
Become thy welcome shelter, where the pure
Wind gives its freshness to thy roving bands,
And languid weakness finds its only cure;
Where few their wants, and bounded their desires
And life all spring and action, they display
Man's boldest flights, and highest, warmest fires,
And beauty wears her loveliest array.

Thou climb'st the mountain's crag, and with the
snows
Dwell'st high above the slothful plains; the rock
Thy iron bed; the avalanche's shock
Thou sternly breastest: hunger, cold, and toil
Harden thy steeled nerves, till the frozen soil,
The gnarled oak, the torrent, as it flows
In thunder down its gulf, are not more rude,
More hardy, more resistless, than thy force,
When, waked to madness in thy headlong course,
Thou rushest from thy wintry solitude,
And sweepest frighted nations on thy path,
A whirlwind in the fury of thy wrath,
And, with one curl of thy indignant frown,
Castest the pride of plumed warriors down,
And bear'st them onward, like the storm-filled wave,
In mingled ruin to their bloody grave.

Spirit of Freedom! I would with thee dwell,
Whether on Afric's sand, or Norway's crags,
Or Kansa's prairies, for thou lov'st them well,
And there thy boldest daring never flags;
Or I would launch with thee upon the deep,
And like the petrel make the wave my home,
And careless as the sportive sea-bird roam;
Or with the chamois on the Alp would leap,
And feel myself, upon the snow-clad height,
A portion of that undimmed flow of light
No mist nor cloud can darken. O, with thee,
Spirit of Freedom! deserts, mountains, storms,
Would wear a glow of beauty, and their forms
Would soften into loveliness, and be
Dearest of earth, for there my soul is free.

HOME.

THERE is a spot, a quiet spot, which blooms
On earth's cold, heartless desert. It hath power
To give a sweetness to the darkest hour,
As in the starless midnight from the rose,
Now dipped in dew, a sweeter perfume flows;
And suddenly the wanderer's heart assumes
New courage, and he keeps his course along,
Cheering the darkness with a whispered song:
At every step a purer, fresher air
Salutes him, and the winds of morning bear
Soft odors from the violet beds and vines;
And thus he wanders, till the dawning shines
Above the misty mountains, and a hue
Of vermeil blushes on the cloudless blue,
Like health disporting on the downy cheek.
It is time's fairest moment: as a dove
Shading the earth with azure wings of love,
The sky broods o'er us, and the cool winds speak
The peace of nature, and the waters fall,
From leap to leap, more sweetly musical,
And from the cloudy bosom of the vale
Come, on the dripping pinions of the gale,
The simple melody of early birds
Wooing their mates to love, the low of herds,
And the faint bleating of the new-born lambs,
Pursuing, with light, bounding step, their dams;
Again the shepherd's whistle, and the bark
That shrilly answers to his call; and hark!
As o'er the trees the golden rays appear,
Bursts the last joyous song of chanticleer,
Who moves in stately pomp before his train,
Till, from his emerald neck, and burnished wings,
The playful light a dazzling beauty flings,
As if the stars had lit their fires again.
So sweetly to the wanderer o'er the plain,
The rose, the jessamine, and every flower

That spreads its leaflets in the dewy hour,
And catches in its bell, night's viewless rain,
In tempered balm their rich aroma shower;
And with this charm the morning on his eye
Looks from her portals in the eastern sky,
And throws her blushes o'er the sleeping earth,
And wakes it to a fresh and lovely birth.
O, such a charm adorns that fairest spot,
Where noise and revelry disturb me not,
But all the spirits that console me come,
And o'er me spread a peaceful canopy,
And stand with messages of kindness by,
And one sweet dove, with eyes that look me blessed,
Sits brooding all my treasures in her nest,
Without one slightest wish the world to roam,
Or leave me, and that quiet dwelling,—home.

LOVE AT EVENING.

It was the hour of moonlight, and the bells
Had rung their curfew tones, and they were still;
The echo died around the distant hill,
Sinking in faint and fainter falls and swells,
Accordant with the fitful wind, that blew
Over the new-mown meadow, where the dew
Stood twinkling on the closely shaven stems,
Glittering as 't were a carpet sown with gems;
And from the winding river there arose
A mist, that curled in volumed folds, and gave
A snowy mantle to the stealing wave,
Like that which fancy, love-enchanted, throws
Over the form it doats on with a feeling
Of most endeared fondness, blind to all
That is not light and loveliness, concealing
The tints of weakness with a darkest pall:
And as the moon descending on the cloud
Gives it a rainbow livery, and hues

All softness and all beauty, so imbues
The fond eye of affection with all charms
The image of its awe: and he is proud,
Ay, prouder than the proudest, when his arms
Around that form of loveliness are flung,
And when those melting eyes are on him hung,
And when those lips are moving in sweet tones,
That tell, whate'er the words be, that she owns
No other for her love; and then the sigh
Struggles within her bosom, and her eye
Is wet with rising tears, and then the smile
Plays sweetly on her parting lips awhile,
And then she hangs upon his arm, and tells,
Her heart how happy, — and that fond heart swells
To give its feelings utterance, and she sings
Sweetly, as when the lark at morning springs
From out a dewy thicket, and away
Winnows his easy flight to meet the day;
And thus their eyes are blended, and they gaze
A moment on each other, and then turn
To where the countless fires of ether burn,
And look from heaven with soft and soothing rays;
A moment with uplifted brow they pour
The swelling current of devotion o'er,
And then, descending from that upward flight,
Again their eyes in tender looks unite,
Again they speak in undertones, as still
As are the winds that rustle on the hill,
Then side by side, in links of fondness prest,
Steal silently unto their hallowed rest.

Silent she stood before me, in the light
And majesty of beauty; and her eye
Was teeming with the visions of her soul; —
She stood before me in a veil of white,
The image of her bosom's purity,
And loveliness enveloped her, as bright

As when, at set of sun, the clouds unroll,
Pavilioning the dusky throne of night.
There is a spirit in the kindling glance
Of pure and lofty beauty, which doth quell
Each darker passion; and as heroes fell
Before the terror of Minerva's lance,
So beauty, armed with virtue, bows the soul
With a commanding, but a sweet control,
Making the heart all holiness and love,
And lifting it to worlds that shine above,
Until, subdued, we humbly bend before
The idol of our worship to adore.

Star of the pensive! "melancholy star,"
That, from the bosom of the deep ascending,
Shines on the curling waves, like mourner bending
Over the ruins of the joys that were;
Or lone, deserted mother sweetly tending
Her hushed babe in its cradle, often blending
Her plaintive song and sigh repressed,—sweet star!
I love the eye that looks on me so far
From all this want, and wretchedness, and woe,
From out that home of pure serenity
Above the winds and clouds. When tempests blow,
The sailor through the darkness looks to thee;—
Thou art the star of love, and fond hearts gaze
With feeling awe upon thy trembling rays,
And dream that other eyes are resting there;
And O what light around the bosom plays,
When, dwelling on the beautiful and fair,
We think that eyes beloved those beauties share!

"O, there is a bliss in tears!"—in tears that flow
From out a heart where tender feelings dwell,

That heaveth with involuntary swell
Of joy or grief for others' weal or woe.
The highest pleasures fortune can bestow,
The proudest deeds that victory can tell,
The charms that beauty weaveth in her spell,
These holy, happy tears how far below!
Yes, I would steal me from life's gaudy show,
And seek a covert in a silent shade,
And where the cheating lights of being glow,
See glory after glory dimly fade,
And knowing all my brighter visions o'er,
Deep in my bosom's core my sorrows lay,
And thence the fountains of repentance pour,
Gush after gush, in purer streams away.

VAUCLUSE.

THE laurel throws its locks around thy grave,
As freshly as when erst thou lingered there,
And plucked the early flowers to crown thy hair,
Or gathered cresses from the glassy wave,
That winds through hills of olive, vine, and grain,
Stealing away from Vaucluse' lonely dell,
Now murmuring scantily, now in the swell
Of April foaming onward to the plain, —
Laura! Thy consecrated bough is bright,
As when thy Petrarch tuned his soft lute by,
And lit his torch in that dissolving light,
Which darted from his only sun, — thine eye;
Thy leaf is still as green, thy flower as gay,
Thy berry of as deep a tint, as when
Thou moved a goddess in the walks of men,
And o'er thy poet held unbounded sway.
Methinks I hear, as from the hills descend
The deepening shadows and the blue smoke curls,
And waving forests with the light winds bend,
And flows the brook in softer leaps and whirls, —

Methinks I hear that voice of love complaining,
In faint and broken accents, of his hours
Of lonely sorrow, and of thy disdaining
And half-averted glances, till the bowers
Are pregnant with the hymn, and every rose
With fresher dew, as if in weeping, flows,
And every lily seems to wear a hue
Of paler tenderness, and deeper glows
The pink's carnation, and a purer blue
Melts on the modest rosemary, the wind
Whispers a sweeter echo, and the stream
Spouts stiller from its well; while from behind
The snow-clad alpine summits rolls the moon,
Careering onward to her cloudless noon,
In fullest orb of silver, and her beam
Casts o'er the vale long shadows from the pine,
The rock, the spire, the castle, and away,
Beyond thy towers, Avignon! proudly shine
The broad Rhone's foaming channels, in their play
Through green and willowed islands, while they
sweep,
Descending on their bold, resistless way,
And heaving high their crest in wild array,
With all a torrent's grandeur, to the deep.

LIGHT OF LOVE.

Fair as the first-blown rose, but oh! as fleeting,
Soft as the down upon a cygnet's breast,
Sweet as the air, when gales and flowers are meet-
ing,
Bright as the jewel on a sultan's vest,
Dear as the infant smiling when caressed,
Mild as the wind, at dawn in April, blowing,
Calm as the innocent heart, and oh! as blest,
Pure as the spring from mountain granite flowing,

Gay as the tulip in its starred bed glowing,
As clouds that curtain round the west at even,
O'er earth a canopy of glory throwing,
And heralding the radiant path to heaven.

Sweet as the sound, when waves, in calm, retreating,
Roll back, in gurgling ripples, from the shore,
When in the curling well still waters meeting,
Clear, from the spout, the molten crystal pour;
Sweet as at distance heard the cascade's roar,
Or ocean on the lone rock faintly dashing,
Or dying thunders, when the storm is o'er,
And dim-seen lightnings far away are flashing;
Sweet as when spring is garlanding the trees,
The birds in all the flush of life are singing,
And as the light leaves twinkle in the breeze,
The woods with melody and joy are ringing,
When beds of mint and flowering fields of clover
Are redolent of nature's balmiest store,
And the cool wind, from rivers, hurries over
And gathers sweets that Hybla never bore.

Fair as the cloudless moon o'er night presiding,
When earth, and sea, and air are hushed and still,
Along the burning dome of nature riding,
Crowning with liquid lustre rock and hill,
Pencilling with her silver beam the rill
That o'er the wave-worn marble falling plays,
Sheeting with light the cascade at the mill,
And paving ocean with her tremulous rays,
Through the closed lids of dewy violets stealing,
And gemming, with clear drops, the mead and grove;
Such is the light the native heart of feeling
Throws round the stainless object of his love.

FLOWER OF A SOUTHERN GARDEN.

Flower of a Southern garden newly blowing,
Fair as a lily bending on its stem,
Whose curled and yellow locks, in ringlets flowing,
Need not the lustre of a diadem;
Than all the wealth of Ind, a brighter gem;
Than all the pearls, that bud in Oman's sea,
Than all the corals waving over them,
Purer the living light that circles thee;
And through thy tender cheek's transparency
The vermeil tint of life is lightly flushing,
Or, at the faintest touch of modesty,
In one deep crimson tide is wildly rushing;
Like rose-leaves, when the morning's breath is
brushing
Away the seeds of pearl the night-cloud shed,
So thy twin opening lips are purely blushing,
Ripe with the softest dew and clearest red;
Purer than crystal in its virgin bed,
Than fountains bubbling in a granite cave,
Than sheeted snow, that wraps a mountain's head,
Or lilies glancing through a stainless wave,
Purer the snow that mantles o'er thy breast,
And rests upon thy forehead; — O, with thee
The hours might flit away so sweetly blest,
That time would melt into eternity!

Go with me to the desert loneliness
Of forest and of mountain, — we will share
The joys, that only purify and bless,
And make a paradise of feeling there;
And daily thou shalt be more sweet and fair,
And still shalt take a more celestial hue,
Like spirits melting in the midway air,
Till lost and blended in the arch of blue:
Alone, not lonely, we will wander through
Thickets of blooming shrubs and mantling vines,

Happy as bees amid the summer dew,
Or song-birds, when the fresh spring morning shines;
And when departing life shall wing its flight,
And render back the gift which God has given,
Be then to me a seraph form of light,
And bear my fleeting soul away to Heaven.

ROSE OF MY HEART.

Rose of my heart! I 've raised for thee a bower,
For thee have bent the pliant osier round,
For thee have carpeted with turf the ground,
And trained a canopy to shield thy flower,
So that the warmest sun can have no power
To dry the dew from off thy leaf, and pale
Thy living carmine, but a woven veil
Of full-green vines shall guard from heat and shower.
Rose of my heart! here, in this dim alcove,
No worm shall nestle, and no wandering bee
Shall suck thy sweets, no blight shall wither thee,
But thou shalt show the freshest hue of love.
Like the red stream, that from Adonis flowed,
And made the snow carnation, thou shalt blush,
And fays shall wander from their bright abode
To flit enchanted round thy loaded bush.
Bowed with thy fragrant burden, thou shalt bend
Thy slender twigs and thorny branches low:
Vermilion and the purest foam shall blend;
These shall be pale, and those in youth's first glow:
Their tints shall form one sweetest harmony,
And on some leaves the damask shall prevail,
Whose colors melt, like the soft symphony
Of flutes and voices in the distant dale.
The bosom of that flower shall be as white,
As hearts that love, and love alone, are pure,
Its tip shall blush, as beautiful and bright

As are the gayest streaks of dawning light,
Or rubies set within a brimming ewer.
Rose of my heart! there thou shalt ever bloom,
Safe in the shelter of my perfect love,
And when they lay thee in the dark, cold tomb,
I 'll find thee out a better bower above.

CATANIA.

CATANIA! on thy famed and classic shore
I long to plant my foot, and stand between
A paradise, all blooming, gay, and green,
And thy earth-circled ocean's gentle roar,
Along whose peaceful waves the sunbeams pour,
From stainless skies, deep amber, and imbue
The ruffled waters with an iris hue,
Like torchlight sparkling in a vault of ore,—
And turning I behold thy fields of grain
Waving in yellow floods o'er vale and plain,
And meadows mantled in a waste of flowers,
And hills whereon the golden orange glows,
And purpling with the ripe vine's nectared bowers,
And breathing with the myrtle and the rose;
And higher still flame-crested Ætna towering,
A belt of giant oak and chestnut waves
In gloomy verdure, like the cypress lowering
With shade of solemn night o'er Eastern graves;
And loftier, in its virgin robe of white,
The snow-cap, pillowed on the cloudless sky,
Seems like a floating column of pure light,
And round its pointed cone dark volumes lie
Rolled from the volcan's jaws, and sheets of flame
Dart on their path to heaven, and flowing o'er
The glowing torrent rolls its flashing stream,
And from the mountain's womb comes forth a sullen
roar.

SONNETS.

I.

I STAND upon the mountains, 'mid a sea
Of rocks, and woods, and waters, vales and plains,
Where smiling Freedom clad in russet reigns,
Beneath a cloudless, deep-blue canopy,
Whereon, in sovereign pomp and majesty,
The lord of day ascends his noontide throne,
And looks o'er all, himself unviewed alone,
Such is the burning brightness of his eye;
And here with upward breast and daring wing,
And glance that dwells undazzled on the blaze,
And finds its home in those unclouded rays,
From off these rocky battlements I spring,
And soaring to a more ethereal height,
My pinions lift me on to heaven's own world of light.

II.

MONARCH of mountains! whose serenest brow,
O'er clouds and storms uplifted, courts the sky,
And gazes on the all-pervading eye,
To which, in heartfelt awe, wide nations bow,
As Him from whom their life and being flow,—
Monarch of mountains! at thy feet I lay
The tribute of my wonder, and there pay
The homage of a soul, to whom the bow
Of glory, that encircles thee when night
Comes on in iris-splendor, and thy height
Glows with unnumbered hues and seems on fire,
And o'er thy pure snows rolls a wave of light,—
To whom these glories are a high delight,
An inspiration, and a deep desire,
And would be heaven, could I but hear an angel's lyre.

III.

My country, — at the sound of that dear name
The wanderer's heart awakens, nerved and bold
Before him stand the deeds and days of old,
The tombs of ages, and the rolls of fame
Sculptured on columns, where the living flame
Of Freedom lights anew its fading ray,
And glows in emulation of that day,
When on their foes they stamped the brand of shame:
Yes, at the thought of these bright trophies leaps
The spirit in his bosom, and he turns
His longing eye to where his parent sleeps,
And high on rocks his country's beacon burns;
And though the world be gayest, and sweet forms
Of love and beauty call him, he would fly,
And walk delighted in her mountain storms,
And man his soul with valor at her cry,
And in the fiercest shock of battle die.

IV.

Now to my task: — be firm, — the work requires
Cool reason, deep reflection, — and the glow
Of heart, that pours itself in restless flow,
Must sleep, and fancy quench her beaming fires,
And all my longings, hopes, and wild desires
Must seek their slumberous pillow and be still;
But energy must mantle o'er my will,
And give the patient toil that never tires:
For Nature stands before me, and invites
My spirit to her sanctuary, and draws
Aside her pictured veil, from where she writes
In living letters her eternal laws;
And as I stand amid the countless wheels,
That roll the car of being on its way,
A deep serene my silent bosom feels,
I seem a portion of the viewless ray,
And o'er me flows the light of pure, unfading day.

V.

COME forth, fair waters, from the classic spring,
And let me quaff your nectar, that my soul
May lift itself upon a bolder wing,
And spurn awhile this being's base control.
How many a cup of inspiration stole
The bards from out thy sparkling well, and sung
Strains high, and worthy of the kindling bowl,
Till all Aonia and Hesperia rung!
And on the green isles of the ocean sprung
A wilder race of minstrels, like the storm
Which beats their rocky bulwarks; there they strung
A louder harp, and showed a prouder form;
And sending o'er the sea their song, our shore
Shall catch the sound, and silent sleep no more.

VI.

FAREWELL, sad flowers, that on a desert blow,
Farewell! I plucked you from the Muses' bower,
And wove you in a garland, which an hour
Might on my aching eye enchantment throw.
Your leaves are pale and withered, and your flow
Of perfume wasted, your alluring power
Has vanished like the fleeting April shower, —
Too lovely flowers to spread your leaves below.
Sweet flowers! though withered, all the joy I know
Is when I breathe your balm, your wreath intwine;
And earth can only this delight bestow,
That sometimes all your loveliness is mine;
And then my frozen heart awhile will glow,
And life have moments, in its path, divine!

VII.

WOULD I were but a spirit, veiled in light,
Wafted by winds of heaven from flower to flower,
Catching, from bending blades, the crystal shower,
When earth, impearled, awakened new and bright;

Would I were set to guide some rolling sphere,
Amid the glories of eternal day,
Hymning aloud a sweet, celestial lay
That immortality alone can hear;
Would I were but the messenger of love,
To bear from soul to kindred soul the sigh,
To kiss the tears that fall from beauty's eye,
And watch the ringdove in the lonely grove;
Then sounds of melody might ever flow
From lips that with the fire of feeling glow.

AN ODE TO MUSIC.

Ἔσπετε νῦν μοι, Μοῦσαι, Ὀλύμπια δώματ' ἔχουσαι.
Iliad, B. 484.

I.

DESCEND, and with thy breath inspire my soul;
Descend, and o'er my lyre
Diffuse thy living fire;
O, bid its chords a strain of grandeur roll!
Touched by thy hand their trembling accents ring;
Borne on thy sounding pinions through the sky,
To Heaven the notes in burning ardor spring,
And as the tones in softened whispers die,
Love seems to flutter round on his Aurora-wing.

II.

O Muse! who erst in Tempe's flowery vale
Wert wont to tune thy harp and breathe thy soul,
And o'er Peneus pour thy dying wail;
Who, when loud-roaring thunders rocked the pole,
Burst from the dell and 'mid the growling storm
Involved in lurid gloom thy shining form;
And while the tempest o'er Olympus frowned,
And lightnings glittered round the throne of Jove,
Thy lyre, with hurried notes and awful sound,
Seemed like the voice that rung through dark Dodona's grove.

III.

Reclined amid the woods that waved around
Castalia's crystal fount and murmuring stream,
While ever-blooming flowerets decked the ground,
And brightened in the summer's softened beam,
Thy virgins nine, with lyres of burnished gold,
Around thy sylvan throne their descant rolled,
And through the mountain glen, the pensive shade,
A mellow echo would the strain prolong,
And as around the hollow cliffs it played,
A thousand heavenly harps seemed answering to the
song.

IV.

Urania o'er her star-bespangled lyre
With touch of majesty diffused her soul;
A thousand tones, that in the breast inspire
Exalted feelings, o'er the wires 'gan roll; —
She sang of night, that clothed the infant world,
In strains as solemn as its dark profound, —
How at the call of Jove the mist unfurled,
And o'er the swelling vault, the glowing sky,
The new-born stars hung out their lamps on high,
And rolled their mighty orbs to music's sweetest
sound.

V.

Majestic Clio touched her silver wire,
And through time's lengthened vista moved a train,
In dignity sublime; — the patriot's fire
Kindled its torch in heaven's resplendent ray,
And 'mid contention rose to heaven again.
In brightness glowing like the orb of day
The warrior drove his chariot o'er the slain,
And dyed its wheels in gore; — the battle's yell,
The dying groan, the shout of victory,
Now like the tempest-gust in horror swell,
Now like the sighing breeze in silence melt away.

VI.

But when Erato brushed her flowery lute,
What strains of sweetness whispered in the wind!
Soft as at evening when the shepherd's flute,
To tones of melting love alone resigned,
Breathes through the windings of the silent vale,
Complaining accents tremble on the gale,
Or notes of ecstasy serenely roll.
So when the smiling Muse of Cupid sung,
Her melody sighed out the sorrowing soul,
Or o'er her silken chords sweet notes of gladness
rung.

VII.

But O Melpomene! thy lyre of woe,
To what a mournful pitch its keys were strung,
And when thou bads't its tones of sorrow flow!
Each weeping Muse, enamored, o'er thee hung:
How sweet, how heavenly sweet, when faintly rose
The song of grief, and at its dying close
The soul seemed melting in the trembling breast;
The eye in dews of pity flowed away,
And every heart, by sorrow's load opprest,
To infant softness sunk, as breathed thy mournful
lay.

VIII.

But when, Calliope, thy loud harp rang,
In Epic grandeur rose the lofty strain;
The clash of arms, the trumpet's awful clang
Mixed with the roar of conflict on the plain;
The ardent warrior bade his coursers wheel,
Trampling in dust the feeble and the brave,
Destruction flashed upon his glittering steel,
While round his brow encrimsoned laurels waved,
And o'er him shrilly shrieked the demon of the
grave.

IX.

Euterpe glanced her fingers o'er her lute,
And lightly waked it to a cheerful strain
Then laid it by, and took the mellow flute,
Whose softly flowing warble filled the plain:
It was a lay that roused the drooping soul,
And bade the tear of sorrow cease to flow;
From shady woods the nymphs enchanted stole,
While laughing Cupids bent the silver bow,
Fluttering like fays that flit in Luna's softened glow.

X.

The rage of Pindar filled the sounding air,
As Polyhymnia tried her skill divine;
The shaggy lion roused him from his lair,
And bade his blood-stained eyes in fury shine;
The famished eagle poised his waving wings,
Whetting his thirsty beak, — while Murder rose,
With hand that grasps a dirk, with eye that glows
In gloomy madness o'er the throne of kings,
And, as she bade her tones of horror swell,
The demon shook his steel with wild exulting yell.

XI.

How light the strain when, decked in vernal bloom,
Thalia tuned her lyre of melody,
And when Terpsichore, with iris-plume,
Bade o'er her lute her rosy fingers fly;
'T was pleasure all: — the fawns in mingled choirs,
Glanced on the willing nymphs their wanton fires,
Joy shook his glittering pinions as he flew;
The shout of rapture and the song of bliss,
The sportive titter and the melting kiss,
All blended with the smile, that shone like early dew.

XII.

Their music ceased, — and rising from thy throne,
Thou took'st thy harp that on the laurel hung,

And bending o'er its chords to try their tone,
A faintly trembling murmur o'er them rung:
At each sweet sound that broke upon the ear,
Started the listening throng, and gazed and smiled;
The satyr, leaning on his ivy spear,
Peeped forth delighted from the flowery wild,
And, while thou tunedst the keys, the raptured soul
Hung o'er the flying tones that on the zephyrs stole.

XIII.

This prelude o'er, a solemn strain arose,
As strayed thy fingers slowly o'er the wire;
How grand the diapason, — and its close,
As when to heaven the organ notes aspire,
And through the gloomy aisle, the lofty nave,
Swell out the anthem pealing o'er the grave!
Low muttering thunders seemed to roar around,
And rising whirlwinds whispered in the ear;
The warrior started at the solemn sound,
Half drew his sword, and slowly shook his spear;
The tiger couched, and gazed with burning eye,
In horror growled, and lashed his waving tail;
The serpent rustled like the dying gale,
And bade his tongue in purple ardor fly,
Quivering like lurid flames beneath the midnight sky.

XIV.

The fury of the storm is howling by,
The whirlwinds rush, the bursting thunders roll,
Grim horror settles o'er the lowering sky,
And ruin flashes on the shuddering soul:
So burst with sudden swell thy awful strain,
And every blast of war was on the gale;
The maddening warriors mingled on the plain,
Loud rose the yell, and rang the clanging mail;
The victor's dripping chariot crushed the slain;
The raging tiger with terrific roar
Sprang on his prey, and dyed his claws in gore;

Rising on spires that shone with varied hue,—
Bright crimson, burnished gold, and livid blue,—
The serpent, hissing in his burning ire,
Glanced on his flying foe, and fixed his tooth of fire.

XV.

Struck by thy bounding quill, a mellow lay
Rang o'er the harp, and softly died away:
As poured the descant in the warrior's ear,
The roar of conflict ceased along the plain,
The foes exulting trampled on the slain,
And shook in mingled dance the glimmering spear;
In listless ease reclined, the tiger lay,
And fondly sported with his bleeding prey;
At times the serpent waved his quivering tail,
Then coiled his folds, and, all to peace resigned,
Listened the strain that sported in the wind,
And hissed his pleasure, shrill as sounds the infant's
wail.

XVI.

At last a murmur trembled on the lyre,
Soft as the dirge that echoes o'er the bier:
Robbed of his spirit bold, his daring fire,
The vanquished warrior dropped a tender tear,
Leant on his bloody sword and breathed a sigh;
And as the tiger spread his claws of gold,
Fawned round thy form and purred his ecstasy,
His emerald eyes in languid softness rolled;
The serpent, falling gently from his spire,
Glided with easy sweep along the plain,
In graceful windings wantoned round thy lyre,
And kissed the trembling chord that breathed the
soothing strain.

THE JUDGMENT.

HARK! the Judgment trump has blown!
  How it rolls along the air!
Time and Hope for ever flown,
  Sinners for your doom prepare.

Slowly o'er the lurid sky
  Rolls a dark, terrific storm,
Showing to the startled eye
  On its skirts a giant form.

Hark! the rattling hail descends,
  See! the forky lightnings glow,
As that form in anger bends,
  Frowning on the world below.

Riding on the whirlwind's wing,
  Canopied in clouds he flies;
With his voice the mountains ring,
  With his presence glow the skies.

Earthquakes roar and rock the ground,
  Tyrants bow before his rod,
Nations tremble at the sound,
  When they hear the voice of God.

Lo! the God! He comes in wrath:
  Vengeance drives his iron car,
Lightnings pave his flaming path,
  As he hurries to the war.

"I have waited long and spared
  Ingrates, on my bounty fed;—
Now my red right arm is bared,
  Now your day of hope is fled.

"I have bid my sun to shine,
  I have bid my dews to fall,
I have sent my love divine, —
  You have spurned and wasted all.

"Now the day of trial o'er,
  I my fatal shaft let fly;
Mercy can endure no more, —
  Time must end and you must die."

Ripe with sin the harvest bends; —
  See the mighty reaper stand!
There his burning scythe he sends,
  And with fury sweeps the land.

See the fields and forests glow!
  See the mounting flame aspire!
Hark the sinner's yell of woe,
  Gasping in a world of fire!

Helpless wretches! whither fly?
  In what den a shelter find?
See! the blasting bolt is nigh,
  Flame before, and wrath behind.

Like the chaff by whirlwinds driven,
  Like the earthquake-shattered rock,
Like the oak by tempest riven,
  Torn and splintered with the shock;

So they fly, a quivering throng,
  Urged by shame, despair, and fear;
Hurried by the sword along,
  Flashing, falling on their rear.

Hear the crackling whirlwind roar;
  Sheets of flame ascend the sky;
Now the feeble cry is o'er,
  Quenched in dark eternity.

Now the hills and mountains melt,
Rocks in flashing torrents run,
To earth's heart the rage is felt, —
Now the work of wrath is done.

Curling like a lettered scroll,
Crisped and crackling in the flame,
Now heaven's vaulted arches roll;
Falls the universal frame.

Now the circling blue has fled,
Suns wax faint and stars grow dim,
Heaven and earth away have sped,
Time's last trump their dying hymn.

Matter now has ceased to be,
All is pure ethereal light;
Saints, from all that bound them free,
To the empyrean wing their flight.

In that fount their beings blend,
All their thoughts, their views, the same;
See creation's essence end
In one flood of viewless flame!

A TRIBUTE TO THE BRAVE.

THOUGH furled be the banner of blood on the plain,
And rusted the sabre once crimsoned with gore;
Though hushed be the ravens that croaked o'er the
slain,
And calmed into silence the battle's loud roar;
Though Peace with her rosy smile gladden the vales,
And Commerce unshackled dance over the wave;
Though music and song may enliven the gales,
And Joy crown with roses and myrtle the brave;

Like spirits that start from the sleep of the dead,
Our heroes shall rouse, when the larum shall blow;
Then Freedom's broad flag on the wind shall be
spread,
And Valor's sword flash in the face of the foe.
Our Eagle shall rise 'mid the whirlwinds of war,
And dart through the dun-cloud of battle his eye, —
Shall spread his wide wings on the tempest afar
O'er spirits of valor that conquer or die.
And ne'er shall the rage of the conflict be o'er,
And ne'er shall the warm blood of life cease to flow,
And still 'mid the smoke of the battle shall soar
Our Eagle — till scattered and fled be the foe.
When Peace shall disarm War's dark brow of its
frown,
And roses shall bloom on the soldier's rude grave, —
Then Honor shall weave of the laurel a crown,
That Beauty shall bind on the brow of the brave.

THE SENATE OF CALLIMACHI.*

AN ODE.

In Callimachi's halls are met
The chieftains of a noble line;
The fathers' spirit lingers yet,
To aid them in their high design;
The spirit that, in ancient days,
Called forth the boldest Spartan band,
With their own shields and breasts to raise
A living bulwark round their land.

The sound that erst in Hellas rang,
When War his brazen trumpet blew,

---

* So it was written in the first accounts of the Peloponnesian Senate. The true name is Calamata. I prefer the name in the text. It has in it an omen: Καλὴ μάχη, "glorious victory."

When shields returned the hollow clang,
And ready feet to battle flew, —
That sound in Sparta's vale is raised;
The Turkish bar and bolt are riven;
The fire that erst on Œta blazed,
In bolder eddies curls to heaven.

That flame o'er Spartan valor burned,
The brave three-hundred's funeral pyre!
Though now in Grecian earth inurned,
Their fame shall Grecian hearts inspire;
It blazes on the sacred rock,
It flashes o'er the hallowed glen;
Advance, ye Greeks! and breast the shock,
And show the world ye still are men.

The sons of sires, who knew no fear
When threatening foemen scaled their walls,
The light shall see, the sound shall hear,
And throng to Callimachi's halls:
The altar of their country burns;
They pledge their oath to liberty;
Their fathers answer from their urns,
"Be like us, sons, and ye are free."

On old Messene's soil are met
The sons of Aristomenes;
Your ancient wrongs and feuds forget
In wrongs so foul, so deep, as these:
A new Aristodemus flings
His iron gauntlet on the foe;
At once, a nation's valor springs
To deal the liberating blow.

Who would not glow in such a cause?
Who not exult in such a name?
Blest be the sword each Maynote draws
To lop away his bonds and shame:
The fire is kindled in his soul;
The spirit flashes in his eye;

A nation's blended voices roll
The vow of freedom to the sky.

Leap from your tombs, ye men who stood
At Pylæ and at Marathon;
The sire shall find his boiling blood
Throb in the bosom of his son:
Haste, demigods! with shield and spear,
And hover o'er the coming fight;
O, let the rocks of Sparta hear
The gathering word, "Unite! unite!"

A PLATONIC BACCHANAL SONG.

Fill high the bowl of life for me, —
Let roses mantle round its brim,
While heart is warm and thought is free,
Ere beauty's light is waning dim, —
Fill high with brightest draughts of soul,
And let it flow with feeling o'er,
And love, the sparkling cup, he stole
From heaven, to give it briskness, pour.
O, fill the bowl of life for me,
And wreathe its dripping brim with flowers,
And I will drink, as lightly flee
Our early, unreturning hours.
Fill high the bowl of life with wine,
That swelled the grape of Eden's grove,
Ere human life, in its decline,
Had strewed with thorns the path of love, —
Fill high from virtue's crystal fount,
That springs beneath the throne of Heaven,
And sparkles brightly o'er the mount
From which our fallen souls were driven.
O, fill the bowl of life with wine,
The wine that charmed the gods above,
And round its brim a garland twine,
That blossomed in the bower of love.

Fill high the bowl of life with spirit,
Drawn from the living sun of soul,
And let the wing of genius bear it,
Deep-glowing, like a kindled coal, —
Fill high from that ethereal treasure,
And let me quaff the flowing fire,
And know awhile the boundless pleasure
That Heaven-lit fancy can inspire.
O, fill the bowl of life with spirit,
And give it brimming o'er to me,
And as I quaff, I seem to inherit
The glow of immortality.
Fill high the bowl of life with thought
From that unfathomable well,
Which sages long and long have sought
To sound, but none its depths can tell, —
Fill high from that dark, stainless wave,
Which mounts and flows for ever on,
And rising proudly o'er the grave,
There finds its noblest course begun.
O, fill the bowl of life with thought,
And I will drink the bumper up,
And find, whate'er my wish had sought.
In that the purest, sweetest cup.

HERE 's to her who wore
The myrtle-wreath that bound me;
Here 's to her who bore
The twine of bay that crowned me: —
O, had not her light
So brightly shone upon me,
Still the cloud of night
Had darkly brooded on me;
There was in her eye
A spirit that inspired me;
Still to do or die,
The electric sparkle fired me;

And though the ice of death
Should chill the heart within me,
The music of her breath
Back to life again would win me;
So here 's to her who wore
The myrtle-wreath that bound me;
The girl who kindly bore
The twine of bay that crowned me.

No more the iron chain
Of doubt and fear inthralls me;
I lift my wing again,
For 't is her voice that calls me;
Still higher, higher still,
In search of glory soaring,
I feel my bosom thrill
To the song her voice is pouring;
And though I stretch my flight,
Where heaven alone is o'er me,
I see her form of light
Still floating on before me:
O, when foes the direst move
In columns to assail us,
Let us hear the voice of love,
And our courage cannot fail us:
So here 's to her, &c.

And when my drowsy soul
A heedless moment slumbers,
Away the vapors roll
At the magic of her numbers;
Back to life again I start,
At her thrilling summons waking,
Every link that bound my heart
Down to earth, indignant breaking;
Then I follow where she flies,
Like a shooting star, before me,
And her fascinating eyes
Shed their fire in flashes o'er me:

O, cold the heart could sleep
When her silver trumpet called it,
And the soul that would not leap
When her flowery chain enthralled it:
So here's to her who wore
The myrtle-wreath that bound me;
The girl who kindly bore
The twine of bay that crowned me.

DITHYRAMBIC.

FILL the cup for me,
Fill the cup of pleasure;
Wake the fairy lyre
To its wildest measure.
Melancholy's gloom
Now is stealing on me,
But the cup and lyre
Can chase the demon from me.
        Fill the cup for me,
        Fill the cup of pleasure;
        Wake the fairy lyre
        To its wildest measure.

In the shades of night,
When every eye is closing,
On the moonlight bank
All in peace reposing,
There is naught so sweet
As the cup of pleasure,
And the lyre that breathes
In its wildest measure.
        Fill the cup, &c.

This the smiling star
That guides me o'er life's ocean,
This the heavenly light
That wakes my heart's devotion:

'T is when Beauty's smile
Gives the cup of pleasure,
And awakes the lyre
To its wildest measure.
Fill the cup, &c.

If the fiend of sorrow
With his gloom affright thee,
There may come to-morrow
One who will delight thee:
'T is the fair, whose smile
Beams with sweetest pleasure,
And whose hand awakes
The lyre's delightful measure.
Fill the cup, &c.

Form of Beauty! bind
Pleasure's wreath of roses
Round this brow of mine,
Where every joy reposes:
Yes, my heart can bound
To mirth's enlivening measure,
When the lyre is tuned,
And smiles the cup of Pleasure.
Fill the cup, &c.

Drive dull care away, —
Why should gloom depress thee?
Life may frown to-day,
But joy will soon caress thee.
While there 's time, my friend,
Drink the cup of Pleasure,
And awake the lyre
To its wildest measure.
Fill the cup for me,
Fill the cup of Pleasure,
Wake the fairy lyre
To its wildest measure.

THE SERENADE.

Softly the moonlight
Is shed on the lake,
Cool is the summer night,—
Wake! O awake!
Faintly the curfew
Is heard from afar,
List ye! O list!
To the lively guitar.

Trees cast a mellow shade
Over the vale,
Sweetly the serenade
Breathes in the gale,
Softly and tenderly
Over the lake,
Gayly and cheerily,—
Wake! O awake!

See the light pinnace
Draws nigh to the shore,
Swiftly it glides
At the heave of the oar,
Cheerily plays
On its buoyant car,
Nearer and nearer,
The lively guitar.

Now the wind rises
And ruffles the pine,
Ripples foam-crested
Like diamonds shine,
They flash, where the waters
The white pebbles lave,
In the wake of the moon,
As it crosses the wave.

Bounding from billow
To billow, the boat
Like a wild swan is seen
On the waters to float;
And the light dripping oars
Bear it smoothly along
In time to the air
Of the gondolier's song.

And high on the stern
Stands the young and the brave,
As love-led he crosses
The star-spangled wave,
And blends with the murmur
Of water and grove
The tones of the night,
That are sacred to love.

His gold-hilted sword
At his bright belt is hung,
His mantle of silk
On his shoulder is flung,
And high waves the feather,
That dances and plays
On his cap where the buckle
And rosary blaze.

The maid from her lattice
Looks down on the lake,
To see the foam sparkle,
The bright billow break,
And to hear in his boat,
Where he shines like a star,
Her lover so tenderly
Touch his guitar.

She opens her lattice,
And sits in the glow

Of the moonlight and starlight,
A statue of snow;
And she sings in a voice
That is broken with sighs,
And she darts on her lover
The light of her eyes.

His love-speaking pantomime
Tells her his soul, —
How wild in that sunny clime
Hearts and eyes roll.
She waves with her white hand
Her white fazzolet,
And her burning thoughts flash
From her eyes' living jet.

The moonlight is hid
In a vapor of snow;
Her voice and his rebeck
Alternately flow;
Re-echoed they swell
From the rock on the hill;
They sing their farewell,
And the music is still.

TO THE HOUSTONIA CERULEA.*

How often, modest flower,
I mark thy tender blossoms, where they spread
Along the turfy slope, their starry bed,
Hung heavy with the shower.

---

* A very delicate and humble flower of New England, blossoming early in spring, and often covering large patches of turf with a white or pale blue carpet. The botanical allusions in this piece are repeated, and perhaps it will not be fully relished by those who have not examined the structure of the flower.

Thou comest in the dawn
Of Nature's promise, when the sod of May
Is speckled with its earliest array,
And strewest with bloom the lawn.

'T is but a few brief days,
I saw the green hill in its fold of snow;
But now thy slender stems arise, and blow
In April's fitful rays.

I love thee, delicate
And humble as thou art: thy dress of white,
And blue, and all the tints where these unite,
Or wrapped in spiral plait,

Or to the glancing sun,
Shining through checkered cloud, and dewy shower,
Unfolding thy fair cross. Yes, tender flower,
Thy blended colors run,

And meet in harmony,
Commingling, like the rainbow tints; thy urn
Of yellow rises with a graceful turn,
And as a golden eye

Its softly swelling throat
Shines in the centre of thy circle, where
Thy downy stigma rises slim and fair,
And catches as they float,

A cloud of living air,
The atom seeds of fertilizing dust,
That hover, as thy lurking anthers burst;
And oh! how purely there

Thy snowy circle, rayed
With crosslets, bends its pearly whiteness round,
And how thy spreading lips are trimly bound,
With such a mellow shade

As in the vaulted blue
Deepens at starry midnight, or grows pale
When mantled in the full-moon's silver veil,
That calm, ethereal hue.

I love thee, modest flower!
And I do find it happiness to tread,
With careful step, along thy studded bed,
At morning's freshest hour,

Or when the day declines,
And evening comes with dewy footsteps on,
And, now his golden hall of slumber won,
The setting sun resigns

His empire of the sky,
And the cool breeze awakes her fluttering train.
I walk through thy parterres, and not in vain,
For to my downward eye,

Sweet flower! thou tell'st how hearts
As pure and tender as thy leaf, as low
And humble as thy stem, will surely know
The joy that peace imparts.

ON FINDING THE ANEMONE HEPATICA,

THE EARLIEST FLOWER OF SPRING.

Beside a fading bank of snow
A lovely Anemone blew,
Unfolding to the sun's bright glow
Its leaves of heaven's serenest hue;

The snowy stamens gemmed them o'er,
The pleasing contrast caught my eye,
As on the ocean's sandy shore
The purple shells and corals lie.

I saw the flower, — what tumults rose
Within my heart, what ecstasy!
The captive soul no brighter glows,
When hailing life and liberty.

'T is Spring, I cried, pale Winter 's fled,
The earliest wreath of flowers is blown;
The blossoms withered long and dead
Will soon proclaim their tyrant flown.

How smiles the sun in yonder sky,
How pure the vault of ether swells,
How sweet to hear on mountain high
The tinkle of the shepherd-bells!

The meadows don their green array,
The streams in purer currents flow;
On sunny knolls the lambkins play,
And sport amid the vales below.

The humble Anemone blows,
The blue-bird now is on the wing;
How soon will breathe the blushing rose,
How soon will all around be spring!

A TULIP blossomed, one morning in May,
By the side of a sanded alley;
Its leaves were dressed in a rich array,
Like the clouds at the earliest dawn of day,
When the mist rolls over the valley:
The dew had descended the night before,
And lay in its velvet bosom,
And its spreading urn was flowing o'er,
And the crystal heightened the tints it bore
On its yellow and crimson blossom.

A sweet red-rose, on its bending thorn,
Its bud was newly spreading,
And the flowing effulgence of early morn
Its beams on its breast was shedding;
The petals were heavy with dripping tears,
That twinkled in pearly brightness,
And the thrush in its covert thrilled my ears
With a varied song of lightness.

A lily, in mantle of purest snow,
Hung over a silent fountain,
And the wave, in its calm and quiet flow,
Displayed its silken leaves below,
Like the drift on the windy mountain;
It bowed with the moisture the night had wept,
When the stars shone over the billow,
And white-winged spirits their vigils kept,
Where beauty and innocence sweetly slept
On its pure and thornless pillow.

A hyacinth lifted its purple bell
From the slender leaves around it;
It curved its cup in a flowing swell,
And a starry circle crowned it;
The deep-blue cincture that robed it seemed
The gloomiest garb of sorrow,
As if on its eye no brightness beamed,
And it never in clearer moments dreamed
Of a fair and a calm to-morrow.

A daisy peeped from the tufted sod,
In its bashful modesty drooping;
Where often the morn, as I lightly trod,
In bounding youth, the fallow clod,
Had over it seen me stooping;
It looked in my face with a dewy eye
From its ring of ruby lashes,
And it seemed that a brighter was lurking by,
The fires of whose ebony lustre fly
Like summer's dazzling flashes.

And the wind, with a soft and silent wing,
Brushed over this wild of flowers,
And it wakened the birds, who began to sing
Their hymn to the season of love and spring,
In the shade of the bending bowers;
And it culled their full nectareous store,
In its lightly fluttering motion,
As when from Hybla's murmuring shore
The evening breeze from her thyme-beds bore
Their sweetness over the ocean.

A few years since, a small lake in a wildly romantic situation in the northern part of Vermont was unfortunately drained by the bursting of one of the banks that confined it. The following stanzas are intended for a description of that event.

A LAKE once lay, where the thunder-clouds sail,
On the lofty mountain's breast,
Whose ripple, when raised by the rustling gale,
Was so gentle, it seemed at rest;
The pine waved round, and the dark cliff frowned,
Their shadow was gloomy as night;
But when the sun shone, on his noonday throne,
The lake seemed a mirror of light.
There the red-finned trout like a flash darted by,
And the pickerel moved like the glance of an eye.

When the wind breathed soft at the dawning of day,
When the morning-birds warbled around,
And the rainbow shone on the scarce seen spray,
No lovelier place could be found:
O, this scene was as dear to mine eye and mine ear,
As the glance and the song of my love,
And the lake was as bright, and as pure to the sight,
As the bosom of angels above:
The surface flashed with a golden glow,
And a forest of verdure seemed waving below.

The year rolled away, and I saw it no more
Till the spring bloomed sweetly again,
Till the birch first unfolded its leaves on the shore,
And the robin first warbled its strain :
But no lake smiled there, with its bosom fair,
'T was a dell all with bushes o'ergrown,
From my dream of delight, like a sleeper at night,
I awoke and I found me alone.
Through the vale it had burst with the swiftness of
wind,
And left but a path of destruction behind.

The leaves were all dead on the wave-loving willow,
It whispered no more in the wind;
No moonbeam slept on the water's soft pillow,
Or smiled like the tranquillized mind;
The flower-bush there was the fox's lair,
And the whippoorwill sung all alone,
Where the moonbeams pale, glancing through the
vale,
Just gleamed on the moss-gray stone.
Where the trout once darted, the adder crept,
And the rattlesnake coiled where the Naiad wept.

By the moon's chill light, the white pebble shone
On the beach, where the wave once rolled,
And the lustre gleamed on the water-worn stone,
But told to the eye it was cold:
No rippling wave that beach shall lave,
No white foam shall toss on that shore,
And the billow's flash, and its scarce heard dash,
Shall be known in that valley no more.
For the wave, shall be heard the serpent's breath,
For the dash of the billow, the hiss of death.

Where the foam once sparkled, the cedar-bush waved,
And the reed rustled sweet in the gale;
And the rock that the water so silently laved
Was hid by the gray lichen's veil;

There the dark fern flings on the night-wind's wings
Its leaves like the dancing feather,
And the whippoorwill's note seemed gently to float
From the deep purple bloom of the heather.
Where the surface glittered, the weed grew wild,
And the flower blossomed sweet, where the wave
once smiled.

So when life first dawns on the infant soul,
'T is as pure as the lake's clear wave;
Not a passion is there but can brook control,
Not a thought that is pleasure's slave:
But youth comes on, and this purity 's gone,
Fair innocence smiles there no more,
And cold is the guest, that lives in that breast,
As the stone on this desolate shore;
A poison floats in its balmiest breath,
And where the flower smiles is the serpent of death.

THE MERMAID.

I.

THE waning moon looked cold and pale,
Just rising o'er the eastern wave,
And faintly moaned the evening gale,
That swept along the gloomy cave:
The waves that wildly rose and fell,
On all the rocks the white foam flung,
And like the distant funeral knell,
Within her grot the Mermaid sung.

II.

It was a strain of witchery
So sweet, yet mournful to my ear,
It lit the smile, it waked the sigh,
Then started pity's pearly tear;
There was a ruffle in my breast,
It was not joy, it was not pain,

'T was wild as yonder billow's crest,
That tosses o'er the heaving main.

III.

Along the wave the moon's cold light
With trembling radiance feebly shone;
A lustre neither faint nor bright
Sparkled on yonder watery stone:
There, seated on her sea-beat throne,
The Mermaid eyed the dashing wave,
Then waked her wild harp's melting tone,
And breathed the music of the grave.

IV.

Her silken tresses, all unbound,
Played loosely on the evening gale;
She cast a mournful look around,
Then sweetly woke her wild harp's wail;
And, as her marble fingers flew
Along the chords, such music flowed,
Her cheek assumed a varied hue,
Where grief grew pale, where pleasure glowed.

V.

The sound rose sweetly on the wind,
It was a strain of melancholy, —
It soothed each tumult of the mind,
And hushed the wildest laugh of folly.
It flowed so softly o'er the main,
And spread so calmly, widely 'round;
The air seemed living with the strain,
And every zephyr breathed the sound.

VI.

The seal, that sported on the shore,
His gambols ceased, and pricked his ear;
He heeded not the billow's roar, —
That strain was all he seemed to hear.

As through the surf the dolphins flew,
They stopped and played around her throne;
It seemed, Arion woke anew
His harp to some celestial tone.

VII.

With what a thrilling ecstasy
I heard the music of her lyre;
The very soul of melody
Seemed warbling on the trembling wire:
O, never o'er her infant dear
The mother half so fondly hung,
As when I bent my soul to hear
Those heavenly strains the Mermaid sung.

LINES

ON VIEWING, ONE SUMMER EVENING, THE HOUSE OF MY BIRTH IN A STATE OF DESERTION.

The crescent moon with pallid light
Was silvering o'er the brow of night;
With downy wing the summer breeze
Sported amid the rustling trees,
Waving the leaves that lightly flew,
And kissing off the night-fallen dew.
Along the gently winding vale,
Its surface ruffled by the gale,
The softly flowing rivulet strayed,
While o'er its wave the moonbeam played,
Smiling, as calmly stealing by,
Like tears of joy in beauty's eye.

Through the wood my fancy loved,
Rapt in kindling thought, I roved;
Not a zephyr shook the spray,
To brush the trembling gems away;
Not a warble met my ear,
All was silent far and near,

Still as cypress boughs, that wave
Slowly o'er the lonely grave,
And weave their deep, impressive gloom, —
Fit emblem of the dreary tomb.

Down a glen, where, half unseen,
Banked with turf of deepest green,
Flowed a winding rill along,
Tinkling like the milkmaid's song;
Where the moon's reflected ray
Smiling on the surface lay,
Seeming to sleep in soft repose,
Like morning dew-drops on the rose;
Where the evening splendors fade
In the maple's quiet shade;
Lonely, desolate appears,
Pale as in the vale of years,
The mansion where my infant eye
First saw the rocks, the woods, the sky.
O, it was a lovely sight,
Though obscured by shades of night;
And though the ivy-mantled wall
At intervals was heard to fall,
Breaking with faintly rattling sound
The quiet hush that reigned around.

Through the walks, where privets blew
And purple lilacs wildly grew,
'Mid entangling weeds and briers,
And the rye-grass' waving spires,
'Neath the pear-tree, where, as Spring
Bade her untaught music ring,
Purest blooms of snowy white
Charmed the fond-reposing sight,
And gales of incense whispered by
Gentle as the lover's sigh, —
I wandered slow, and fondly viewed
This scene in evening tears bedewed,
And felt around my heart the throe
Of tender grief and melting woe,

To see a spot so sweet, so dear,
Now laid on desolation's bier,
And view a scene of loveliness
In ruin's wildest, roughest dress.

With trembling hand I oped the door,
And wandered o'er the mouldering floor;
Along the slowly crumbling wall,
Where wintry fires were wont to fall
And smile with beams of ruddy light,
Chasing away the gloom of night,
Naught was seen but shadows drear,
And sights that filled my soul with fear:
Darkened by trickling autumn rains,
That left their wild, fantastic stains,
Seeming, as stars with feeble ray
Reflected o'er the ceiling play,
Spirits that swiftly flutter by,
And glance like visions on my eye.
And there the slowly creeping snail
Drew o'er the wall its slimy veil;
Its silken web the spider wove
To trap the flies that idly rove;
While, slumbering through the summer's day,
The bat in some lone corner lay,
Till, started by my solemn tread,
He flapped his wings around my head,
And, darting through the broken pane,
Sailed on the evening breeze again.

The moonbeam shone along the room,
Like starlight glistening on a tomb;
The clock was still, — its sweet-toned bell
No longer rung Time's funeral knell,
No more its index seemed to say
How swift the moments flew away.
All was lonely, all was still,
The thrush was silent on the hill,
The sheep-bell's shrilly tinkling note
Was heard no longer in the cote,

No breathing soul the silence broke,
No flageolet its sweetness woke,
No voice was singing in the vale,
No echo floated on the gale;
'T was hushed, but when with droning sound
The slow-winged beetle hummed around.

Resting on a broken chair,
Relic of the ruin there,
By the window I reclined
And listened to the moaning wind,
That whispered through the broken pane.
Mournful as the funeral strain.
O'er my head the woodbine blew,
All its flowers were wet with dew,
And sweeter fragrance flowed around,
Than ever charmed enchanted ground;
So sweet the scent, that Eden's gale
Seemed breathing through the desert vale.
Ivy hung its tendrils there,
And trembled in the dewy air,
Twisting around the shattered frame,
Where still a rudely sculptured name
Half hid in lichens caught my eye,
And told me of the years gone by.

Beneath my eye, and in the shade
An aged elm, low bending, made,
A modest rose-bush reared its head,
And far around its sweetness shed.
Two damask flowers, with leaflets pale,
Were lightly trembling on the gale,
And, as the moonbeam o'er them shone,
Seemed like two mourners left alone
Amid those scenes, where gay delight,
Frolic ever dancing light,
Woke their shouts of rapture wild,
And cheerfulness serenely smiled.
All, — all were gone. Like insects gay,
That sport them in the summer ray,

Young Happiness, so sweetly blown,
With hurrying wing away had flown,
Vanished in night the vision fair,
And left these two to wither there.

Soon I glanced my roving eye
On a sprig of rosemary;
Hid in grass that rankly grew,
There the humble floweret blew,
Bashful 'neath the rose's shade
All its modest hues displayed;
As the maiden sweet as May,
With her eye of heavenly ray,
Shrinking from the world's rude storm,
Hides in shades obscure her form.
On its lip of paly blue,
Smiled in peace a pearl of dew;
'T was a melancholy flower,
Such as in affliction's hour
O'er the heaving turf I 'd throw,
To deck the friend that rests below.

Glancing farther o'er the scene,
Gay with flowers and soft with green;
But now beneath the moon's pale light
All seemed one color to the sight.
Such the mellow fading tint,
When the fays their footsteps print,
Where the tiny billows break
On the gently heaving lake:
'T was not ebon, 't was not green,
Mingled hues that melt between;
As when beside the taper's ray
The maiden weeps the hours away,
And seen at distance faintly glows,
Her grief-worn cheek's decaying rose,
Till every soft and winning charm
Dissolves into a sylphid form.

O'er the slowly winding flood,
'Mid the shadows of the wood,
And in the meadow spread before
The ruined mansion's broken door,
I saw in gently veering flight
The insect lightning of the night,
Shining with a feeble ray,
As it slowly sailed away,
Or twinkling with a sudden spark,
Spangling the scenery wild and dark.
So the meteor light of fame
Glows with such a fickle flame,
So all happiness below
Is an insect's transient glow:
For a time it sweetly smiles,
Dressed in fancy's dearest wiles;
Mirth amid his rosy bowers
Laughs away the gliding hours,
The moments of a short-lived day
That steals like air unseen away;
Love entwines his silken chain,
And breathes his soft, enchanting strain;
Joy awakes his twisted shell
To the notes that please him well;
Hope's gay colors richly blend,
And tell of sports that never end;
While jovial Pleasure's golden dawn
Sparkles awhile, and all is gone.

Farther still I turned my eyes,
Where the waving forests rise,
Where the hills with easy swell,
Rising from the lowly dell,
Smile beneath the pallid ray,
Till they fade in mist away.
Upward to the sky I turned,
Where the stars serenely burned,
And around the lonely pole
Saw the Bear its lustre roll.

There amid the lofty blue,
Veiled in robe of silver hue,
Luna showed her crescent pale,
And trembled through her misty veil:
Round her orb the halo shone
Lovely as the milky zone,
When, in winter's cloudless night,
It spreads o'er heaven its belt of light.
"Silvery planet! kindly shed
On thy humble votary's head
Thy serenest rays, and shine
On my brow with beam divine.
Light me through this world of sorrow,
Till I find a fair to-morrow;
Till the woes that rack my breast
Slumber in an infant's rest.
When my corpse is lowly laid
Where the yews inweave their shade,
Through the boughs that slowly wave,
Smile serenely on my grave.

"Never will thy pallid ray
O'er such lovely waters play,
Never shine on fairer bowers
Through the evening's quiet hours,
Nor shed thy flood of spotless light
On scenes more beauteous or more bright."

Land of my nativity!
How thou charm'st the wearied eye!
O, thou hast a genial balm,
That can the saddest bosom calm!
Smiling in the dewy dawn,
When the songsters o'er the lawn
Open their mellifluous throats
And warble their enchanting notes,
Glowing when the noon-tide beam
Gilds the flowery bordered stream,
And charming at the close of day,
When the twilight fades away.

Mountains swelling to the sky,
Forests frowning on the eye,
Waving woodlands, meadows gay,
Streamlets where the minnows play,
Winding valleys, swelling hills,
Crystal fountains, tinkling rills,
Smile in morning's rosy light,
And melt amid the shades of night.
Such thy scenes, for ever dear,
Whether far away or near;
Whether smiling on the eye,
Or in the hues of memory.
When I leave this desert vale,
Thou wilt ever bid me wail,
Always wake the parting sigh,
And draw the tear-drop from my eye.

THE PARTING OF WILLIAM AND MARY.

"We part, perhaps to meet no more:
To distant lands from thee I go;
Far, far beyond the ocean's roar,
For thee my tears will ever flow:

"An exile from my native land,
I long must plough the raging main:
Alas! no Mary's gentle hand
Shall soothe my bosom's inward pain.

"Thou weep'st, my love:—how dear those tears,
What treasures to thy William's heart!
They banish all his anxious fears,—
They blunt the point of sorrow's dart,—

"They tell me Mary loves me still,
And grieves to bid her last adieu:
O, guard her, Heaven, from every ill,
And keep her to her William true!"

"And wilt thou, William, think no more,
When far beyond the raging main,
How Mary lingers on this shore,
And strains to catch thy sail in vain?

"O William! let thy wishes rise
And send them o'er the wave to me:
The Power that rules in yonder skies
Will hear the vows of constancy."

"Yes, I will think when far away,
How thou art weeping on this shore;
Dark be the hour, and cursed the day,
When I shall muse on thee no more.

"But hark! the signal! we must part:—
While life remains, let us be true;
Yes, though I feel a bursting heart,
I now must bid my last adieu."

Her drooping head his Mary laid
Upon the youth she loved so well:
He gently kissed the sinking maid,
And breathed upon her lips *farewell;*

Then tore him from her fond embrace,
And dashed the tear-drops from his eye;
Just gazed upon her angel-face,
Then turned and marked the streamers fly.

He shouted, as he leaped on board,
To hide his bosom's inward pain;
The sails were set,—the loud winds roared,—
The ship ploughed foaming to the main.

"VANITY OF VANITIES, ALL IS VANITY."

On Reggio's classic shore I stood,
And looked across the wave below,
And saw the sea, a glassy flood,
In all the hues of morning glow;*
Groves waved aloft on sunward hills,
Their leaves were green and tipped with gold,
And all the dazzling pomp that fills
The sunset skies was round them rolled;
Arches on arches, proudly piled,
Seemed towering to the deep-blue sky,
And ruins lay deserted, wild,
And torrents foamed and thundered by;
And flowery meadows soft and green
In living emerald met the light,
And o'er their dewy turf were seen,
In countless gems, the drops of night;
And gardens, full of freshest flowers,
Unfurled the pictured veil of Spring,
And round the gay and perfumed bowers
Sweet-warbling birds were on the wing;
And many a tall and stately spire
Rose to the clouds, that loosely curled,
And, kindled each with solar fire,
Seemed beings of a brighter world;
And mountains reared their giant head,
And lifted high their peak of snow,
And o'er its wide, majestic bed
The ocean seemed to ebb and flow;
And all the wonders of the skies
And earth and sea were thrown around,
And all were stained in deepest dyes,
And vast as Being's utmost bound;
And on the magic scene I gazed,
And as behind the hills arose

* The Fata Morgana.

The golden sun, awhile it blazed
In brighter tints, and then it closed,
And all the changing pageant passed,
In faint and fainter hues, away,
Until a tender green, at last,
Glassed o'er the still and waveless bay,
And Reggio's towers, Messina's wall,
The hills, the woods, the frequent sail
That trembled on the stream, were all
The relics of the fairy tale.

'T was evening, and the sun went down,
Deep crimsoned in the frowning sky,
And Night, in robe of dusky brown,
Hung out her lurid veil on high;
A mist crept o'er the lonely wild,
That heaved, a sandy ocean, round,
And loosely lay, in billows piled,
To the horizon's farthest bound;
The sun, as if involved in blood,
Shone through the fog with direful beam,
And from behind the hills a flood
Of liquid purple poured its stream,
And o'er the dusty desert flowed,
Until, as kindled by the rays,
The heated plain intensely glowed,
Like some wide forest in a blaze;
And riding o'er the distant waste
The burning sand-spout stalked along,
And as the horrid phantom passed,
The driver keener plied his thong,
And shrieked, as on the Simoom roared,
As if the gathered fiends of hell,
Around in vengeful armies poured,
Had rung the world's decisive knell;
But far away a bright Oase *
Shone sweetly in the eastern sky,

* The Mirage of the Desert.

As fair as in the magic glass
Groves, lawns, and hills, and waters lie;
A lake in mirrored brightness lay,
Spread like an overflowing Nile,
Its peaceful rippling seemed to play,
And curl in Summer's sweetest smile;
The sunset tinged the surface o'er,
And here it lay in sheeted gold,
And there the ruffled stream, before
The evening breeze, in emerald rolled;
And many a white and platted sail
Dropped softly down the silent tide,
Or as the rising winds prevail,
Careening low was seen to glide;
And there the fisher plied his oar,
And spread his net, and hung his pole,
And drove with palm boughs to the shore,
In crowds, the gayly glittering shoal;
And birds were ever on the wing,
Or lightly plashing in the flood,
And, gorgeous as an Eastern king,
In stately pomp the flammant stood;
And herds of lowing buffaloes,
And light gazelles, came down to drink,
And there the river-horse arose,
And stalked a giant to the brink;
And shepherds drove their pastured flocks
To taste the cool, refreshing wave,
And on the heathy-mantled rocks
The goats their tender bleating gave:
And o'er the green and rice-clad plain,
In coats of crimson, gold, and blue,
The small birds trilled their mellow strain,
And revelled in the falling dew;
And there the palm its pillar heaves,
And spreads its umbelled crown of flowers,
And broad and pointed glossy leaves,
Whose shade the idle camp embowers;
And there the aged sit and tell
Their tales, as high the light smoke curls,

And eye the dance, around the well,
Of fiery youths and black-eyed girls,
Or where in many a leap and curve
They keenly rush around the ring,
And with an aim that cannot swerve,
In eager strife, the jerreed fling;
And there beside the bubbling fount
The date its welcome shadow threw,
And many a child was seen to mount,
And pluck the fruit that on it grew;
And with its broad and pendent boughs,
The thickly tufted sycamore,
The image of profound repose,
Waved silently along the shore;
And mangroves bent their limbs to taste
The wave, that calmly floated by,
And showed beneath, as purely glassed,
A softer image of the sky;
And groves of myrtle sweetly blew,
And hung their boughs with spikes of snow,
And beds of flowering cassia threw
A splendor like the morning glow;
And o'er the wild, that stretched away
To meet the sands, now steeped with rain,
The lilies, in their proud array,
With pictured brightness gemmed the plain
And roses, damask, white, and red,
Stood breathing perfume on the rocks,
And there the dry acacia spread
Its deep, unfading yellow locks;
And gardens brighter bloomed the while
Around the silver-tiled kiosk,
And brighter shone with sacred smile
The gilded crescent on the mosque;
And over all calm evening drew
A tender, softly dimming veil,
And mellowed down each gayer hue
To tints that seemed divinely pale;
It was a lovely resting-place,
The traveller's home, the pilgrim's well,

Where he might sit at ease and trace
His wanderings, and his dangers tell;
It rose at once upon their sight,
Like Paradise from Heaven descending,
And there, with keen and eager light,
Each look, in panting hope, was bending;
An island on the pathless waste,
It caught the weary camel's eye,
And on he flew in wildest haste,
As if to drink the wave, and die;
And there the fainting Bedouin gazed,
As if the cup of life were given,
And then with thankful look he raised
His withered hands in prayer to Heaven;
And as he hurried on his road
O'er burning sand, and flinty rock,
Before his eye the phantom flowed,
A flattering, but delusive mock;
Its brightest tints grew wan and pale,
Its fairer features faded dim,
Till in a dark and lonely vale
A mist alone was seen to swim;
And as the tear in anguish stole,
The last and faintest beam of day
Fled, and the dream was seen to roll
And vanish in the night away;
And cold the wild Harmattan blew,
And rolled the dusty billow by,
But still no welcome rain nor dew
Came down to soothe their misery;
Parched, burnt, in agony they tread
The waste, in hopeless longing, o'er,
A frowning sky above their head,
A shoreless sea of sand before.

And life is but a fairy tale:
Its fondest and its brightest hours
Are transient as the passing gale,
Or drops of dew that melt in flowers;

And life is but a fleeting dream,
A shadow of a pictured sky,
The airy phantom of a stream,
That flattering smiles, and hurries by;
The mists that hover o'er the deep,*
And seem the storm-beat sailor's home,
And, still retiring, always keep
Their station on the farthest foam;
Till imaged out, his woods and hills,
His father's cot, the village spire,
And all his heated fancy wills,
And all his eager hopes desire,
The white chalk coast that fronts the billow,
The boat that trimly scuds below,
The brook that glides beneath the willow,
With lulling chime and quiet flow;
Till all he loves, and all he longs
To meet and fold his arms around,
Come crowding in alluring throngs,
And every charm of home is found;
And round the ship the meadow lies,
That filled his hand with flowers in May,
And as the billows onward rise,
They spread and blossom green and gay;
But if he stoop to pluck the grass,
That waves in frolic mimicry,
Away the darling phantoms pass,
And leave alone the bitter sea:
And life is but a painted bow,
That crowns our days to come with smiles,
The mingled tints of Heaven, that throw
Their pomp on glory's airy piles;
But when we run to catch the gay
And glittering pageant, all is o'er,
And all its bright and rich array
Can draw us fondly on no more;
'T is like the moon who shines so clear
Above the mountains and the groves,

* The Mirage of the Ocean.

And seems to float along so near
The boy, he grasps the moon he loves,
And dreams it is some sweet, bright face,
Who smiles in such a pleasant sky,
And he would think it heaven to pass
His still, soft nights that maiden by;
He sits upon the grassy bank,
And rests his face upon his hand,
And looks intent, as if he drank
The light that silvers sea and land;
And though she smiles so sweetly on
Her fond and loving shepherd boy,
The same bright face is ever won
By those who make the night their joy.
O, life and all its charms decay!
Alluring, cheating, on they go;
The stream for ever steals away
In one irrevocable flow;
Its dearest charms, the charms of love,
Are fairest in their bud, and die
Whene'er their tender bloom we move;
We touch the leaves, they withered lie.
At distance all how gay, how sweet,
A very land of fairy blisses,
Where smiles, and tears, and soft words meet,
And willing lips unite in kisses;
But when we touch the magic shore,
The glow is gone, the charm is fled;
We find the dearest hues it wore
Are but the light around the dead,
And cold the hymeneal chain
That binds their cheated hearts in one,
And on, with many a step of pain,
Their weary race is sadly run;
And still, as on they plod their way,
They find, as life's gay dreams depart,
To close their being's toilsome day,
Naught left them but a broken heart.

THE FAIREST ROSE IS FAR AWA'.

The morn is blinking o'er the hills
With softened light and colors gay;
Through grove and valley sweetly trills
The melody of early day;
The dewy roses blooming fair
Glitter around her father's ha',
But still my Mary is not there,—
The fairest rose is far awa'.

The cooling zephyrs gently blow
Along the dew-bespangled mead,—
In every field the owsen low,—
The careless shepherd tunes his reed;
And while the roses blossom fair,
My lute with softly dying fa'
Laments that Mary is not there,—
The fairest rose is far awa'.

The thrush is singing on the hills,
And charms the groves that wave around,
And through the vale the winding rills
Awake a softly murmuring sound;
The robin tunes his mellow throat
Where glittering roses sweetly blaw,
But grieves that Mary hears him not,—
The fairest rose is far awa'.

Why breathe thy melody in vain,
Thou lovely songster of the morn?
Why pour thy ever-varying strain
Amid the sprays of yonder thorn?
Do not the roses blooming fair,
At morning's dawn or evening's fa',
Tell thee of one that is not there,—
The fairest rose that 's far awa'?

THE FLOWER OF THE VALLEY.

Sweet flower of the valley, why droop'st thou so low?
Ah! why is thy beauty all faded and gone?
Ah! who could destroy thee,—who wield the sad blow,—
Who rifle *thy* charms in their earliest dawn?

So gay was the morning that rose as you blew,
So fragrant the zephyrs that fluttered around,
So soft didst thou smile through thy mantle of dew,
No lovelier *flower* in the valley was found.

But see, on the turf all thy beauties are laid,
Thy leaves, they are scattered, thy sweetness is gone:
Thy colors — once gay as the rainbow — now fade
As fast as the hues that enliven the dawn.

Sweet flower! once the sweetest that bloomed in the vale,—
Sweet flower! we will weep, for thy beauties are fled,—
For those charms that are gone we will pour the sad wail,
And chant o'er thy ruins the dirge of the dead.

LINES

WRITTEN ON HEARING A LADY SING IN THE TOWER OF MONTEVIDEO, NEAR HARTFORD.

The soft dews of twilight are steeping the plain,
And gemming the boughs of the willow;
The eve-star is lighting its twinkle again,
To shine on the foam of the billow.

The south breeze is brushing the breast of the lake,
That swells with a light heaving motion,
And its ripple is heard on the pebbles to break
Like the slumbering wave of the ocean.

The gale on its pinions of gossamer flies
Through the boughs of the low bending willow,
And sweeping the forest, it mournfully sighs
O'er the turf of my flowery pillow.

It bears on its wing, from the dark, lonely tower,
O'er the mead, and the wave's "playful motion,"
The song of the maid, who at eve's balmy hour
Sings her sweet breathing strain of devotion:

Like the hymn of a seraph, it floats through the grove,
And sighs o'er the slope of the mountain;
How sweet, how enchanting, its warble of love!
How it lulls, like the glow of the fountain!

As I listen, I fancy the dew-dropping cloud
That glows with a lovely "to-morrow,"
An angel conceals in its ebony shroud,
Whose harp breathes her accent of sorrow.

Once, on a cloudless summer-day,
Beneath a mantling vine I lay,
When Cupid came by chance that way,
And aimed at me an arrow.

He laid the dart upon the bow,
And drew the horn and sinew so,
And said, "My friend, you soon will know,
How keenly stings my arrow."

His cheek was gay, his eye was bright,
And shot a piercing, bitter light:

He drew the nerve all tense and tight,
  And then let fly his arrow.

The bow twanged sharp, and with a bound
At once its mark the weapon found;
I tingled with the fiery wound
  Of that soul-kindling arrow.

He flapped his wings, away he flew,
And, turning backward, looked me through,
And slyly laughed, as forth I drew
  The heart-encrimsoned arrow.

I felt my blood like lava glow,
I writhed, and twined, and wrestled so,
As madmen in their dying throe, —
  I broke and cursed the arrow.

It is indeed a cruel thing,
When early youth is on the wing,
To feel, and keenly feel, the sting
  Of such a poisoned arrow.

My heart too firmly trusted, fondly gave
Itself to all its tenderness a slave;
I had no wish but thee, and only thee;
I saw no joy, no hope, beyond thy smile;
I knew no happiness, but only while
Thy love-lit eyes were kindly turned on me.

I took the tender image to my breast,
I made it there a dear, a cherished guest,
I laid it on the pillow of my soul;
I gave it all my feeling, and around
The fond idea all my heart-strings bound;
In that one point I blent my being's whole.

But thou hast gone, and left me here to bear
The weight of loneliness; thou thinkest not, where
Bright forms caress thee, of my bosom torn
By thee so coldly; but I cannot rend
Thy image from my heart, I cannot blend
Hate with the love so long, so fondly borne.

I feel my spirit falter, and my frame
Trembling and faint with weakness, but the flame
Of passion burns as brightly:—I will lay
My forehead on my pillow, and resign
My bosom to its torture, nor repine,
And let the fire consume my life away.

How beautiful is Night!
A smile is on her brow;
Her eyes of dewy light
Look out, serenely bright,
Upon the waves below:
The waters, in their flow,
Just murmur, and the air
Hath scarce a breath to show
A spirit moving there:
The world is purely fair,
The winds are hushed and still;
The moonlight on the hill
Is sleeping, and her ray
Along the falling rill,
In lightly dancing play,
Soft winding, steals away:
A cool and silent breath,
From waterfalls and streams,
Comes o'er my ear, like dreams,
Which, in the pictured death
Of slumber, on the soul
Delicious whispers roll;

And lead, in mazy light,
Before the spirit's eye,
Sweet visions of delight,
In trains of beauty, by.

How fair and calm is Night!
Amid the dewy bowers
She guides the silent Hours,
With fairy steps, along,
And round the floating throng
A cloudy vesture throws;
And loosely on the air
She spreads their raven hair
To every wind that blows:
They seem to hover by,
Between me and the sky,
Each with a golden zone,
A waving robe of snow,
A veil, whose folds are thrown
In undulating flow,
Like clouds, when breezes blow;
So to my fancy's view
The sylphid people play
Around the vaulted blue,
And then they melt away,
And leave the sky all bright,
With lamps of living light;
And as I fondly gaze,
Where countless cressets blaze,
I look to heaven and say,
"How beautiful is Night!"

Often, when at night delaying,
Where the winding river flows,
On the silent waters playing
How the star of beauty glows!

In the clear wave brightly sparkling,
Brightly as the love-lit eye,
Now again its beams are darkling,
As the clouds athwart it fly:
With a soft and tender feeling
When I whisper out my song,
While the mellow brook is stealing
Silently the sand along.

There is in that twinkling planet
More than all the stars can boast,
And my fond eye loves to scan it,
Like a light-house on a coast,
Where the budding Spring is ever
Pranking out her wooing bowers,
And the locks of beauty never
Float without a crown of flowers,
And her eye is ever straying
Round and round with kindling beam,
Like her own bright planet playing
Sweetly on the silent stream.

Now the star is near the mountain
Slowly setting in the west,
Shining on a crisping fountain,
Or a lakelet's ruffled breast;
Now its maiden brightness mingles
With the mist that hovers there,
Rising from the woody dingles,
Like a streaming tress of hair;

Now a form is imaged round it,
'T is the form that I adore;
Every charm of earth has crowned it,
Fairer, beauty never wore:
Oh! how dear that tender feeling,
When the rays of beauty play,
Where the mellow brook is stealing,
Lighted by the moon, away.

SONG.

O, PURE is the wind,
As it blows o'er the mountain;
And clear is the wave,
As it flows from the fountain;
And sweet are the flowers
In the green meadow blooming;
And gay are the bowers,
When the soft air perfuming.
  O go, dearest, go
  To the heath, and the mountain,
  Where the blue violets blow
  On the brink of the fountain;
  Where nothing but death
  Our affection can sever,
  And till life's latest breath
  Love shall bind us for ever.

O, bright is the morn,
When it breaks on the valley;
And shrill is the horn,
When the wild huntsmen sally;
And clear shines the dew,
As the hounds hurry o'er it;
And light blows the wind,
As the sail flies before it.
  O go, dearest, go, &c.

O, soft is the mist,
When it curls round the island;
And dark is the cloud,
As it hangs on the highland;
And sweet chimes the rill,
O'er the white pebble flowing;
And quick glides the boat,
O'er the smooth water rowing.
  O go, dearest, go, &c.

O, fleet is the deer
Through the blue heather springing,
And loud is the shout
Through the wild valley ringing;
And soft is the flute,
O'er the lake faintly sighing,
When the wide air is mute,
And the night-wind is dying.
O go, dearest, go, &c.

O go, dearest, go
To the heath and the mountain;
Where the heart shall be pure,
As the clear-flowing fountain;
Where the soul shall be free,
As the winds that blow o'er us,
And the sunset of life
Smile in beauty before us.
O, go, dearest, go
To the heath, and the mountain,
Where the blue violets blow
On the brink of the fountain;
Where nothing but death
Our affection can sever,
And till life's latest breath
Love shall bind us for ever.

THE LAND OF THE BLEST.

The sunset is calm on the face of the deep,
And bright is the last look of day in the west,
And broadly the beams of its parting glance sweep,
Like the path that conducts to the land of the blest:
All golden and green is the sea, as it flows
In billows just heaving its tide to the shore;
And crimson and blue is the sky, as it glows
With the colors which tell us that daylight is o'er.

I sit on a rock that hangs over the wave,
And the foam heaves and tosses its snow-wreaths below,
And the flakes, gilt with sunbeams, the flowing tide pave,
Like the gems that in gardens of sorcery grow:
I sit on the rock, and I watch the light fade
Still fainter and fainter away in the west,
And I dream I can catch, through the mantle of shade,
A glimpse of the dim, distant land of the blest.

And I long for a home in that land of the soul,
Where hearts always warm glow with friendship and love,
And days ever cloudless still cheerily roll,
Like the age of eternity blazing above:
There, with friendships unbroken, and loves ever true,
Life flows on, one gay dream of pleasure and rest;
And green is the fresh turf, the sky purely blue,
That mantle and arch o'er the land of the blest.

The last line of light is now crossing the sea,
And the first star is lighting its lamp in the sky;
It seems that a sweet voice is calling to me,
Like a bird on that pathway of brightness to fly:
"Far over the wave is a green sunny isle,
Where the last cloud of evening now shines in the west;
'T is the island that Spring ever woos with her smile;
O, seek it, — the bright, happy land of the blest!"

My heart was a mirror, that showed every treasure
Of beauty and loveliness life can display;
It reflected each beautiful blossom of pleasure,
But turned from the dark looks of bigots away;
It was living and moving with loveliest creatures,
In smiles or in tears, as the soft spirit chose;
Now shining with brightest and ruddiest features,
Now pale as the snow of the dwarf mountain-rose.

These visions of sweetness for ever were playing,
Like butterflies fanning the still summer air;
Some sported a moment, some, never decaying,
In deep hues of love are still lingering there:
At times some fair spirit, descending from Heaven,
Would shroud all the rest in the blaze of its light;
Then wood nymphs and fays o'er the mirror were driven,
Like the fire-swarms that kindle the darkness of night.

But the winds and the storms broke the mirror, and severed
Full many a beautiful angel in twain;
And the tempest raged on, till the fragments were shivered
And scattered, like dust, as it rolls o'er the plain:
One piece, which the storm, in its madness, neglected
Away, on the wings of the whirlwind, to bear,
One fragment was left, and that fragment reflected
All the beauty that MARY threw carelessly there.

O, NOW 's the hour, when air is sweet,
And birds are all in tune,
To seek with me the cool retreat,
In bright and merry June;

When every rose-bush has a nest,
And every thorn a flower,
And every thing on earth is blest,
This sweet and holy hour.

O come, my dear, when evening flings
Her veil of purple round,
And zephyr, on his dewy wings,
Sweeps o'er the flowery ground;
When every bird of day is still,
And stars are bright above,
O come, my dear, and we will fill
Our cup, and drink of love.

We 'll fill it from the pure blue sky,
And from the glowing west,
And catch its spirit in thine eye,
And in the small bird's nest;
And take its sweetness from the flowers,
Its freshness from the spring,
Its coolness from the dewy hours,
When night-hawks take the wing.

Then we will wander far away,
Along the flowery vale,
Where winds the brook, in sparkling play,
And freshly blows the gale;
And we will sit beneath the shade
That maples weave above,
And, on the mossy pillow laid,
Will drink the cup of love.

O, WILT thou go with me, love,
And seek the lonely glen?
O, wilt thou leave for me, love,
The smiles of other men? —

The birds are there aye singing,
And the woods are full of glee,
And love shall there be flinging
His roses over thee.

O, wilt thou go with me, dear,
And share my humble lot?
O, wilt thou live with me, dear,
Within a lowly cot?—
Though beauty hath enshrouded thee
With all that 's sweet and fair,
The sorrows that have clouded thee
Shall all be wanting there.

O, wilt thou go with me, Anne,
To yonder mountain side,
And, happy there in me, Anne,
Ne'er sigh for aught beside?—
O, Heaven shall there be over us,
Unclouded, pure, and bright,
And wings of love shall cover us,
And all around be light.

Yes, thou wilt go with me, love,
I see it in thy smile,
And I will be to thee, love,
Thy shelter all the while;
And thou shalt spread thy bloom around,
And be all sweet and fair,
And every sight and touch and sound
Shall be ecstatic there.

Yes, thou wilt go with me, dear,
The cot shall be thy home,
And never near its roof, dear,
Shall want or sorrow come;
O, I will be the parent dove,
That hovers o'er her nest,
And we will know how sweet is love
Caressing and caressed.

Yes, thou wilt go with me, Anne,
Though seas are now between,
And thou wilt dwell with me, Anne,
In woodlands flowered and green;
I cannot cross the sea to thee,
I do not love that shore,
So cross the ocean, dear, to me,
And we will part no more.

HERE the air is sweet,
Fresh from the roses newly blowing;
Here the waters meet,
Down the grassy valley flowing;
Here the bands of ivy twine,
Here the bells in yellow shine
On the flowering gelsemine,
Round the woven trellis growing.

Here the flitting breeze
Wafts afar the musky treasure,
And the wanton bees
Sip the honeyed fount of pleasure;
Here the loving spirits dwell,
Here they sit, and weave their spell,
And within the blossom's bell
Tune their soul-dissolving measure.

Here the wind is balm,
Laden with the breath of roses;
Here the air is calm,
And the sleeping noon-flower closes;
Now the sun is setting bright,
And his arch of purple light
Heralding the summer night,
Earth in dreams of bliss reposes.

Here 's a magic bower:
O'er it budding vines are creeping,
And a dewy shower,
By, a bank of turf is steeping;
Though the fallen winds are mute,
Faintly from the sweet-blown flute,
Tones, that with the stillness suit,
Harmonies of love are keeping.

I am here alone:
Far has fled my flowery dreaming,
All its beauty flown
Like a bow by moonlight gleaming;
Fancy's day of love is o'er,
All its rich and golden store
Ne'er can charm my spirit more
With its false, but fairy seeming.

THE WANDERING SPIRIT.

There 's a voice that is heard in the depth of the sky,
Where nothing is seen but the blue-tinted heaven;
That voice with the wind rolls its mellowness by,
And a few notes alone to our fond ears are given:
The spirit who sings it still hastens away,
He is doomed round the wide earth for ever to roam,
He may settle a moment, but never will stay,
For he ne'er found, and never will find, here a home.

There is grief in the voice, as it comes through the air,
Like the low-moaning wind in the calmness of even,
Or the tone, as we dream, of the angels, who bear
The pure soul, that rises to mingle with heaven;
It was clear when it first came, but quickly afar
It murmured and died, like the wave on the shore,
When the mariner hails the benevolent star,
That rises and smiles, and the tempest is o'er.

O, that voice is the dirge that for ever is sung
O'er the wreck and the ruin of beauty and love,
But in ears that are deaf is its melody flung,
There are none who will listen, but pure ones above :
O, earth is no place for the spirit who feels
Every wound of the heart with the pang of despair;
He will mourn, and be never at home, till he steals
To the skies, and the bright world that welcomes
him there.

FAREWELL TO MY LYRE.

Lyre of my soul! the parting hour draws nigh,
The hour that tears thy votary away, —
The hour when death shall close my fading eye,
And wrap in earth my cold and lifeless clay.

I feel his icy fingers chill my heart,
And curdle all the blood that warms my breast;
Charm of my darkest moments! soon we part, —
Soon shall thy chords in endless silence rest.

What if thy sounds have charmed the coldest ear, —
What if they breathed like melody divine, —
What if they stole the fair one's purest tear,
Or bade the downcast eye with pleasure shine!

Still I must sink in death's unbroken sleep,
And coldly slumber 'neath the hallowed ground;
And thou must all thy chords in silence keep,
Nor sweetly wake them to the feeblest sound.

Sleep in yon cypress shade, — its heavy gloom
Becomes the awful stillness of the grave;
Rest, where, above yon maiden's early tomb,
The willow's boughs in sorrow seem to wave.

There should the fainting zephyr, whispering by,
Awake one note along thy tuneful string,
O, be it sadder than the mourner's sigh,
And in my ear like funeral dirges ring.

Let not a trill of joy invade my ear,
This gloomy hour asks nothing of delight:
Let all be like the pall that shades the bier,
Or like the darkest canopy of night.

Let no sweet songster pour its witching spell —
No voice of comfort to my spirit come;
Naught but the echo of the passing-bell,
The hollow murmur of the muffled drum.

And yet I seem to hear thy seraph strain
Pour like a gentle stream along the gale:
It ceases, — now its music wakes again,
And breathes as sweetly as the turtle's wail.

Ah, I would brush thy chords and faintly wake
To sounds of joy thy melody awhile, —
Would charm my heart a moment ere it break,
And gild my dying features with a smile:

But no! my hand refuses: 't is but clay, —
The touch of death has withered all its powers;
Soon will its wings my spirit waft away
From thee, thou charmer of my darkest hours!

Farewell, thou lyre of sweetest minstrelsy!
Distraction calls, its sufferer must obey;
The ruthless hand of dark adversity
Has chilled my soul, and torn thy chords away:

The mist of death, that hovers o'er my eyes,
Withdraws thy lovely image from my view;
Like fancy's midnight dream, th' illusion flies, —
Lyre of my soul, adieu! a long adieu.

CARE-WORN, and sunk in deep despondency,
I bless the hours that lay my thought at rest:
I woo the covert of a midnight sky,
But sink in feverish dreams, by doubt distrest.

The pleasing morning of my early days,
My opening fortune's bright and flattering bloom,
Gone are they all, and mute the voice of praise:
How hard to one who shone, this cruel doom!

Would I were in some lonely desert born,
And 'neath the sordid roof my being drew;
Were nursed by poverty the most forlorn,
And ne'er one ray of hope or pleasure knew.

Then had my soul been never taught to rise;
Then had I never dreamed of power or fame;
No pictured scene of bliss deceived my eyes,
Nor glory lighted in my breast its flame.

What to the wretch like me this towering mind!
'T is but a curse, — a pang that racks the soul.
Better in humble life to be resigned
To ceaseless toil, as round the seasons roll.

Happy the life that in a peaceful stream,
Obscure, unnoticed, through the vale has flowed;
The heart that ne'er was charmed by fortune's gleam,
Is ever sweet contentment's blest abode.

But can I leave the scenes my fancy drew
In colors rich as heaven, and strong as light;
Can I avert from fame my longing view,
And plunge again amid my native night?

Hard is the pang that rends these links away,
And humbling to my soul to rise no more;
How cruel to abandon wisdom's ray,
And find my hopes, my fame, my prospects o'er!

Yes, I must yield, — but slowly I retire;
O, can I dim the light that science gave?
O, can I quench my bosom's ardent fire?
Welcome, ye paths, that lead me to my grave.

ANACREONTICS.

I.

Ἡ γῆ μέλαινα πίνει. Anac. Od. ϑ.

EARTH is a thirsty drinker,
The trees drink from its bosom,
The ocean drinks the wet winds,
The fiery sun the ocean,
The moon drinks in the sun's light.
Then why, my friends, be angry,
Because I love to drink too.

II.

FULL-bosomed maids of Chio!
Around your auburn tresses
The woven roses twining,
Now sport in circling dances.
The moon is on the ocean,
The light, loose clouds around her
Their fleecy heaps are piling,
And gird her with a halo:
No longer from the billow
The fresh sea-wind is stealing;
His pinions wet with night-dew,
And bathed in liquid odors,
He slumbers on the flower-bed,
And lies till morning wake him.
Then come, ye maids of Chio!
And while your dark eyes sparkle,
Full eyes of living brightness,
Weave in your mazy dances

The flowery chain of Ero,
And round our yielding bosoms
Its rings of roses linking,
Give us those glowing kisses,
That drop the tempting treasures
Of Aphrodite's nectar.

III.

Dear girl of Mytilene!
Thy dark locks loosely flowing,
Thy full, round, jet eye sparkling
With soul-subduing glances,
Thy brown cheek flushed and glowing,
Thy lips, like opening rose-buds
Their earliest balm exhaling,
Thy slender hands of coral,
Whose light and fairy fingers,
The cittern sweetly tuning,
Awake the song of Sappho,
And echo, "Lovely Phaon!
Adored, but cruel Phaon!"
Dear girl of Mytilene!
Beneath the bending vine-bower,
That hangs its loaded clusters
Full-swoln with purple nectar,
And o'er the vaulted trellis
Its tendrils, wildly ramping,
With broad, green leaves inwoven,
Shut out the star and moonlight, —
Dear girl of Mytilene!
As in that secret bower
Thy love-lorn song is flowing,
The shepherd, on the moss bank
All silvered o'er with moonlight,
Beside a dimpling fountain,
Shall play upon his tabret,
Responsive to thy echoes,
The dying song of Sappho
To loved, but cruel Phaon.

HORATIAN.

"Quem tu, Melpomene, semel." — Horat. Od. L. IV. 3.

Fairest of all, bright Urania!
Who, on Helicon's top, sing to the golden stars,
When Night draws all her curtains round,
And far over the hills shines the moon's mellow light;
First she gilds the tall mountain-top,
Then on glittering streams, and the wide-spreading plain,
And the dark waves of the tossing sea,
Pours all her mellowest beams, till earth and ocean smile.
Fairest of all, bright Urania!
Sing to thy golden-stringed lyre, sing the sweet song of Heaven.

Come on your sky-blue wings, ye Paphian doves!
And o'er me drop the pure Idalian dews,
Come, fan the air with silken pinions,
Pluck with tender bill the roses,
While they open in the thickets,
Heavy with the tears of morning:
Bear them on the faltering breezes,
As they waken with Aurora,
Lightly brushing o'er the meadow,
Kissing, as they pass, the lilies;
Sighing through the silent forest,
Waking from their nightly slumbers
All its murmuring tones and echoes;
Floating o'er the sleeping ocean,
When without a wave or billow,
Like a green and golden mirror,

In the morning light it glows;
Bear these nectar-breathing blossoms,
Hovering round on rustling pinions,
Drop them on my mossy pillow,
Till a heap of crimson sweetness
Buries in its down my head.
O come, ye Paphian doves! from Cyprus come;
Close o'er the smiling queen of love and joy
Your wavy pinions, that a canopy
Of living sapphire, gold, and amethyst,
Emerald and hyacinth and orient pearl,
Cool her and shield her in its moving shade.
The Paphian Goddess, on her sea-born car
Of polished shell, sails lightly on the wind:
Before her chirp the bounding sparrows,
As they draw the lovely burden
With a trace of gauzy film:
She nearer comes and sends before
Her harbinger, the breath of roses,
Sweeter than the spicy gales
That blow from Araby, the blest;
Where, resting on white coffee-beds,
Or groves of frankincense and myrrh,
They drink the airs of Paradise;
Sweeter than a languid zephyr,
From a flowering myrtle thicket,
Which, beside the briny billow,
Sucks the essences of love,
And by the secret arts of Nature,
To the most refined sweetness,
Floating in a cloud of ether,
Turns the salt and bitter wave.
Drop on my head those thrilling dews,
So oft in childhood's tender hours
You poured in kindling showers around.
But no, — my brow is cold, —
Passion's fire is spent, —
The dews no sooner touch my forehead,
Than they freeze to crystal drops,
d scornful bound away.

I once thought of writing a poem in the irregular measure of Thalaba, the scene to be laid in Peru, among the Incas. I however wrote only the following *morceaux*.

MAN is born to die,
And so are nations. Thus I mused,
As on the Inca's pyramid
I sat and gazed around.
Here, methought, a royal race,
To whom a nation bowed,
As if they were the sons of Heaven,
Came and paid their adoration
To the all-o'erseeing sun.
And where is now that royal race?
Gone, and mingled with the ages
That have passed away.
Here a countless multitude
Of self-made slaves, through weary years,
Toiled and built this stately pile.
Years on years have rolled away,
Since they who built it lived.
Still it rears its massy front,
And stands unmoved, in proud defiance,
'Gainst the scythe of time
And ruin's crumbling hand;
While the same winds bleach the bones
Of the poor slave, that toiled,
And the great king, who bade.

'T WAS midnight, — and the full round moon
Was riding in the midway heaven,
And poured her faint but spotless light
Around the pillow where he lay.
On the tender grass, and half-shut flowers,
That closed their leaves against the nightly air,
The dews, that hung in falling drops,
Sparkled with a feeble ray.
Sleep poured out her poppy dews,
And spread her gauzy mantle o'er him;

Like an infant in its cradle,
There in innocence he lay,
Unconscious of impending harm.
Sudden from the ground he starts,
And feels it rock beneath his feet,
And like the ocean roll.
From the north, a growling sound
Rushes on his ear.
Louder, louder, on it comes,
Like the never-ending din
Of some wide waterfall,
That in the desert pours its ceaseless flood;
Or like the roar of ocean
When the tempest rages,
And on a reef of broken rocks
The billows chafing, bursting, foam;
Or like the rush of myriad horsemen
When to conflict fierce they ride,
And 'neath the thundering tramp
Quivers the embattled plain.
Never ending, still increasing,
On it comes, and now beneath him
Bellows like the groans of hell:
Instant to the ground he falls,
And long entranced is lost.
Hark! the volcan's thunder
Rolling o'er the hills.
As at midnight, when the storm
Rears its front in Heaven,
And sheds a thicker darkness o'er the gloom,
Bursts the thunderbolt,
And shakes the solid ground:
So the volcan's thunder rolls.
See the lightning's flash
Quivering in the sky.
Long red streams of flaring light
Rise and lick the stars.
From the crater's mouth
Rolls the fiery flood:

Down the rocks it sweeps its way,
And the ice of ages
In an instant melts,
And bursts a torrent to the plains below.
Slower rolls the fiery flood, —
From cliff to cliff it tumbles,
And like the mingled roar of thousand cataracts,
Deeper, deeper strikes the ear.
  Hast thou seen Niobe's statue
Stand in speechless agony,
With eye upraised, and clasped hand,
As if to curse the bolt of Heaven?
So Atalpa stood.

THE night draws on,
And closer o'er the wave
Her sombre curtain spreads.
The dark-blue Heaven swells o'er the sea,
And rests its pillars on the tossing deep.
The star of evening
Has lit its lamp,
And, hanging o'er the western wave,
Sparkles upon the foam below.
How calmly steal the winds along the main,
And heave the water round the cleaving prow!
The sail swells lightly overhead,
And the streamer scarcely flutters; all is still,
But the petrel, as he circles round,
And skims the wave with snowy wing.

'T IS midnight, and the moon
Has lit her lamp in heaven.
Around her silver throne
The twinkling stars grow pale,
So bright she pours her beams.
Below her, o'er the sea,
Spread like a floor of glass
Unruffled by the winds,
Her image travels on.

As the mariner looks at the wake of the ship,
He sees a long track of light behind,
And the sparkling foam a world of gems.
I hear the voice of mirth,
The song of love, and the flute's soft note
Floating o'er the wave.
A white sail steers its course against the moon
And seems a sheet of snow.
Beneath its shade the music breathes, —
'T is the ship of joy that sails.
Streamers of silk wave on the topmast,
Shining with purple and gold.
So light the west wind blows, —
The sails flap and the cordage creaks;
While, moving to the sound of flutes,
The long white oars in order strike,
And cut the marble main.

THE morn is young in heaven,
And the light is spread over the mountains;
The sky is blue above,
And the earth is green below;
The mist rolls over the rocks,
And curls its light folds in the valley;
The grass is wet with dew,
A gem is on every twinkling blade;
The song of the birds has awaked the sleeper,
And he starts on his journey anew.

NEW ENGLAND.

HAIL to the land whereon we tread,
Our fondest boast!
The sepulchre of mighty dead,
The truest hearts that ever bled,
Who sleep on glory's brightest bed,
A fearless host:

No slave is here; — our unchained feet
Walk freely, as the waves that beat
    Our coast.

Our fathers crossed the ocean's wave
    To seek this shore;
They left behind the coward slave
To welter in his living grave;
With hearts unbent, high, steady, brave,
    They sternly bore
Such toils as meaner souls had quelled;
But souls like these, such toils impelled
    To soar.

Hail to the morn when first they stood
    On Bunker's height!
And fearless stemmed the invading flood,
And wrote our dearest rights in blood,
And mowed in ranks the hireling brood,
    In desperate fight:
O, 't was a proud, exulting day,
For ev'n our fallen fortunes lay
    In light.

There is no other land like thee,
    No dearer shore;
Thou art the shelter of the free;
The home, the port of liberty
Thou hast been, and shalt ever be,
    Till time is o'er.
Ere I forget to think upon
My land, shall mother curse the son
    She bore.

Thou art the firm, unshaken rock,
    On which we rest;
And rising from thy hardy stock,
Thy sons the tyrant's frown shall mock,
And slavery's galling chains unlock,

And free the oppressed:
All, who the wreath of freedom twine,
Beneath the shadow of the vine
Are blessed.

We love thy rude and rocky shore,
And here we stand:
Let foreign navies hasten o'er,
And on our heads their fury pour,
And peal their cannon's loudest roar,
And storm our land:
They still shall find, our lives are given
To die for home; — and leant on Heaven
Our hand.

NAVAL ODE.

OUR walls are on the sea,
And they ride along the wave,
Manned with sailors, bold and free,
And the lofty and the brave
Hoist their flag to the sport of the gale;
With an even march they sweep
O'er the bosom of the deep,
And their order trimly keep,
As they sail.

Though so gallantly we ride,
Yet we do not seek the fight;
We have justice on our side,
And we battle in our right,
For our homes, and our altars, and sires:
Then we kindle in our cause,
And awhile a solemn pause —
When the cannon's iron jaws
Spout their fires.

We abhor the waste of life,
And the massacre of war;
We detest the brutal strife
In the van of Glory's car;
But we never will shrink from the foe:
This, when battle's lightning runs
Through his horror-speaking guns,
And his brazen thunder stuns,
He shall know.

We have met them on the deep,
With Decatur and with Hull,
Where our fallen comrades sleep
In their glory's proudest full;
For our homes we will meet them again:
Let their boasted navies frown,
As they proudly bear them down;
We will conquer, burn, or drown,
On the main.

We, too, have hearts of oak,
And the hour of strife may come,
With its hurricane of smoke,
Hissing ball and bursting bomb,
And the death-shot may launch through our crew;
But our spirits feel no dread,
And we bear our ship ahead,
For we know that honor's bed
Is our due.

Then come on, ye gallant tars!
With your matches in your hand,
And parade beneath our stars,
With a free and noble stand,
As you wait for the moment of death:
Hark the word! the foe is nigh,
And at once their war-dogs fly,
But, with bosoms throbbing high,
Yield your breath.

Do your duty, gallant boys!
And you homeward shall return
To partake your country's joys,
When the lights of triumph burn,
And the warm toast is drank to the brave
Then when country calls again,
Be your march along the main,
And in glory spread her reign
O'er the wave.

THOU art endeared to me by all
The ties of kindred minds,
And thou hast twined my heart in all
The chains that beauty binds;
The man who could deceive thee,
And, when the prize was won,
Could ruin, scorn, and leave thee,
Must have a heart of stone.

For but one look of kindness given
By thee, my heart would brave
The coldest, darkest frowns of Heaven,
The terrors of the grave:
O, death cannot affright me,
When thou art smiling by;
I ask no star to light me,
But the sparkle of thine eye.

But all thy bloom and loveliness
How soon will fade away!
Thy beauty and thy comeliness
Will moulder into clay:
O, when thy charms have taken wing,
And all thy light is gone,
How fondly still my heart would cling
To thee, and thee alone!

THE FRENCHMAN'S DARLING.*

The rose may sparkle in the morn,
And blush and brighten on its thorn;
The gaudy tulip proudly spread
Its glories o'er the enamelled bed;
The iris imitate the bow,
That sunbeams on a tempest throw;
All these may shine around, — but yet
I love my darling mignonette.

I ask no deep-encrimsoned flower
From India's never-fading bower;
No lotus,† where it closely weaves
The Ganges with its azure leaves;
I ask no pensive bud of woe, ‡
That gives the night its wreath of snow;
All these may have a charm, — but yet
Thy charm is more, sweet mignonette.

No lily, § that with gold-specked urn
Seems like a chandelier to burn,
Where wide Savanna's waters flow
Beneath a forest bower of snow; ||
No palm with bending tufts of fire,
No spiced vanilla, I desire;
These you may fondly twine, — but yet
I fondlier twine my mignonette.

The Scot may love his thistle-down,
Its prickly leaves, and purple crown;
And Erin on her shamrock smile,
The beauty of her emerald isle;

* Reseda odorata, the Mignonette.
† Nymphæa cerulea, the Sacred Lotus.
‡ Nyctanthes Arbor-tristis, Night Jessamine.
§ Lilium superbum.
|| Magnolia grandiflora.

The holly twine its glossy braid,
A starry wreath for Albion's head:
We love the modest *violette*,*
And dearer still the *mignonette*

ADIEU ! fair flower, though frail:
I gazed on thee awhile,
And thought I saw thee smile,
And woo the passing gale;
And thou didst shine the while,
In early beauty bright,
And in thy maiden light
Who would have dreamed of guile?
The cankerworm will blight
Thy colors, now so gay,
And they will pass away,
Like drops that fall by night,
Before the eye of day:
It nestles in thy core,
And thou wilt charm no more
The winds that round thee play;
But all thy sweetness o'er,
Thy leaves will droop and fall,
And darkness spread its pall
Where all was bright before.
And when thy beauty all
Has faded, they will turn
Away, and coldly spurn
Thy love, and thou wilt call
Unnoticed, and wilt mourn,
That in the flush of spring,
When hope was on the wing,
And virtue from her urn

---

* Viola tricolor, the Pansy Violet; — the flower of Napoleon.

Her choicest dews might fling,
  And drop her richest wave,
  That thou didst dig thy grave,
And barb, for death, a sting.

WE met in cheerless hours, my dear,
  When life had waned with me,
And all that once had charmed me here
Was gone, but only thee, my dear,—
  Was gone, but only thee.

I loved thee with the glow of youth,
  But with a purer flame;
I vowed, before the shrine of truth,
To be for aye the same, my dear,
  To be for aye the same.

For youthful passion soon decays,
  It flashes and it dies;
But my fond feeling shone with rays
That kindle in the skies, my dear,
  That kindle in the skies.

Thou wert too young to read my heart,
  Or love the spirit's light;
Thou saidst, "Gay boyhood can impart
A pleasure doubly bright, my dear,
  A pleasure doubly bright."

It was the fondness of the eye,
  That led thy heart away;
And not the hues that deeper lie
Than boyhood bright and gay, my dear,
  Than boyhood bright and gay.

So farewell, love, for dear to me
Thy heart shall be for ever;
And though I cannot live with thee,
O, I 'll forget thee never, dear,
O, I 'll forget thee never.

O, LOVE was made to mourn,
Its home is not below;
While in this being's bourn,
It still must weep in woe.

Its home is in the skies;
A wanderer with men,
It turns its longing eyes
To find that home again.

But there are forms so bright,
So fair, they seem its own;
They glow, like stars at night,
When clouds away have flown.

And there we fondly turn,
And think, that love's pure fire
Will ever brightly burn,
The spirit's vestal pyre.

But oh! how short the light,
How soon it fades away!
And all our heart's delight,
Enchantments, — where are they?

The glow, the bloom, are fled,
O, never to return;
And hope to heaven has sped,
For love was made to mourn.

TRANSLATION OF A LATIN ODE.

WINTER now has flown away,
  And the snow has left the hills;
Spring, with cheek all flushed and gay,
  Now her urn with fragrance fills.

Now the ploughman's heart is high,
  As he drives his team along,
Turning every furrow by
  To the melody of song.

Now the meadow laughs with flowers,
  And the woods a balsam pour;
Zephyrs breathe through rosy bowers,
  Where they nod along the shore.

Now the brook, that lately stole
  Murmuring in an icy chain,
Freshens, as its waters roll,
  With sweet waves, the grassy plain

Now the pastured bullocks drink,
  Where full rivers kiss their brim;
And where poplars crown the brink,
  Rustic flutes and voices hymn.

Now the girls, in festal glee,
  Garlanded with roses, play;
Gathering blossoms, like the bee,
  Light they sport the summer day.

When she thus, on Enna's plain,
  Crowned with myrtle, chanced to rove,
Pluto, from her frighted train,
  Stole the idol of his love.

Fairest Spring! at thy return,
  Meadows breathe the balm of flowers,
And the wheels of day's god burn
  Brightest in the train of hours.

THE SABBATH.

A SAPPHIC.

SWEET is the morning when the Sabbath-day dawns,
And earth and sky spread lovelier before me;
When not a breath stirs, in its whispering motion,
                    Garden or forest,
Which does not seem to partake in the holy
Peace of the pure hearts, where passion slumbers,
Care is composed, and the thoughts all awaken
                    Bright with devotion.
Sweeter the lark sings on that sunny morning,
Livelier the wren chirps round the shingled cottage,
Deeper the robin swells his throat, and pours forth
                    Hymns to his Maker.
Sweetly the bell sounds far in the distance,
Rising and falling with the winds, and rolling
Over hill and mountain, like the tones that summon
                    Pure souls to heaven.
Sweet comes the music of the rustic voices,
When in the oak grove, or the low-browed temple,
Hymning and praising HIM whose name is HOLY,
                    Hearts glow with rapture.
Sweet is the clear tone, where the breath of incense,
Longings of clean hearts, prayers by pure lips spoken,
Swell on the light winds, through the arching branches;
                    Sweet as when organs,
In the dark choir of the lofty-vaulted minster,

Pour forth the deep stream of harmony, and roll
round
Pillar and altar, fretted roof and tall arch,
Sounds like the echoes
Which, in the still night, after storms have beaten
Wild on the roof-tree, round the distant mountains,
Mellow, but majestic, send on the soothed ear
Calmness and slumber.
Sweet is the Sabbath, to the heart who loves it,
As the day when heaven's gates opened on this
dark world,
When the KING OF GLORY, mounted on a bright
cloud,
Conquering ascended.

O EVENING! thou art lovely: — in thy dress
Of sober gray I woo thee, when thy star
Comes o'er the hazy hills, that rise afar,
When tender thoughts upon my spirit press,
And with the whispering gales and fanning airs
The quiet swelling of my bosom pairs;
And by the lake that lieth motionless,
Low in the secret hollow, where the shade,
By bending elms and drooping willows made,
Displays its peaceful canopy, and gives
A moving picture to the lymph below,
Where float the sapphire sky, the clouds of snow,
The evening streaks, and every swarm that lives
And murmurs in the dun air, and the leaves
That quiver in the breath of night, and shine
With slowly gathered drops, and boughs that play,
Rising and falling gently, he who grieves
For some deep-wounding sorrow, as is mine,
In such a lonely shade his head may lay,
And on the scented grass and flowers recline,
And gaze upon the lingering light of day.

Empress of night! I saw thee through the rack,
That *fleeced* * the face of heaven, careering by,
And launch again upon a cloudless sky,
A beam of glory setting in thy track;
Like vessel in her course along the sea,
Now voyaging through islands, now away
On the wide ocean, in her liberty
Rejoicing; or like falcon on her wing
Skirting the mountain shadows, as they fling
Gloom o'er the world beneath them, now at play,
On broad, exulting pinions, in the clear
Blue noon-vault, where nor speck nor mist appear,
And bathing in the deepest flood of day; —
So seemed thy round, full orb to hold its flight,
Ascending proudly to its highest throne,
Mellowing the dun obscurity of night,
And walking in its majesty alone;
Now through its waving veil of white clouds beaming
With softer light, now pouring on their snow,
Floating like heaps of foam, an iris glow;
Now from a narrow rift in glory streaming
With columned rays, as when through arches shine
Thy beams on some looped wall or broken shrine,
That prouder swell in thy uncertain gleaming;
And now undimmed, unshrouded, on the high
O'erbending vault of sapphire, as an eye
Soothing the brow of heaven, it pours abroad
Brightness o'er vale and mountain, gilds the rock,
Silvers the winding river, tips the wave
With flowing amber, where its foam-wreaths lave
The ocean's bulwark, seeming to unlock
The pure and calm benignity of God.

* I have used this word in a new sense, but easily understood, I presume.

STAR of the dewy morning! from thy sphere
Of light and purity, before the hue
Of dawn has tinged thy lofty throne of blue,
Before the purple, gold, and crimson stain
The soft transparence of that heavenly plain,
Before the warbling birds salute the ear,
While yet the hills are dark, before the glow
Irradiates yon aerial peak of snow,
And paints the floating clouds, and dyes their veil,
That with the wind swells, like the ruby sail
Of Nautilus, who skims along the deep,
Ere yet the mustering winds the mirror sweep;—
Star of the dewy morning! by thy ray
I love to brush the pearls that gem the lawn,
The while I hasten, ere the bars are drawn
That close the portals of approaching day,
From yonder hill to view the smiling dawn
Shine on the living landscape's proud array;
And while those flashes from the orient play,
Thou sparklest now intensely, now thy beam
Scatters a feebler radiance on the stream,
And as the sun's bright herald gayly flushes,
And from the deep-stained windows of the morn
The rosy nymph of light and darkness born
In all the glow of youth and beauty blushes,
Thy faint and fainter twinkling dies away:
So, when through life's chill night we journey on,
Following the star-like beacon in the skies,
Till, as the long and weary way is done,
At once the doors of heaven before us rise,
A wave of glory from the Eternal Sun,
The beaming welcome of the Holy One,
Mingles with Love's angelic harmonies.

Bow of the fabled huntress! who on high,
Throned in the bright meridian, bend'st thy arch
Towards Day's beaming chariot on its march
Of triumph o'er this pure autumnal sky,
Which, mantled in a soft cerulean dye,
Encircles Nature with its crystal dome,
And, like the matchless Pantheon of Rome,
Shows in its perfect sphere one only eye;—
I mark thy silver crescent purely white
Inlaying yon sublimest azure, where,
Clear and transparent as the viewless air,
And like the empyrean pavement bright and fair,
Expands the softest tinctured arch of light.
Faintly amid this canopy of blue
Thy maiden brightness sweetly trembles through
The golden glories of the orb of day;—
But soon thy sparkling circlet in the west,
Then following, as thou now lead'st on the way,
Shall glitter on the ocean's glassy breast,
And on the mountain's mellow summit play,
And, with the star of beauty by thy side,
Behind yon waving ridge of cedars glide
Serenely to the palace of thy rest.

A REVERIE.

I saw a neat white cottage by a rill,
A limpid rill, that wound along a glade,
Curling and flashing to the sun; a shade
Of willows brooded over it; a hill,
Not distant, heaved its fresh green slope, and smiled
With daisies and with dandelions; oft
I wandered through such meadows when a child,
And loved the turf below, the sky aloft,
So softly green, so clearly, purely blue;
And as the mild wind, breathing odors, flew

Serenely through the grass tufts, and the crown
Of dandelions filled the fields with down,
Or some gay butterfly, on velvet wing,
Flitted around me, in the hearty glee
Of youth just bursting out of infancy,
And nerved with all the buoyancy of Spring;
Wild as the courser, when he bounds away,
And gives his graceful limbs their freest play,
And perks his ears, and waves his flowing tail,
His broad mane proudly heaving on the gale,
Now stops, now, with keen neigh and flashing eye,
Leaps like the winds, and scours and gallops by,—
So, in the bloom of early life I flew,
Where'er the insect roved, the feather blew,
For ever cheated, and for ever still
The creature of a wild and reckless will,
Pursuing after bees and flowers anew.
I saw that neat white cottage, and I thought
That was the shelter I so long had sought,
And there with one companion I might rest
My weary head on humble Quiet's breast;
And see the Year come forth, and dress her bowers,
And o'er the lattice weave her veil of flowers;
And now, in playful wandering down the stream,
Follow its mazy bend, and in a dream
Of holy musing, on its banks of thyme
Reposing, listen to its simple chime,
Through glossy pebbles, over pearly shells;
And, stealing through the sunny meadow, cull
And crown our tresses with the lilies' bells,
And with geraniums fill our bosoms full;
And then return, and seated by the door,
The scarlet woodbine flaunting over head,
Recount our gathered stores of Nature o'er,
From flower to flower by sweet enchantment led;
And then go back to ages past, and dwell
With Contemplation in her holy cell;
And, turning o'er the treasures of the mind,
Talk with the great, the witty, the refined,

And kindle with the ardent; smile and laugh
With Butler and Cervantes; deeply quaff
Rich streams of inspiration from the fount
That flowed on Zion and Aonia's mount;
Hang on the tender tale with melting eye,
Hour after hour unnoticed stealing by;
Or with the patriot rising, feel the swell
Of indignation heaving in the breast,
And weeping go to Marathon and dwell
On barrows, where the brave unhonored rest;—
And from the kindled altar take the coal,
That fires the lip, and animates the soul,
And, mounting upwards on a seraph's wing,
Break from this feeble tenement of clay,
And, wrapt in reveries of glory, spring,
Singing and soaring, to eternal day.

Motherless infant; to the quiet sleep
Of early death descending, thou wilt die
As others sink in slumber, and wilt lie
Erelong within thy narrow grave. To weep
For those who fall like thee befits not,—tears
Are shed on those whom we have watched for years,
Who, in our yielding hearts, have planted deep
The rivets of affection. Thou art fair
And pure as rock-sprung fountains, where they well
Beneath o'erarching roots, and scatter there
Light bubbling dews. Pale infant, thou canst tell
Of pain, but thou art silent, for thy heart
Is calm; Remorse has never barbed a dart
To sting and tear thy vitals,—for to thee
Regret can never come, and thou wilt part
With being as a lock would fall from me.
Thine eyes are closed, thy lip is still and pale,
Thy cheek is deadly wan, or faintly flushed
With hectic gushings; all thy cries are hushed,

Thy breath is silent, as the summer gale
Stealing through withered roses. Thou wilt die,
And never know the thousand ills which wait
The fairest and the brightest, and thine eye
No bitter tears will scald, — thy early fate
Is dealt to thee in mercy; thou wilt go,
Unstained, unspotted, to a better state,
And though thy scanty pilgrimage below
Was weary, often painful, it was free
From *all those stings which long have tortured me.*

IMAGE of calm devotion, on thy brow
The peace of heaven is brooding, and thine eye
Is lifted to its glories; deeply thou
Hast drank of its pure fountain; therefore now
Thy thoughts are centred in the world on high.
Silently, as the midnight hours steal by,
Thy watch is on the firmament, — and there
Thou seest the hills of heaven in prospect lie,
As on the passing gale the light clouds fly,
And heave their fleecy folds, like curls of air,
So thin and so transparent is their veil;
Or dost thou mark some white-winged angel sail
Slowly athwart the moonbeam, shining through
His spiritual form in every lovely hue?
Or do more gentle thoughts than these prevail,
And is there in that fairy sky a bower
Sacred to love and friendship, where the heart
May all its unchecked tenderness impart,
And feel again the bliss of that fond hour,
When first affection budded, and its bloom
Opened to suns and zephyrs, still and warm,
Ere chilled and withered by that coming storm,
Of all our brightest hopes the common doom?
Young as thou art, thy heart must surely know
Bitter and keen-felt sorrows, for the tear

Is brimming on thine eyelids, and their flow
Has stained thy cheeks. I look, and seem to hear
From trembling lips a tone, that winds its way
Into my sympathizing heart. How fair
Thy soft, cherubic features! they were seen
By feeling Fancy in its peopled air,
That teems with all of beauty that hath been.
Backward in waving ringlets flows thy hair
Of auburn glossiness; thy brow of snow,
Smoother than sculptured marble, full and high,
And crowning with its graceful curve thine eye
Pregnant with thought and feeling, and its glow,
When kindled, like a blade of tempered steel;
Those lips, that move so touchingly, and send
Persuasion to the listening youth, and blend
In rapid flow their smiles and tremblings, — all
Around thy face so Grecian and so holy,
That, as I gaze upon its charms, I feel
My rising heart swell with the tears that fall
In tender but delightful melancholy.
Such tears are of a holy kind, that shed
Brightness on those who weep them, like the veil
Of dewy light, whose liquid lustre throws
A clearer tint of beauty on the rose,
Or like the folds of morning mist, that sail
In iris pomp around the mountain's head.
With thy pure spirit, thy enchanted eye
Reading the visioned loveliness of air,
The bright celestial forms that wander there,
And often sweep with sounding pinion by;
With thy soft bosom, melting at the tone
Of tender, fond entreaty, burning still
To reach with tireless step the golden throne
That Truth has planted on her holy hill, —
With one so fair, so sweet, and yet so high
In all her aspirations, I could blend
Thought, wish, and feeling, — Time might hasten by,
And age invade us, Love could never end.

SONNETS.

I.

WINTER is now around me, and the snow
  Has thrown its mantle over herb, tree, flower:
  The icicle has tapestried the bower,
And in a crystal sheet the rivers flow;
And mustering from the north, at evening, blow
  The hollow winds, and through the star-lit hour
  Shake from the icy wood a rattling shower,
That tinkles on the glassy crust below;
And Morning rises in a saffron glow,
  Pouring her splendor through the fretted grove,
In tints that round the heart enchantment throw,
  Like what the Graces in their girdle wove;
And shining on the mountain's frosted brow,
  That o'er the gilded landscape looks afar,
Her kindling beams the virgin mantle strow
  With drops of gold, that twinkle like a star.

II.

ITS bitterness the heart alone can know, —
  The blight, the death of hope, and love, and fame;
  The fire that all can dim, and none can tame;
Departed peace, which time can ne'er bestow;
The tender feelings of unsullied years,
  When earth and heaven are beautiful and bright,
  When nothing dims the eye's serenest light,
And life is fairer seen through innocent tears.
O, who would wear the tedious years away,
  That hang around us like a rusted chain,
Clinging the closer each dull, joyless day,
  And printing all its links in scars of pain,
O, who can feel this bitterness of heart,
  This death-like chill, that curdles all the soul,
This ever-writhing round a venomed dart,
Nor keenly wish to reach life's final goal.

III.

WHAT bird can sing when storms are in the sky,
When flowers and verdure from the turf are gone?
How can the nighted traveller carol on
When winds are loud, and lightning flashes by?
How can the lip smile, when all prospects die,
When earth is but one cold and lifeless waste?
And how can pleasure brighten up the eye,
When hope has, like a lovely night-dream, passed, —
When days are lingering onward dark and slow,
And suns arise, but brightly shine no more, —
When gloom has covered all that charmed below,
And nothing lures us on, — when life is o'er?
The heart has then no fountain of delight,
The eye has then no spirit to illume;
A worse than death has withered with its blight
All hope's fair visions, and all fancy's bloom.

IV.

THE blue heaven spreads before me, with its keen
And countless eyes of brightness, — worlds are there, —
The boldest spirit cannot spring and dare
The peopled universe, that burns between
This earth and Nothing. — Thought can wing its way
Swifter than lightning flashes, or the beam
That hastens on the pinions of the morn;
But quicker than the glowing dart of day
It tires and faints along the starry stream,
A wave of suns through boundless ether borne. —
Though infinite, eternal! yet one power
Sits on the Almighty centre, whither tend
All worlds and beings from time's natal hour,
Till suns and all their satellites shall end.

MAID OF YEMEN.

DARK maid of Yemen! from the tufted grove
Of date-trees, full in bloom, at sunset glowing,
And o'er the drifted sand their shadow throwing, —
Maid of the flashing eye, that kindles love,
Go with me now to yonder myrtle bower,
That flings its perfume on the deep-green wave,
And, gathering from the desert every flower,
Bind in their sweetest links thy willing slave.
Bring snowy rings from beds of coffee, twine
The myrrh and cassia round my offered arms;
O, let the red-rose blend its freshest charms,
And all its breathing odors now be thine!
Maid of the glossy brow, the swelling cheek
Clear as the juice that ripens in the rind
Of Granatine, whose locks flow on the wind,
Like the light-streaming clouds, that often streak
The pure sky of thy country, — maid, whose tone
Tells of a heart that beats with keenest thrill,
Whose glances burn, like serpent eyes, that kill, —
O maid of Yemen! loose thy girded zone,
And spread abroad thy beauty, now the hour
Of tender thought steals on, and we are met
In loneliness and freedom, when the power,
That sported erst amid the Grecian isles,
Against our hearts his point of flame has set,
And, as he twangs his burning bow-string, smiles.

FREEDOM.

O THOU, who dwelt in loftiness,
  Ere man had learned to fall;
Ere penury drank, in bitterness,
  Its wormwood and its gall;
Ere wealth had reared its golden piles
  Where nations bow the knee,

But health, all radiant o'er with smiles,
  Made man unbent and free; —

Thou Spirit! who pervad'st the wild
  And desert wilderness,
But in thy wrath hast never smiled
  Where crouching thousands press;
Who, through the danger and the dread,
  The high-souled hero bore,
Unshook by fear, by glory led,
  Through battle's deepest roar; —

O, thou wilt never come and dwell
  Where men in cities throng;
Where heartless pimps, in triumph, swell,
  To power, a pæan song:
Thou shun'st the base and crawling herd;
  The desert is thy home;
And with the pinions of a bird,
  Thou only there wilt roam.

O Spirit! take me then with thee,
  Where winds of ocean blow;
Till life, replete with ecstasy,
  To inspiration glow:
O, let me wander freely there,
  Till death my being sever;
Then through the brightest fields of air,
  A Spirit, float for ever.

GIVE the Warrior Chief his due,
Him who, to his country true,
Boldly, at her summons, flew,
    Fired with gallantry!
Him who met the foe in fight,
And with death-fires lit the night,
Till his valor turned in flight
    Britain's chivalry.

Crown him with the laurel wreath,
Hail him with the clarion's breath,
Him who, in the face of death,
Battled fearlessly.
Let the bard a chaplet twine,
Deathless gift of song divine,
And the hero's name will shine
Through eternity.

Cherish then the son of song:
He shall proudly bear along,
High above the meaner throng,
Light and Liberty.
Let the voice of music rise,
Let the painter seek his dyes
In the glory of the skies,
For the bold and free.

Let the rostral trumpet blow,
And to Eastern monarchs show
How the fires of freedom glow,
Fires that cannot die.
Then our nation's fame shall thrive,
And to endless ages live,
For the song and pen can give
Immortality.

IL to the land of the free and the bold,
iere honor and justice have planted their throne,
iere the hearts of the meanest can never be sold,
; order and liberty reign there alone!
Hail to the souls that can never be slaves,
Who boast of the rights they have won by the sword,
Who fight for their forefathers' altars and graves,
And soar as the eagle who rescued them soared!

Hail to the land we have cherished so long,—
The soil where the bright tree of liberty grows!
May its root deeper sink, and its branches be strong,
While the wave of the ocean in majesty flows!
Long may we meet and be glad in its shade,
Secure from the tempests that madden the world;
Its leaves shall be green, and its flowers never fade,
And the starred flag, that tops it, be ever unfurled.

Hail to the cradle where liberty drew
The pure air that freemen alone can inhale!
Here the crowd never toiled for the gain of the few,
And the palace ne'er shadowed the cot in the vale:
We swore on our swords and our hearts to unite,
Till the chain should be broken, the slave should be
free,
And the hands that are daring in battle for right,
To welcome as brothers, wherever they be.

Then hail to the nations, who wake from the sleep
Of a long night of darkness, like giants from wine,
To the heroes who rouse in their greatness, and leap
To gather the laurels on liberty's shrine!
Their fetters are broken, their tyrants are fled,
And the hands of the North and the South shall unite
To raise, o'er the tombs of the glorious dead,
A temple of honor, and crown it with light.

I SAW the sun, at the dawning of day,
Chasing the mantling mist away,
And tinging it over with gold;
The clouds that before his face were driven
Were rich with the deepest hues of heaven,
And in volumes of crimson rolled:
The world was blooming and bright and fair,
But nor life nor love was moving there.

I saw that sun, at his setting hour,
Send over the hills an amber shower
  Of softer and mellower rays;
It bronzed the trunks of the moss-grown wood,
And bathed their leaves in a golden flood,
  As he sank in his fullest blaze:
The world was dewy and calm and fair,
But nor life nor love was moving there.

I saw the moon, at the noon of night,
Crowning the sky serenely bright,
  And gilding the waves below;
Clear in her beam the white frost shone,
As if over the fields were loosely thrown
  A sparkling sheet of snow:
The world was silent and pure and fair,
But nor life nor love was moving there.

I saw, on her gay and purple wing,
The light and laughing spirit of Spring,
  Strewing the earth with flowers;
The leafless shrubs were hung with bloom,
And an airy wave of soft perfume
  Was poured from the budding bowers:
The world was smiling and sweet and fair,
But nor life nor love was moving there.

I saw through the shade of a maple grove,
In the light of her youth and beauty, move
  The fancied queen of my soul;
From her bright and quenchless orbs of blue
The arrows of thought and feeling flew,
  And the tears of compassion stole:
O, she was the image of all that is fair,
And life and love were moving there.

Two flowers were budding on one stem,
Imbued with fragrance, fresh with dew,
And bent with many a trickling gem,
That trembled as the west wind blew;
And softly shone their crimson through
That veil of crystal purity,
And as the thrush around them flew,
He clearer piped his melody.

Two fledglings, in a ring-dove's nest,
With tender bill, and feeble wing,
Sat brooding on their downy breast,
And they had just begun to sing,
And as they saw their mother bring,
With tireless love, the food she bore,
They made the woods around them ring
The infant note they carolled o'er.

I saw, along the ocean, sail
Two barks, that flew before the wind;
The canvas swelling to the gale,
They left a foaming wake behind,
And low the bellying sheet inclined,
As freshly blew the sweeping blast;
But still the pilot kept in mind,
There was a peaceful port at last.

I saw, along the cloudless sky,
Two stars adorn the brow of night;
They shone serenely on my eye,
With pure and unoffending light;
The beam was mellower than bright,
Like gems that twinkle in their mine;
It soothed and tranquillized the sight,
And seemed a spark of love divine.

I saw two sisters, — they were one
In beauty, sweetness, age, and soul:

Their bosom was the stainless throne
  Where virtue held supreme control,
Their hearts were pointed to the pole
  By God to erring mortals given,
The bright, the pure, the happy goal,
  That waits the fair and good in heaven.

I FOUND thee on an apple-tree,*
  Poor sickly and untimely flower!
'T is not the time for thee to be
  A garland to the sunny bower;
Thou shouldst have waited for the hour
  When April dances o'er the plain;
Without her soft, refreshing shower,
  Thy purple leaf is spread in vain.

The bough is freshly green around
  With all the tender hue of May;
But short thy stinted being's bound:
  One wind will blow thy leaves away,
One frost will all thy honors lay,
  And seared and brown thy tint will be,
And never on an Autumn's day
  The fruit will ripen after thee.

Sad emblem of the timid mind,
  The delicate, the shrinking form,
The heart too tender, too refined,
  To dwell in life's unpitying storm:
But there shall come a still, a warm,
  A fragrant, an eternal Spring,
Where envy never can deform,
  Nor power its chill, cold fetter fling.

* Written on finding a tuft of blossoms, September, 1821, — the consequence of a violent southeast storm, which had destroyed the foliage exposed to it.

SWEET, sainted haunt of early days!*
With thee my lingering spirit stays,
And muses on the balmy hours,
When forth I wandered after showers;
When bushy knoll, and meadow green,
Were spangled with the dewy sheen,
And evening calmly came along,
And gave my ear the rustic song.

Sweet, sainted haunt! those days are flown,
And I am left, to steal alone,
In tears, along a foreign shore,
And look the boundless ocean o'er
For thy dear spot, and all that threw
Enchantment on my simple view:
But truth has told my heart too well,
That joy can never with me dwell;
For early hopes and loves are dead,
And every charm of home has fled.

I have here attempted to imitate a favorite pastoral measure of the Italian and Spanish poets. In this age of *terza* and *ottava rime*, of *hexameters*, *sapphics*, and *anacreontics*, I can surely be pardoned for imitating a measure in some degree associated with those of our language in rhyme and accent.

I SAW, upon a mountain,
A violet newly springing,
And round the broken rocks a perfume shedding;
It grew beside a fountain,
Its bubbling water flinging,
And down a turfy slope its current spreading,
And greenest grass imbedding;
There the sunbeams poured their glory,

* Suggested by reading an Ode to Vale Crucis Abbey, by William Stanley Roscoe, Esq.

At morn in golden brightness;
And many a song of lightness
The careless shepherd sung, and many a story
He told of love despairing,
Himself in all their joy and sorrow sharing.

I loved that quiet valley,
When sultry noon was firing
The cloudless sky, that o'er my head was glowing;
And in a cool, dark alley,
In solitude retiring,
Where bending elms their tufted boughs were throwing,
And softest gales were blowing, —
There I breathed my bosom's anguish
In many a strain of sorrow,
And from the dove would borrow
Her melancholy tones and dying languish,
When with the zephyr blending,
That murmurs through the reeds before it bending.

In lonely peace reposing,
I gazed upon the ocean,
That in the distant view was proudly swelling;
I lay till day was closing,
And with a softer motion
The ringdove fluttered round his airy dwelling,
Still to his turtle telling
The tender love he bore her;
And like a fond one sighing,
As if his heart was dying,
He sat among the boughs that trembled o'er her;
The while, in eddies whirling,
The mellow brook in day's last light was curling.

The wind was faintly sighing,
The boughs were lightly dancing,
And down its stony bed the brook was chiming;
And now the wind was dying,

The leaves were dimly glancing,
The loaded vine, that o'er the elm was climbing,
Still with the light air timing,
In a slower curve were waving
Its clusters freshly breathing,
And with its foliage wreathing,
Like hyacinths the early meadow paving,
And in the dewy morning
With richest hues the grassy plain adorning.

The moon was on the ocean;
The billows, proudly swelling,
Heaved to her light their tops in foamy brightness;
With slow, majestic motion,
O'er Tethys' coral dwelling
They curled their glassy ridge in snowy whiteness,
Tossing with downy lightness;
And loud and long their roaring,
Like peals of distant thunder,
Or mountains rent asunder,
When high in air the volcan's flame is soaring,
Wide o'er the dark waste rolling,
Seemed like a knell the sailor's ruin tolling.

Through leaves and boughs inwoven,
My grassy pillow shading,
Her silver orb in broken light was gleaming;
Now, where the rock was cloven,
Through fleecy vapor wading,
Her virgin fire, in deeper distance beaming,
In one full flood was streaming:
With tender, smeet emotion,
My bosom gently swelling,
I sought my quiet dwelling,
And raised to heaven my heart's intense devotion,
Walking beneath the mellow brightness, flowing
From countless gems in yon blue ether glowing.

I WILL go to the grave where my child has gone,
And strew its turf with flowers;
He was my loved and only one,
The charm of my lonely hours:
O, he was life in its freshest bloom,
He cheered me many a day;
His smile and his beauty lit my gloom,
And chased its night away.

Day after day, like an opening flower,
His mother's pride he grew;
He seemed like an infant germ of power,
So bright he met my view:
I saw, in his gay, exulting face,
The future greatness glow;
And I thought his light infantine grace
To manhood's might would grow.

I read, in every word and smile,
The father's look and tone;
And I hung on those dear eyes, the while,
As when first our hearts were one:
So bright a vision could not last,
That dear illusion fled;
Like a rainbow-cloud away it passed
To the cold and voiceless dead.

But there is a home where dear ones meet,
And blend their innocent love;
Where hours of happiness never fleet,
In the peaceful world above;
Where the links, that bind our souls by death,
Shall never be broken more,
But a better life, with its quickening breath,
Shall every charm restore:
Then cease, ye bitter tears, to fall;
My heart its grief shall bear,
Till I hear, from Heaven, the tender call
Of love invite me there.

THE CARRIER PIGEON.

Come hither, thou beautiful rover,
  Thou wanderer of earth and of air;
Who bearest the sighs of the lover,
  And bringest him news of his fair:
Bend hither thy light-waving pinion,
  And show me the gloss of thy neck;
O, perch on my hand, dearest minion,
  And turn up thy bright eye, and peck.

Here is bread, of the whitest and sweetest,
  And there is a sip of red wine;
Though thy wing is the lightest and fleetest,
  'T will be fleeter when nerved by the vine:
I have written, on rose-scented paper,
  With thy wing-quill, a soft billet-doux,
I have melted the wax in love's taper,
  'T is the color of true hearts, sky-blue.

I have fastened it under thy pinion,
  With a blue ribbon round thy soft neck;
So go from me, beautiful minion,
  While the pure ether shows not a speck.
Like a cloud in the dim distance fleeting,
  Like an arrow, he hurries away:
And farther and farther retreating,
  He is lost in the clear blue of day.

These weeping skies, these weeping skies,
  They weep so much, that I weep too;
And every thing, like Mary's eyes,
  Around, above, below, looks *blue.*
Such days as these will never do,
  My Muse can never soar again;
Her wings are wetted through and through,
  She tries to fly, but all in vain.

Love brought a wreath, a laurel wreath,
  And it was steeped in fog, not dew;
The little urchin drooped beneath,
  And gladly down his burden threw.
"The Sylphs have sent a wreath to you."
  He laughed as he his errand told.
"What makes it look so very *blue?*"
  Says Love, "It 's only touched with *mould*."

I twined the wreath around my brow,
  And felt my brain grow numb and chill;
If I had worn the wreath till now,
  My heart had been for ever still.
Oh! skies that weep so much will kill
  The Muses, and their servant, Love;
Their home is on the sunny hill,
  Where naught is *blue* but heaven above.

  Fair breaks the morning on my eye,
After long days of gloom and sorrow;
  Bright is the cloud, as it floats on high,
  Sailing along the purpling sky,
Like the sign, at night, of a clear to-morrow.

  Light blows the wind along the sea,
Heaving the wave with peaceful motion;
  Gayly the mariner carols, free
  As a heart that is light and strong can be,
When afloat, like a bird, on the boundless ocean.

  Dimmer and dimmer grows the shore,
Laid, like a fold, on the water's pillow;
  Steadily glides, the gale before,
  The ship, in its fullest canvas, o'er
The glassy breast of the rolling billow.

Riding along, like a mighty ark,
The gallant vessel skims the water,
Leaving behind a foaming mark,
Like a whale, when he flies before the bark,
Impelled in the crimson path of slaughter.

O, how delightfully on my eye
Comes the clear morn of sunny brightness!
Higher and bluer swells the sky,
With a swifter wing the gannets fly,
And the billow heaves with a purer whiteness.

Give me but winds that steadily blow,
Sending the ship, like a dart, o'er the ocean;
Then shall my life's blood lighter flow,
And my eye shall beam with a brighter glow,
And my heart shall swell in its deep devotion.

Country and friends I leave behind,
Flying, on wings, the ocean over:
Come, with a fleeter foot, thou wind,
And bear me on, till my heart shall find
The home that awaits the restless rover.

Now the setting sun is glowing,
Far along the golden sea;
Many an ocean wave is flowing,
Dearest, 'tween thy home and me;
To my lonely bosom showing,
I shall never meet with thee.

Now my heart is madly beating,
As I linger on the west,
Where the golden sun, retreating,
Blazes on the billow's breast;
Bright and fair, but oh! as fleeting,
Was the smile that made me blest.

Now that orb is dimly stealing
  To his palace in the deep;
Homeward now the gannets wheeling
  O'er the rolling ocean sweep:
But in me the pang of feeling
  Time can never lay asleep.

Let me onward, o'er the ocean,
  Distance cannot cure my ill;
Rise, ye waves, in wildest motion,
  But my heart is throbbing still;
Let it burn with full devotion, —
  Deeper, — it will sooner kill.

SONG OF THE REIM-KENNAR.

Eagle of the far Northwest!
  Thou, who bear'st the thunderer's bow,
Thou, who com'st with lightning crest,
  And with eye of swarthy glow;
Thou, who lashest with thy wing,
  Wild in rage, the foaming deep,
Till the warring billows spring,
  And the upturned waters leap;
Thou, who send'st thy scream of wrath,
  Like a nation's dying cry,
Sweeping on thy surging path,
  Like the roar of tempest, by;
When thy scream is wild in ire,
  When thy wing is swift as death,
At my bidding, quench thy fire!
  At my bidding, hush thy breath!

Thou hast met the mountain pine, —
  And the towering wood is low;
Thou hast spread those wings of thine, —
  Ocean steeds their prowess know;

When the bark in triumph rides
  Proudly in its press of sail,
Lo! thy pinions lash the tides,
  And the stoutest seamen quail;
Where aloft the tower of might
  Crowns in pride the cloud-capt rock,
There thou bend'st thy maddening flight,
  And it shivers in the shock;
Though the clouds before thee fly,
  Though thou rulest rock and tower,
Thou shalt lay thy fury by,
  When thou hear'st my spell of power.

At the uttering of my spell,
  Faint and fall the flying deer;
Bloodhounds cease their muttered yell,
  When the mighty sound is near;
Then the wild hawks stoop their wing,
  Then the wolves their howling hush,
Then around the magic ring
  Glaring fiends and goblins rush:
Thou, who scorn'st the scream and yell
  Echoed from the midnight wreck,
Sneering with the laugh of hell
  As the wild waves sweep the deck;
Thou, who hear'st, with shouts of glee,
  Crushing roof and pillar fall,—
Thou shalt listen unto me,—
  Me, who rule and conquer all.

From thy fury on the deep,
  From thy madness on the shore,
Where the wailing widows weep
  Those who sink to rise no more,
From the ravage of the wood,
  From the sweeping of the plain,
From the swelling of the flood,
  Come, and hear my Runic strain.
Let thy giant wing be still,
  Let the ocean cease to roar,

Settle on that lonely hill,
  Dart thy bolt, and flash no more; —
Thou, who, from the far Northwest,
  Scour'st the wild sea in thy course,
Fold thy rapid wings in rest,
  Conquered by my magic force.

Eagle of the far Northwest!
  Thou hast furled thy sweeping sail,
Thou hast closed thy wings in rest,
  For my charm and spell prevail:
Now I bid thee steal away,
  O'er the calmly rolling wave;
Go, and till I call thee, stay
  Slumbering in thy icy cave:
Sweet and silent be thy sleep,
  On the rock beneath the pole;
Let thy rest be still and deep,
  Till thou feel'st my strong control:
I can rouse thee with my spell,
  Bird of might and bird of flame!
Then one word thy rage can quell,
  And thy wildest fury tame.

The wave is resting on the sea,
Or only ripples into smiles,
That curl and twinkle silently
Around the cocoa-tufted isles;
Beneath the Moro's frowning walls
The faintest chime of ocean falls,
As if the rolling tempest-swell,
Subdued by moonlight's magic spell,
Were murmuring its last farewell.
And now the distant breath of flutes,
Or tinkling of the light guitars,

The mellow sound of love, that suits
The silent winds and drowsy stars,
When each discordant note is still,
And all the hum of day at rest,
And tender tones more inly thrill
The yet unstained and virgin breast, —
These sounds, that tell the heart's devotion,
Come floating upward from the ocean,
As, skimming through the flaky foam,
The light canoes are calmly driven
By winds, that send them to their home,
So soft, they seem the gales of heaven.

But yet the reckless pirate keeps
His tiger watch, while nature sleeps,
And in his thirsting hope unsheathes
The sword that glares with sullen flame;
With firm-set teeth he sternly breathes
His curses on each better name;
Careless he stands, prepared to strike
Friend, stranger, foe, for gain, alike.
As wolves who gather in the wood,
And lurk till chance their prey has given,
Then, burning in their thirst for blood,
With fiendlike yells are madly driven:
So cowers the pirate in his cave,
Till far away the snowy sail
Moves calmly o'er the mirrored wave,
And flutters in the dying gale;
Then, with a demon swell of heart,
He hurries from the guilty shore,
And stealing on it, like a dart,
He dyes that snowy sail in gore.

THERE 's a valley that lies in the bosom of hills,
Where the wind ever calmly and silently blows,
And a stream, that collects from the mountain its rills,
Over pebbles and shells in a clear current flows,
Whose waters through meadows go stealing away,
Reflecting the willows that grow on their brim,
And shun, under evergreen thickets, the day,
Where the noon-hours, when brightest, like twilight are dim;
Where the brook sleeps as still, in its ebony well,
As the hush of a bee in the bell of a flower,
Or the life that is waiting to burst from its shell,
And charm with its melody meadow and bower;
Where the leaves, that are platted and woven above,
Shut out every glimpse of the sun and the sky,
And the flowers are as pale as a mourner in love,
And ever are wet like the lids of her eye;
Where sorrow for ever her vigil might keep,
And silence be still as the dead in their grave;
Where the heart that is rifled and broken might weep,
And mingle its tears with the motionless wave.
In the shade of a valley so lonely and still,
I could live in a quiet and fanciful dream;
Not a wish of my heart would go over the hill,
But life glide away like the flow of the stream.

I WOULD follow the sun when the north winds arise,
And Autumn has taken its blue from the skies;
I would go, with the birds and the flowers in their train,
Like a sylph, o'er the wide-rolling waves of the main,

And seek on a warmer and lovelier shore
A home, till the dark storms of winter are o'er.

'T is pleasant to stray in a tropical grove,
Where flowers, fruits, and foliage are blended above,
Where the sky, as it opens so vividly through,
Is pure as a spirit in mantle of blue,
Where the wind comes perfumed from the orange and lime,
And the myrtle is ever in bloom in that clime,
Where the citron its green and its gold ever wears,
And the birds are for ever caressing in pairs: —
O, 't is pleasant awhile in those groves to remain,
Till Spring comes to visit and charm us again.

But I never could stay when the winter has fled,
And the flowers of the valley awake from the dead,
When April has moistened the earth with its shower,
And May is enamelling meadow and bower,
When the woods are in leaf, and the orchards are blooming,
And the hill in the gray mist of morning is looming,
When the air is as sweet from the pear-tree and clover,
As a wind that has travelled rich Araby over,
When the thickets are living with music and wooing,
And the light wings of swallows their mates are pursuing: —
O, when mountain birds call me, I cannot remain,
So away to the land of my fathers again!

THE PIRATE LOVER.

THOU hast gone from thy lover,
  Thou lord of the sea!
The illusion is over,
  That bound me to thee;
I cannot regret thee,
  Though dearest thou wert,
Nor can I forget thee,
  Thou lord of my heart!

I loved thee too deeply
  To hate thee and live;
I am blind to the brightest
  My country can give;
But I cannot behold thee
  In plunder and gore,
And thy MINNA can fold thee
  In fondness no more.

Far over the billow
  Thy black vessel rides;
The wave is thy pillow,
  Thy pathway the tides;
Thy cannon are pointed,
  Thy red flag on high,
Thy crew are undaunted,
  But yet thou must die.

I thought thou wert brave
  As the sea-kings of old;
But thy heart is a slave,
  And a vassal to gold:
My faith can be plighted
  To none but the free;
Thy low heart has blighted
  My fond hopes in thee.

I will not upbraid thee;
  I leave thee to bear
The shame thou hast made thee,
  Its danger and care:
As thy banner is streaming
  Far over the sea,
O, my fond heart is dreaming,
  And breaking for thee.

My heart thou hast broken,
  Thou lord of the wave!
Thou hast left me a token
  To rest in my grave:
Though false, mean, and cruel,
  Thou still must be dear,
And thy name, like a jewel,
  Be treasured up here.

THE FAREWELL.

MUST hearts who love so dearly part,
  And must they bid adieu?
And must those eyes, in weeping, dart
  Their last and fondest view?
How cruel comes the parting day,
  When we have parted never,
And one must wander far away,
  To come no more for ever!

They lived securely in their glen,
  Like doves they fondly loved,
And never had their feet, till then,
  Beyond their mountains roved;
But far away the trumpet calls
  To danger and to death;
How cold and heavy on them falls
  That trumpet's warning breath!

For war is now upon their shores,
  And *he* must meet the foe,
Must go where battle's thunder roars,
  And brave men slumber low;
Go, where the sleep of death comes on
  The proudest hearts, who dare
To grasp the wreath by valor won,
  And glory's banquet share.

O, bright the wreath the warrior twines!
  But dark the heart it covers,
For like a blasting fire it shines
  On widowed wives and lovers:
How glorious is the front of fight,
  When first the gun has spoken!
But dimly gleams its after light,
  For many a heart is broken.

Yes, they must part, who loved so long,
  And part for ever too;
How many bitter feelings throng
  Around that last adieu!
Their hands are pressed, their bosoms meet,
  That look — what words can tell?
And faint the voice, when they repeat
  That cold, that wild FAREWELL.

LET us love while life is young,
  And the vital stream is glowing;
When the heart is newly strung,
  And the tide of health is flowing.

Let us pluck the Paphian rose,
  When its bud is first unfolding;
Ere its withered petals close,
  In the misty darkness moulding.

Pluck it, when the morning dew
  Twinkles on the new-blown flower,
And the vernal sky of blue
  Opens through the melting shower.

Pluck it, when the air is sweet,
  And the winds no more are chilling;
When the loving swallows meet,
  And the soft-eyed doves are billing.

Weave it in a wreath of bloom,
  Let it bind our hearts together;
Now when life is all perfume,
  Warm and bright as April weather;

Now when life is dancing on,
  Like a brook, where flowers are blowing,
Curling upward to the sun,
  Or in mirrored beauty flowing;

Ere those waving locks of jet,
  By the touch of age, are thinning,
While the cheek is blooming yet,
  And the eye is bright and winning.

Love in life's delightful spring, —
  You will find returning passion;
Wait till youth has taken wing, —
  Love will then be out of fashion.

If you have a bosom bright
  Longer than the form around it,
Beauty never will requite
  Love like that, but only wound it.

Thy charms are all decaying, love,
The smile that once was playing, love,
So pure and bright,
It seemed but light
From day's clear fountain straying, love, —

That smile away is stealing, love,
Thy lip no more revealing, love,
The sweets of soul,
That Cupid stole
To fill his cup of feeling, love.

That lip will shed its sweetness, love,
Thy form will lose its fleetness, love,
Arrayed no more,
As when it wore
The snowy veil of neatness, love.

O, time is stealing by us, love,
And age is drawing nigh us, love;
So let me sip
Thy dewy lip
Before the young hours fly us, love.

The rose of youth is blowing, love,
The tide of health is flowing, love;
Then let me be
Entwined to thee,
As elms and vines are growing, love.

A chain of flowers has twined us, love,
And blest the hours shall find us, love;
Then heart from heart
No more shall part,
Till age and death unbind us, love.

THE LUNATIC GIRL.

'T WAS on a moonshine night like this, we took our last farewell;
And as he gave his parting kiss, I felt my bosom swell;
He said, "Adieu, my Caroline," but I said not a word;
Yet never heart was fond like mine,—how wild that dark bush stirred!

The moon was round, the moon was bright, the moon was riding high;
It was just such a pleasant night, and he was standing by:
The sweet bird sung his roundelay, he mocked me all night long;
'T is winter, and he 's flown away, or I should hear his song.

The moon looks down upon the spring,—she cannot melt it though;
The pretty bird has spread his wing,—he does not love the snow;
The winds blow hard,—they say, at sea, such winds will raise a storm;
I wish my love was here by me,—my heart would keep him warm.

I have a hat of straw for thee; I wove it, and I wept
To think thou wert so far at sea, and I the toy have kept.
I made a basket, which I filled with lilies to the brim;
But plucking them their beauty killed, and so I thought of *him.*

They say the moon loves such as I, — her love is very cold;
She floats so softly through the sky, I'd take her down and fold
My cloak around her snowy face, and warm her on my heart; —
O, no! she needs a warmer place! — How could we ever part!

What can my heart have done, to make me love so much the moon?
My fingers are so cold, they ache, — I shall be frozen soon:
I would not love my lover so, — my tears are never dry;
I hear him call, and I must go, — and so, sweet moon, good by.

Come to my heart, thou stricken deer!
The world has aimed its shaft at thee;
There is a welcome shelter here,
There are no enemies with me.
Thou art too fair and delicate,
To bide the cold and pelting storm:
O, fly the world, that can but hate
The brighter cheek and fairer form.

Fly to my heart, thou mourning dove!
And seek a refuge in my nest;
I'll fold around my wings of love,
And hush thy beating pulse to rest.
I heard the death-shot in the wood,
I saw the fowler clip thy wing;
Thy ruffled wings are dropped with blood,
But here no foe a dart shall bring.

Come to my home, thou bleeding heart!
  And trust thy woes to me alone;
For thou mayst all thy griefs impart,
  And I will take them as my own.
I have a healing balm for thee,
  To stanch thy blood, and soothe thy pain;
For kindly touched by sympathy,
  Thy wound shall never bleed again.

The world may scorn thee, if they please,
  But I will dare to love thee still;
Beneath these darkly sheltering trees,
  I 'll guard thee safe from every ill.
For I have found thee kind and true,
  A tender heart, a melting soul,
And still I see thine eye of blue
  As brightly and as purely roll.

O Mary, my dearest! though waves roll between us,
  The light of thy beauty still lives in my heart;
Though gone all the bright sunny days, that have seen us
  Smiles and whispers and glances of feeling impart;
Though gone are the hours when the universe brightened,
  And glowed with the purest effulgence of love,
When joy, like the flash of a summer cloud, lightened,
  And life seemed as sweet as they say 't is above.

O Mary, dear Mary! I cannot forget thee,
  Though coldness hath parted my spirit from thine;
For ever the moment of bliss when I met thee
  Shall live and be bright in this bosom of mine;

The smile on thy lip, and the words that were spoken,
The glance that revealed me the fire of thy soul,
Like a dream of enchantment that cannot be broken,
Around me in all their first loveliness roll.

O Mary, sweet Mary! O, canst thou forget me,
And think, never think, how we looked and we loved?
O, wilt thou not bid me return there, and let me
Be yet by thy sweetness to ecstasy moved? —
O, bid me return, — and my spirit shall fly then,
Like doves from the storm and the hawk, to their home,
And my heart for no happier dwelling shall sigh then,
But cling to thee, — never, ah! never to roam.

Dove of my heart! I've built a nest
For thee, and for thy young ones too,
Where they may sweetly sleep, caressed
Beneath thy warm and downy breast,
As infants in their cradles do.

I've bent around a limber vine,
To form for thee a cool recess;
I'll scatter roses there, and twine
Above an arch of eglantine,
That all within may charm and bless.

And when the frequent falling showers
Make green the tender turf in May,
I'll go and pluck the young-eyed flowers,
Just opening in the lilac bowers,
And on thy mossy pillow lay.

And when the sky is bright in June,
  I 'll sit within a neighboring shade;
And at the silent hour of noon
I 'll put my mourning voice in tune
  To sigh around the lonely glade.

O, come, thou soft, retiring dove!
  And sit within my downy nest;
I 'll spread my sky-blue wings above,
Then, in the shadow of my love,
  Brood o'er thy young ones, and be blest.

SHE has no heart, but she is fair, —
  The rose, the lily, can't outvie her;
She smiles so sweetly, that the air
  Seems full of light and beauty nigh her.

She has no heart, but yet her face
  So many hues of youth revealing,
With so much liveliness and grace,
  That on my soul 't is ever stealing.

She has no heart, she cannot love,
  But she can kindle love in mine; —
Strange, that the softness of a dove
  Round such a thing of air can twine.

She has no heart, — her eye, though bright,
  Has not the brightness of the soul;
'T is not the pure and tender light,
  That love from seraph beauty stole.

'T is but a wild and witching flame,
  That leads us on awhile through flowers,
Then leaves us, lost in grief and shame,
  To mourn our vain, departed hours.

Go then from me, — thou canst not chain
  A soul whose flight is winged above;
Turn not on me thine eye again;
  Thou hast no heart, thou canst not love.

THE winds of the winter are over,
  The flowers and the green leaves return;
The meadow is mantled in clover,
  The hillock is scented with fern;
The blue-birds are flitting and singing
  Their love-notes in thicket and tree,
But the flowers and the sweet birds are bringing
  No spring and no beauty to me.

My hopes have departed for ever,
  My vision of true love is o'er,
My heart shall awaken — ah! never,
  There 's a spring to my bosom no more;
The roses that crowned me are blighted,
  The garland I cherished is dead;
The faith we had promised and plighted
  Is broken, — my lover has fled.

They saw that my life was decaying,
  For my cheek lost its bloom, and grew pale;
They saw that my spirit was straying,
  But I told not a word of my tale;
Not a whisper revealed my deceiver,
  Not an ear heard me sigh or complain,
For my heart still adored its bereaver,
  And I hoped I should meet him again.

He came, — but another had rifled
  The troth he had plighted to me;
I looked on, and my agony stifled,
  Though it burned like the sting of a bee.

O, the sun is now sinking in billows
That roll, o'er the hills, in the west;
But morning will shine through the willows,
And find me for ever at rest.

THE dark cloud is over, the storm flies away,
The sun glances out at the closing of day;
The air now is freshened with rain and with dew,
And the turf shows a greener and livelier hue;
Though day is departing, the birds are awake,
And in full burst are merry in forest and brake;
The mist hovers over the fountain and rill,
And curls in light folds on the slope of the hill;
The bright arch of beauty its loveliness throws
O'er the cloud, as the west takes the tint of the rose.

New fragrance is flowing from garden and bower,
The flowers are all urns deeply filled with the shower,
And their incense is rising and floating away,
To hallow and sweeten the closing of day;
The lily, in purer and silkier white,
Is gemmed with the tenderest touches of light,
The rose shines with deeper carnation, and breathes
Softer balm, as the maiden her coronal wreathes,
And brighter and clearer the round pearls that drip
From its leaflets to blend with the dew of her lip.

O, there is not a sweeter and lovelier hour,
Than the bright sunny evening that follows a shower!
Like a hand o'er the heart-strings in tenderness thrown,
It tunes every thought to the mellowest tone;

Then the eye flashes keen, though the pressed lip be still,
And hand touches hand with a livelier thrill;
Then soft words, in whispers of fondness, are flowing,
And the cheek with the warm flush of passion is glowing;
There is silence and sweetness in earth and in air,
And the spirit of love and of beauty is there.

THE frenzy of a lover who can tell?
The glow and flush of feeling, when the eye
Dilates o'er beauty, and the burning sigh
Heaves deep, and strong, and frequent, from the swell
Of hearts o'erwrought to rapture, — who can give
The colors to the canvas, that portray,
On cheek, and lip, and brow, the changeful play
Of hope, despair, of ecstasy and pain
Too keen for common hearts to feel and live,
The long, long wish to meet those eyes again,
The disappointed hope deferred, till all
Is hung around with doubt's funereal pall,
And darkness veils the spirit, like the gloom
Thrown in embodied blackness from the tomb?
O, there are feelings which no tongue hath power
To utter, which come o'er him at the hour
When looks of kindness flash into his soul,
And tones that tell affection greet his ear,
And sweet smiles answer, when she leans to hear
His whispered heart! O, then their feelings roll
Wild as the ocean, when the winds have blown
Madly, but now the tempest far has flown,
And on the curling foam, and bursting wave,
The sun in all his pomp of brightness glows,
And stars and flakes of liquid lightning pave
The clefted billows, where they rush and rave

Around the vessel, as she proudly goes,
Leaping impetuous on, from surge to surge,
Like coursers whom the calls of battle urge
Onward, with quivering bound and flashing eye,
To mingle in the thickest fight, and die.

They gazed upon each other. They were young,
In the first bloom of beauty. She was fair: —
Around her marble neck her raven hair
In flowing curls and waving tresses hung;
There was a pensive spirit in her eye,
Whose sparkling jet, beneath a falling lid
Fringed with its long, dark lashes, vainly hid
The fire of love that lit it. She would try
To seem light-hearted, but whene'er she met
The eye that fixed upon her, darkly set
The dawning of her mirth, and deeper glowed
The clear carnation of her tender cheek;
And though she often strove to smile, and speak
Gayly, the quivering lip and accent showed
A fire was in her bosom, whose pure flame
Not time, nor want, nor force, could quench or tame,
But round her heart the torch would ever play,
And eat, through hopeless years, her life away.

Beneath the pensive willow's shade,
As evening melts in yonder sky,
In careless ease inglorious laid,
My dreaming moments hover by.

Why should the mind be racked with care?
Why should the bosom beat with pain?

Our hopes all end in blank despair,
Our strife for power and wealth is vain.

They cannot dry one trickling tear,
They cannot hush one bursting sigh,
They cannot quell the gloomy fear
Of death, or bid its phantoms fly.

Then all in peace inglorious laid,
At dewy evening's quiet dawn,
O, let me trace the mellow shade
Advancing o'er the silent lawn.

Without one wish beyond my lyre,
I'd all my careless hours employ
In music, and awake the wire
To tones of grief and trills of joy.

PARAPHRASE OF ISAIAH XXXIV.*

1 Come near, ye people, to the Almighty Lord;
Come, listen, all ye nations, to his word,
And hear the fiat of his sure decree:
Let the wide earth re-echo to the sound,
The world, and all its fulness, ring around;
For what Jehovah utters — that shall be.

2 Against the nations he has bared his wrath;
Fury and indignation mark his path;
And all their armies backward shrink in dread:
Their hosts to one wide slaughter he hath given,
And by his sweeping sword their cohorts driven,
Shall roll in one deep, bleeding pile of dead.

* The imagery throughout has been adapted as much as possible to Babylon. Wherever a variation from the common translation has been made, the notes to Michaelis's Hebrew Bible have been followed.

3 Their corpses heaped upon the battle-field,
No friend the rites of sepulture shall yield;
There they shall rot, and welter in the sun:
The worm shall be their covering, and their shroud
The stench that rises in a tainted cloud, —
Like rivers from the hills their blood shall run.

4 And all the host of heaven shall waste away,
A sooty steam shall dim the light of day,
And darkness brood o'er all with raven wing;
The sun, the moon, the stars away shall roll,
The skies convolving like a folding scroll,
And there unmingled Night her veil shall fling.

The hosts of heaven shall from their centres rush,
And all their frame, in one tremendous crush,
With trailing flames to earth its arches bend;
As when the vine's sere foliage falling plays,
And ripe figs drop in autumn's lonely days,
So shall those countless worlds of light descend.

5 The purple of their crime has filled the sky,
And stained it with a deep, a guilty die;
And there Jehovah bathes his burning sword:
High o'er Chaldea's land that falchion waves,
A people doomed and destined to their graves;
It falls, — urged onward by the avenging Lord.

6 It falls, — and every soul a victim dies;
In mangled heaps their weltering corpses rise,
The king, the prince, the servant, all are gone:
That sword, with slaughter wearied, drips in gore;
With clots and hair and brains bespattered o'er,
It rests, — the work of vengeance now is done.

Scared by the terrors of the Conqueror's eye,
Like sheep and goats, *a timorous flock*, they fly;
The sword behind them thirsts and flashes still:
It longs on all their carcases to feed,
And as the palpitating victims bleed,
From the warm stream of life to drink its fill.

7, 8 Armies and peasants, camps and cities, all
Doomed to one spreading desolation, fall,
Like bulls and lambs before the lion driven:
The soaked earth steams a hot and feverish cloud,
The gore-fed weeds their crumbling bones enshroud:—
Come near, and see the wrath of injured Heaven.

9 'T is silent, lonely, desolate,—a land
Of molten rocks, of white and dazzling sand,
Where stifling vapors fill the poisoned air;
With pitchy slime its sluggish rivers flow,
And lava-torrents heave and boil and glow;
Bitumen burns, and sulphur flashes there.

10 The quenchless fire shall redden through the night,
And send aloft, by day, a smoky light,
And rolling clouds in heavy folds ascend;
From age to age, the traveller, on his path,
Shuddering shall see that wasted land of wrath,
And back with fearful steps his journey bend.

Ruin is on that city of renown;
Her towers and battlements have thundered down,
The engine of the Lord hath laid them low:
The busy hum of trade, the slave's employ,
The warrior's echoed shout, the glee of joy,
Are hushed in that eternal overthrow.

11, 12 The trumpet shall in vain to battle sound;
No armed host shall proudly throng around
Their captains; all their pomp and power is gone:
The courts and chambers, to the Arab's tread,
Ring, like the vaulted caverns of the dead,
And silence sits upon the monarch's throne.

And there the pelican shall build her nest,
And feed her young ones from her bleeding breast,
And by the bittern's boom the hush be broke;

The owlet sit and mourn in every tower,
And when the day is dark, and tempests lower,
The raven in sepulchral omens croak.

On every tumbling wall and mouldering shrine
The Lord, the unerring Lord, shall stretch his
line,
And in eternal ruin thou shalt lie;
Sure as the plummet settles to the ground,
Thy courts shall echo, with an empty sound,
To the scared wanderer, as he hurries by.

13 And thorns shall choke the palace of her kings,
The bramble and the nettle twine their stings,
And mantle o'er her bulwarks and her walls;
The lurking lizard there shall dwell and breed,
The ostrich on the tall, rank grass shall feed,
That rustling waves in her deserted halls.

14 In the dark watches of the lonely night,
In one infernal chorus shall unite
The wild-cat's yell, the gaunt hyena's howl;
The baboon to his fellow-baboon cry,
The wild blast of the desert whistling by
Ring with the harpy screaming of the owl.

15 There shall the viper nestle, and shall lay
Her filmy eggs, and there her young shall play;
There she shall coil, and watch beneath the
shade,
And on the traveller, darting, fix her sting;
And there the vulture fold his sooty wing,
Beside his mate in sordid slumber laid.

16, 17 Go read the fatal volume of the Lord;
Go listen to his sure, unerring word:
"Thou, Babylon, shalt rise in glory—never;
But I will sweep my besom over thee,
And all thy pomp shall fade, and thou shalt be
A desolation and a hiss for ever."

RELIGION.

Sweet and soul-composing star
Twinkling in the heavens afar, —
Who through being's lonely night
Guid'st me with unerring light,
And though clouds awhile may roll
O'er thy brightness and my soul,
Soon the vapor flits away,
And the world again is day, —

Thou, with pure, consoling beam,
Shin'st on life's unquiet stream;
And thy ray of beauty guides
O'er the dark and tossing tides,
Rising with a smiling form
From the bosom of the storm,
Till, the gloom and tempest past,
Safe we reach thy home at last.

When I weep in grief alone,
Every fond endearment flown,
When the gay world has no power
In this dark and lonely hour,
Still thy calm and lovely beam,
Bright as morning on a stream,
Drops a light upon my breast,
Hushing every pulse to rest.

Life is poor and faint below;
Never can its joy bestow
Pleasure on the pure in heart, —
They pursue a better part:
O'er this dark and turbid sea,
Hastening onward after thee,
Stayed by calms, by tempests driven,
All their hope, their aim is Heaven.

"The heavens declare the glory of God, and the firmament showeth his handiwork."

In wisdom God hath made the world,
And still upholds its wondrous frame;
The planets, in their orbits whirled,
Roll round their endless path the same.

The same unchanging laws control
The suns that sparkle in the skies, —
The waves that now in calmness roll,
And now in wildest tempest rise.

The winds obey his word, and go
Where'er his mandate sends them forth;
They now in balmy zephyrs flow,
Now whistle from the icy North.

The rain descends, the fields are green,
And smile to catch the falling showers;
The clouds are gone, and earth is seen
To mourn in summer's scorching hours.

Lightnings await his voice, and fly
On wings of flame athwart the storm;
Whose midnight volume, rolling by,
Lifts, like a tower, its giant form.

The spring is but his smile of love,
The tempest but his angry frown;
His music charms us in the grove,
And then he pours his torrents down.

The dew, the rain, the frost, the snow,
And night and day, his power proclaim;
And all their varying changes show
The hand that guides them still the same.

"Suffer little children to come unto me, and forbid them not, for of such is the kingdom of Heaven."

THERE is an infant, pillowed sweetly,
Asleep upon its mother's breast;
A cloak is wrapped around it neatly,
And it is smiling in its rest;
A halo seems to hover o'er it,
An emanation of the skies,
And the glad heart of her who bore it
Reads peace around its sleeping eyes.

The emblem of angelic spirits,
Who live beyond the arching blue,
Where every stainless soul inherits
Delight, eternal ages through;
The same pure light around it flowing,
The same soft smile is imaged there,
The same bright, burning heart is glowing,
As in the forms divinely fair.

To all who reach the gate of Heaven,
And o'er its starry threshold go,
A heart as pure, as soft, is given,
It burns with holy feeling so;
With love unstained their eye is beaming,
Love for their God and all he made;
Such, deem I, is the infant dreaming,
Upon its tender pillow laid.

Be like the infant — pure, unspotted,
As fountains bubbling from their spring —
Before the sheet of life is blotted,
Or Peace, the dove, has taken wing;
Be like the infant, — soft and tender,
As flowers that just begin to blow;
And God will be your kind defender,
Where'er you rest, where'er you go.

HOLY DYING.

CALM is the parting hour,
When death with sovereign power
Throws o'er the righteous soul his heavy chain:
Nor doubt, nor dread attend,
While round him loved ones bend;
But peace celestial mocks the body's pain.

He sees the links of earth
Part; and his final birth
To perfect holiness, with raptured eye:
Behind, a vale of tears,
In cloud and shade appears;
Before, the heaven-bright fields of promise lie.

His friends hang round and weep,
While, like an infant's sleep,
The chilling lethargy of death steals on;
And o'er his eye the glaze
Falls, and the spirit's blaze
Flashes for once, and all of earth is done.

How silent, like the breath
Of morning, was that death!
No agony nor torturing thought was there:
And what a holy smile
Plays round those lips the while,
And how, like heaven's own arch, that brow is fair!

O, may my footsteps tread
This path, by virtue led,
And God's own day-star, till I sink in dust;
And when I lay me down
To sleep, O, may the crown
Shine on my eye, that circles round the just!

S. M.

A. M. FISHER.

I.

We ask no flowers to deck thy tomb;
Thy name, in purer light, shall bloom,
When every flower of earth is dead,
And all that bloom below are fled.

To thee the light of mind was given,
The centre of thy soul was heaven;
In early youth, the spirit came,
And wrapped thee in its wings of flame.

The lambent light that round thee flowed
Rose to its high and bright abode,
And bore thy restless eye afar,
To read the fate of sun and star.

Fain would we think the chain is broke,
That bound thy spirit to its yoke;
That now no mist of earth can blind
Thy bright, thy pure, and perfect mind.

Thy grave is on a foreign strand,
Thy tomb is in a distant land,
No kinsman came, no friend was near,
To close thine eye, and deck thy bier.

But friends will gather round thy tomb,
And long lament thy early doom,
And thither Science oft repair,
To plant her choicest laurels there.

II.

THE brightest blossom soonest dies,
The purest dew will early rise
  To mingle with the viewless air;
The fairest rose will soon decay,
The softest beauty pass away,
  And all be dark and lonely there.

The brightest souls are soonest gone,
The proudest race is quickest won,
  And genius finds, in youth, a grave;
The hand that sent it from above
Recalls it in its fondest love,
  And takes the choicest gift it gave.

Mind cannot linger long below,
And keep unstained its virgin snow;
  Earth will assert its base control:
Happy the life that soon is o'er,—
Pain ne'er can bow the spirit more,
  No force can crush the tender soul.

A few short years, but oh! how bright
With pure, serene and mellow light,—
  No hour, no moment spent in vain.
Better, than base eternity,
To live these transient years, like thee,
  In light, and die without a stain.

CARMEN SECULARE.

INTO the gulf of past eternity
  Another year, in all its pride, has rolled,
And soon its brightest pageantry shall be
  Lost in the long-forgotten days of old;

Oblivion draws around its darkest fold
  To hide the pomp that millions gazed upon
The curfew of departed joys has tolled,
  Another circle in our life is run,
  And nearer draws the goal, where all of earth is won.

A year has ended, — let the good man pause,
  And think, for he can think, of all its crime
And toil and suffering. Nature has her laws,
  That will not brook infringement; in all time,
All circumstance, all state, in every clime,
  She holds aloft the same avenging sword;
And, sitting on her boundless throne sublime,
  The vials of her wrath, with justice stored,
  Shall, in her own good hour, on all that's ill be poured.

And kings, who hug themselves in sordid ease,
  And revel in their vassals' blood and tears,
Who grasp at all can sense or passion please,
  And build their strength on others' wants and fears, —
For them, the heaped-up vengeance of long years,
  Poised like a snow-cliff on a mountain's brow,
Wild as the sounding avalanche careers,
  Or oceans rushing in their stormy flow,
  Shall bury all their power in one wide overthrow.

Revenge may hold her breath awhile, but still
  The spirit boils within, and soon will burst,
Like lavas from their vaults; — the long-checked will
  Breaks out with deeper fury, fed and nurst
By ever-growing outrage, till the worst
  And reddest scourge of tyranny unbinds
The rusted links of cent'ries, which, long cursed
  But dreaded, now the vassel rends, and finds
  At once his galled limbs free and chainless as the winds.

Sovereigns may band in holy leagues, and lock
Their fetters on a continent, which springs
To claim its birthright, — they may coldly mock
The strivings of young Liberty, as things
That are to them but toys to play with; — kings
Have long enough made men their play, — the hour
When wrath shall wake, and triumph clap her wings
Over the broken images of power,
Draws nigh, and they who rear the haught crest soon will cower.

The dawning year beheld a nation rise,
Free in a glorious seeming, — but it fell.
Where was the Roman fire? Italian skies
Shone over them as purely; and the swell
Of that wide gulf, where ancient glories dwell,
Rolled with as bright a tint on Baiæ's coast.
Though Rome's dark ruins frowned, as by a spell,
At once before the German's hireling host
They sunk, and, in one hour, forgot their proudest boast.

They sunk, but yet in nobler souls lives still
A feeling, fetters, swords, can never quell;
Brute force may crush the heart, but cannot kill;
The mind that thinks, no terrors can compel,
But it will speak at length, and boldly tell
The world its weakness and its rights; the night,
Our race so long has groped through, since man fell
From his imagined Eden of delight,
Must, will erelong retire from Truth's fast-dawning light.

For mind has dared assert its native claim,
And bigot rage, and superstitious dread,
And priesthood robed in purple, cannot tame
Its strong uprisings. Power, with hydra head,
On vice and self, as on a Lerne, fed,
Awhile may bind the nations to its car:

In thousand hearts a Hercules is bred,
  The fearless champion of a coming war,
  When Liberty, at last, shall break her dungeon bar,

And, in the vigor of her youth, go forth,
  Unshackled and undaunted, and shall call,
With the clear summons of her trump, the North
  To send its nerved sons on to scale the wall,
Whereon the Cross and Crescent shadow all,
  That cradled glory in the olden time;
And sack the Czar's firm bulwarks, wherein stall
  Slavery, and beastly ignorance, and crime,
  And sense, that drags its folds in pleasure's foulest slime.

And on the sea, whose bright green waves should roll
  Without the stain of innocent blood, nor bear
The burden of rank avarice to the goal
  Where toil and stripes await it, — where thieves dare
Their darkest deeds of rapine, — she will there
  Ride in her car of vengeance, and proclaim
To every plunderer, be it they who bear
  The ocean's lord, or dogs unknown to fame,
  That her strong arm shall soon their blood-drunk boasting tame.

Go forth, ye navies, o'er the ocean go,
  Where havoc riots on the pirate's deck,
Where steals along the cowering bark of woe,
  And bid those dens of torture float a wreck;
And as you first the Invincible did check,
  So let him feel the force of Nature's sway.
Would they might rouse, who worship at the beck
  Of Europe's *would-be* lord, and rend away
  The veil that hides from Greece the glories of that day,

Of which all hearts are proud, the brightest hour
 In all the round of ages, which will stand
A monument of light, the sacred dower
 Of never-dying truth. The tyrant's hand
Awhile may dim the glories of that land,
 And doom it to be trampled on, but still
There we shall image out the Spartan band,
 There we shall gaze on Freedom's holy hill,
 And from her kindling founts the cup that fires us fill.

Where sleeps the fire that erst in Pylæ burned?
 Where lurks the spirit of that godlike age?
Shall the bright soul for ever rest inurned?
 Is there no hand to check the Tartar's rage?
Shall Turk on light and love and freedom wage
 A war, that swept whole nations like a flame?
Shall Europe never in that cause engage,
 And wipe from off her shores that blot and shame?—
 Her feeblest arm might now the glutted vulture tame.

But shall we mourn because those fanes are low
 Where Gods were knelt to, and where lust was right?
There was a gladness in the overthrow
 Of temples, where Religion had no light;
And though the Cross still left the land in night,
 And bound the spirit in as cold a chain,
Yet we can still exult, and boldly write,
 "Idols and idol-worshippers again
 On lands where Truth has poured her light shall never reign."

There is a twilight dawning on the world,
 The herald of a full and perfect day,
When Liberty's wide flag shall be unfurled,
 And kings shall bow to her superior sway:

Already she is on her august way,
  And marching upward to her final goal;
Nations the warning of her voice obey,
  Away the clouds of fear and error roll,
  The chain is broke that bound the thralled and fettered soul.

That chain is off a continent, where man
  Begins anew his being, — where a course,
Brighter than ever Greek or Roman ran,
  Spreads its wide list before him. From a source
Unstained and deep, with strong, resistless force
  The unchecked wave of enterprise rolls on:
Hope gilds it o'er with sunbeams; wild and hoarse
  As storm-lashed oceans, till the plain is won,
  Then in majestic might its calm, full waters run.

Here Liberty shall build her proudest fane,
  Loftier than snow-topped Andes, and its dome
Shall cast a burning brightness o'er the main,
  And all who seek a purer, calmer home
Shall steer their bounding barks across the foam,
  And furl their sails on Freedom's chosen shore; —
Here all that Law has in her choicest tome,
  And all the climes of Greece and Latium bore,
  Nature from her full stores around our hearts shall pour.

Here shall the energy of mind be shown,
  In all its widest daring, — naught can check
The generous spirit, which away hath thrown
  The yoke that galls and curbs, the toys that deck;
Prescription cannot bow him at her beck,
  Nor rooted wrong command, nor force control;
He is not of the sordid slaves, who reck
  The statesman's gilded bribe and stinted dole; —
  In vain corruption woos the high, enlightened soul.

We have our sages, who drew down from heaven
The bolt that shivers, and the light that warms;
Who steered the helm of state, when madly driven
It seemed the prey of power and civil storms.
We have our heroes, who have met the swarms
Of hireling butchers, — back the torrent rolled:
Though want and terror took their direst forms,
Proud in their simple freedom, sternly bold,
They stood through trying years, and kept their last strong-hold.

And they were victors, and new light hath risen
From them upon the nations, — here they draw
The energy that breaks their feudal prison;
The light that guides them is our country's law:
Too strong its perfect brightness, — when they saw,
Maddened they rushed upon their lords, and tore
The sceptre from their grasp, — the coward awe
Of crown and mitre crushed their hearts no more, —
They wildly fed the hate, so long they fiercely bore.

They turned upon each other, with an ire
Like that of ravening tigers, till their glut
Of kindred slaughter quenched the maniac fire,
And then again their prison-gate was shut.
They grasped at full and perfect freedom, but
A stronger bar confined them than before;
Fetters of adamantine steel were put
Around their scarce healed limbs; they dragged through gore,
To please a driver's whim, the manacles they wore.

Order alone is freedom. We must bend
Beneath the sanctity of higher power, —
Not transient will, but laws that have no end,
Stamped and enforced in being's earliest hour;

Sanctioned by time, they are the holy dower
Of ages, which from darkness rose to light.
Man first was fearless, then he learned to cower,
And groped through superstition's Stygian night;
Till Science rose, and day shone round him warm and bright.

Few are the clear, strong spirits, who can bear
To look on Truth in her unclouded blaze;
Few are the high, heroic souls, who dare
Above the low pursuit of gain to raise
Their firm, unbending purpose; few can gaze
At Virtue, on her pure and awful throne, —
Ah! few can love the ethereal coin she pays, —
But they must love it, for the souls alone
Who master self can claim our birthright as their own.

And Freedom thus, of old, so often fell
Before Ambition, when the herd, that crawls
Within the crowded haunt, the sordid hell
Where luxury and lust have built their walls,
Sunk in each vice that deadens and inthralls,
Bartered their unprized liberty for gold; —
As the pure stream upon the palate palls,
When wine has fired the senses, so they sold
The rights, that prouder hearts than being dearer hold.

There is a twofold liberty in man,
The liberty of knowledge and of power.
This wanders in the desert with the clan,
Or where aloft the Alpine summits tower.
Limbs knit with iron cannot stoop or cower,
Hands hardened by free toiling cannot bear
The burden of a tyrant. He might pour
Whole hosts around them; they would nobly dare
To guard their desert rocks, or die unconquered there.

The other hath its dwelling with the sage ;—
  Where mind is dark, and appetites prevail,
Where grovels lust, and brutal passions rage,
  The breathings of her spirit naught avail.
Of cultured states 't is the eternal bale,
  That vice will grow with wealth and light, and bow
The strength that reared the fabric ; free hearts quail
  Before that torrent-wave, whose giant flow
  Buries a nation's pride in one deep overthrow.

Cities have been, and vanished ; fanes have sunk,
  Heaped into shapeless ruin ; sands o'erspread
Fields that were Edens ; millions too have shrunk
  To a few starving hundreds, or have fled
From off the page of being. Now the dead
  Are the sole habitants of Babylon ;
Kings, at whose bidding nations toiled and bled,
  Heroes, who many a field of carnage won,
  Their names—their boasted names to utter death
      are done.

Such is the fate of empire :— Ashur rose,
  Where elder thrones and prouder warriors stood ;
Before the Memphian priest his precepts chose,
  Men reasoned greatly of the highest good ;
Before Troy was, or Xanthus rolled in blood,
  Armies were ranged in battle's dread array ;
They fought,— their glory withered in its bud ;
  They perished,— with them ceased their tyrant
      sway ;
  New wars, new heroes came,— their story passed
      away.

They had no bard, and they are dead to fame ;
  But they were brave, were demigods, and yet
The spirit which no threat, no force could tame,
  Which burned the brighter when in conflict met,
The sun of ancient valor long has set,
  Their deeds are swept from memory's teeming page.

How soon the renovated race forget
  The chiefs who ground the nations in their rage!—
  Some lord must rise to curb and crush in every
      age.

Napoleon, Frederic, Charles, and Cromwell,—these
  Swept the earth with a besom dipped in fire.
They would have kings and nations bend their knees;
  Theirs was the untamed thirst of something higher,
An energy of hope, that could not tire,
  The love of self to deeds of might sublimed,
Ambition wrought to habitudes of ire,
  Force, reckless force, unchecked, unbent, untimed,
  An aim to gain a height where power had never
      climbed.

They sought they knew not what, — they set no
      bound
  To their wide-clenching grasp, — their longing
      grew,
As grew their empire, — keenly, as the hound
  Catches the deer-track in the morning dew,
They snuffed the scent of conquest, — victory threw
  Her laurels at their feet, — awhile they gave
Blood to the earth like water, — madly flew
  Their gore-fed eagles. But the wildest wave
  Breaks and subsides at last; — their end was in
      the grave.

Now they are dust and ashes; other swarms
  People the ground they wasted, other men
Rise to be torn and tossed by other storms.
  Ambition sleeps a moment in her den
To gain new breath, and fire, and strength; but then
  She blows the embered coals, and they are flame.
So it must be, for it hath ever been: —
  Age rolls on age, and heroes are the same, —
  The rest, the crowd, the mob, the warlike hunter's
      game;

Food for the sword and cannon, steps to climb
Ambition's ladder, brutes, who walk erect,
Crouching and gloating on the dust and slime,
Where they would creep and wallow, if not checked
By biting wants, that man to man connect,
The strong necessity of care and toil.
Give them their own free scope, and they are wrecked;
For master souls their passions will embroil,
And tyranny at last will twine them in its coil.

THERE is a calm lagoon,
Hid in the bosom of a cypress grove;
Around deep shade, above
The tropic sun pours down the heat of noon.
The aged fathers of the forest wave
Their giant arms athwart the gloom below,
And as the winds in fitful breathing blow,
Their rush is like the tide's resounding flow,
Or sighs above a maiden's early grave.
The long moss hangs its hair,
In hoary festoons, on from tree to tree:
Lianas, twining there,
Ramble around the forest, wild and free;
They wave their bowering canopy,
Impervious to the faintest ray of light;
The softest dew of night
Steals never through its mantling tapestry,
With blue and starry blossoms spangled o'er;
And scarlet fruits, in clusters hung,
Low bending, shine around the winding shore,
Brighter than aught Hesperian gardens bore,
Or Eastern bard, in vine-clad arbor, sung.

And on that calm lagoon
The water-lilies float;

Blue, as the deepest tinctured sky at noon,
Or white, as new-fallen mountain snow,
Or died in carmine, like the stain
Of clouds that on the verge of morning glow,
Or golden, as the setting beam,
When flashing on the burnished stream,
Or veiled in mellow tinctures, like the flow
Of milk and wine dissolving, or the plain
Of ether, when its starry bow
O'erspans the arch of midnight, as a belt,
Or like the pearl and topaz, when they melt
Their soft reflections in the folded chain,
Around the fairest neck of beauty hung, —
So sit they calmly in their cups, or swung
Along the surface of the rippling wave,
Whether the spirits of the air awake,
And sport, with glancing pinions, on the lake,
Or slumber in their silent cave.

All live and move to the poetic eye.
The winds have voices, and the stars of night
Are spirits throned in brightness, keeping watch
O'er earth and its inhabitants; the clouds,
That gird the sun with glory, are a train,
In panoply of gold around him set,
To guard his morning and his evening throne.
The elements are instruments, employed
By unseen hands, to work *their* sovereign will.
They do *their* bidding; — when the storm goes forth,
'T is but the thunderer's car, whereon he rides,
Aloft in triumph, o'er our prostrate heads.
Its roar is but the rumbling of his wheels,
Its flashes are his arrows, and the folds
That curl and heave upon the warring winds,
The dust, that rolls beneath his coursers' feet.

I saw, on the top of a mountain high,
  A gem that shone like fire by night;
It seemed a star, which had left the sky,
  And dropped to sleep on the lonely height;
I climbed the peak, and I found it soon
A lump of ice, in the clear, cold moon.
Can you its hidden sense impart?
'T was a cheerful look, and a broken heart.

SONNET.

Again farewell, — perchance a last adieu!
  Our meeting was in loneliness and tears,
  For life looked frowning on my early years,
And the bright moments of my youth were few.
I longed to meet a bosom, fond and true,
  Where I might find a heart that beat with mine;
  I imaged out a beauty all divine,
And there the homage of my soul I threw.

Vain were those fond illusions! O, as vain
  The light of fame, that drew my spirit on
To climb with patient step the lofty fane,
  Whereon the brightest wreath of mind is won,
And on the proudest height of glory gain
  The twine of bay, that crowns her chosen one.

SONNET.

Why have ye lingered on your way so long,
  Bright visions, who were wont to hear my call,
And with the harmony of dance and song
  Keep round my dreaming couch a festival?

Where are ye gone, with all your eyes of light,
  And where the flowery voice I loved to hear,

When, through the silent watches of the night,
  Ye whispered like an angel in my ear?

O, fly not with the rapid wing of time,
  But with your ancient votary kindly stay;
And while the loftier dreams, that rose sublime
  In years of higher hope, have flown away,
O, with the colors of a softer clime,
  Give your last touches to the dying day.

GENIUS SLUMBERING.

He sleeps, forgetful of his once bright fame;
  He has no feeling of the glory gone;
He has no eye to catch the mounting flame,
  That once in transport drew his spirit on;
He lies in dull oblivious dreams, nor cares
Who the wreathed laurel bears.

And yet not all forgotten sleeps he there;
  There are who still remember how he bore
Upward his daring pinions, till the air
  Seemed living with the crown of light he wore;
There are who, now his early sun has set,
Nor can, nor will forget.

He sleeps, — and yet around the sightless eye,
  And the pressed lip, a darkened glory plays!
Though the high powers in dull oblivion lie,
  There hovers still the light of other days;
Deep in that soul a spirit, not of earth,
Still struggles for its birth.

He will not sleep for ever, but will rise
  Fresh to more daring labors: — now, even now,
As the close shrouding mist of morning flies,
  The gathered slumber leaves his lifted brow;

From his half-opened eye, in fuller beams,
His wakened spirit streams.

Yes, he will break his sleep. The spell is gone,
The deadly charm departed. See him fling
Proudly his fetters by, and hurry on,
Keen as the famished eagle darts her wing;
The goal is still before him, and the prize
Still woos his eager eyes.

He rushes forth to conquer: — shall they take,
They, who with feebler pace still kept their way,
When he forgot the contest — shall they take,
Now he renews the race, the victor's bay?
Still let them strive, — when he collects his might,
He will assert his right.

The spirit cannot always sleep in dust,
Whose essence is ethereal, — they may try
To darken and degrade it, — it may rust
Dimly awhile, but cannot wholly die;
And when it wakens, it will send its fire
Intenser forth, and higher.

GREECE, FROM MOUNT HELICON.

THIS is the land of song: — the very mountains
Are vocal with invisible minstrelsy;
The valleys are the haunt of unseen choirs;
The fountains utter music, and the hills
Are full of pleasant sounds. Before me stands
The temple of the Muses, Helicon,
The seat of their divinity, when Greece
Stood fair and glorious. It is beautiful,
But lonely. Where are now the hallowed shrines,
The pillared porches, and the sun-gilt domes,
Where ancient Genius offered up his prayers,

And kindled, on the altar of his God,
A sacrifice, whose odor was divine,
And breathed of inspiration? — Fallen, broken,
And overgrown with natural wildness, like
The intellect that wanders round these ruins,
With all its brightness veiled.
Now, I have come
On a fond poet's pilgrimage; my foot,
Wearied, yet eager still, shall find its way
Upward to yonder pinnacle of rock,
The mountain's sacred summit, by the side
Of clear Termessus, where it throws itself,
From leap to leap, over the polished stones,
And with a sportive wildness hurries on
To this secluded nook of bays and roses,
This quiet shelter, where the dove of peace
Nestles securely, while the distant roar
Of violence comes from the open plains,
Echoed, but faintly.
Pleasant stream, that erst
Gave water to the shepherd in old times,
When from their cloudy dwelling they descended,
Memory's bright daughters, in the silent night,
Breathing sweet voices, through the slumbering air,
Into his dreaming ear, and told to him
Mysteries, which he revealed in harmonies
Of measured sounds, high oracles that made
The crowd his worshippers, and drew around
The woodmen from their caves, to learn of him
Kindness and love, — clear rolling stream, whose wave
Shines in this gladdening sun like flowing gold
Poured from a fretted urn, so smooth the rocks
That border thee, and so fantastical
Their time-worn hollows, — how it gushes out
From some obscure recess, where it lay hidden
In clustered vines and feathery foliage, wet
With ever-falling dews! and how it bulges
In silvery brightness o'er the polished boss

Of marble, veined like pictures from the hand
Of tasteful art, and yet the very sport
Of frolic nature! what a busy din
Of tinkling waterfalls! and how it blends
With the low murmur of the shaken leaves,
And the still hum of bees! These many sounds,
These murmuring melodies of many voices,
They lap me in oblivion, and I seem
Living in dreams. I wonder not the bards
Who gathered here in worship, and were filled
With the dim feeling of religious awe, —
That they imagined, on the shores of Lethe,
Such murmurs from the beds of amaranth-flowers,
When they went nodding to the odorous winds,
That stole from laurel groves and myrtle shades,
And crisped the waters as they glided on
Over their sands of gold. Such happiness
As now I feel in listening to thy music,
And gazing on thy sparkling waterfalls,
Thy bubbling wells, thy mossy-cinctured lakes,
And rose-crowned islands, where the bird and bee
Nestle and find their home, — such happiness
Elysium well might envy. But I pause,
Even on the threshold, when the far ascent
Calls me to regions where a loftier power
Dwelt on his airy throne.
Then be my guide,
Wandering Termessus, upward through thy vale,
And let me find, beneath the twisted boughs
Of these old evergreens, coolness and shade,
To make my toil the easier. Darkly rolls
Thy current under them, and hollower sounds
Thy hidden roar. I just can catch a glimpse
Of yon deep pool, dark and mysterious,
Sunk in its well of rock; and now from out
A tuft of seeded fern I see thee plunge,
Tinted with golden green, for there a sunbeam
Strays through thy arch of shade. Still as I climb
Thy voice goes with me, like the laborer's song,

To cheer me; and anon I see thee flashing
Through the laburnum thickets, rivalling
Their golden flowers; and then thou rushest by
Crested with foam, the whiter for the darkness
That covers thee; and then I pause and hang
Over a broad, smooth mirror, where the sky
Looks in, and sees itself, as purely blue,
As vast and round, and all its cloudy folds;
Their snowy bosses and their iris fringes
Are there, and all the circling rocks repeat
Their lights and shadows in that vacancy,
So clear, it seems but air. Thou rollest on
Thus brightly, and for ages thou hast kept
This ever-varying, yet eternal way;
And like the voice of a divinity
Thou pourest thy endless song. But now the rocks
That hemmed thee in recede, and, round and fair,
The open vale of Aganippe smiles
To greet me, as a fond and gentle mistress
Welcomes her weary lover, when he comes
At evening to her bower.
                                        Enchanted vale!
Well did the early worshippers of song
Choose thee to be their place of pilgrimage,
That in thy quiet groves and still recesses
They might invoke, with due solemnity,
The boon-inspiring power. Here they would come,
From the blue islands, and the olive-groves
Of Thebes and Athens, and thy laurel-crowned
And golden banks, Alpheus, and the shores
Of far Ionia, where the wooing air
Pants with a softer breath through myrtle groves,
And thee, thou emerald gem, amid the foam
Of ocean, whence thy guardian goddess rose,
To be the world's delight. From every land
That heard the echo of those flowing sounds,
That dropping honey, which, from eloquent lips,
Distilled persuasion, reverently they came,
Clad in white robes, and crowned with wreaths of
    bay,

And bearing golden harps and ivory citterns,
And round the marble temple, and the fountain
Of soft and gentle harmony, uplifted
The joyous pæan, through the bright-eyed day
Singing, till sunset threw its yellow veil
Round thy blue summit, Helicon, and Night
Sat on her purple cloud, and dipped her bough
Of cypress in Nepenthe, and then waved,
Over their leafy beds, oblivion
And holy dreams; — and when their God arose,
And shook his yellow locks in the blue air,
And dropped his shining dews, then they began
Anew their solemn chant, and up the heights
They moved in measured march, bearing their hymns
To Hippocrene and the crowning rocks,
Whence they beheld Parnassus, white and bare,
Glittering among the clouds, a golden throne
Rich with a waste of gems; and, as it rose,
Touched with the sun's first blaze, its forked peak
Seemed like twin spires of flame, curling and trembling
From earth to heaven. They saw, — and then they bowed,
And worshipped in their hearts, — their voices paused,
Their harps were mute, and fearful silence told,
More eloquent than words, their love and awe.

'T was thus of old: now all is desolate,
But fair and lovely. 'T is a wilderness
Of bush and flower, and over it are hung
A few old knotted oaks and untrimmed bays,
That, in their careless dress, are like the hearts
Of this rude land, — beautiful thoughts run wild, —
Courage and tenderness concealed beneath
Ungovernable rage and stern revenge.

Here is a ruin, — once a temple, now
Fallen, shapeless, and o'ergrown, — a mingled pile

Of blocks and broken pillars, fretted ceilings
And sculptured friezes, moulded cornices,
And wreaths and garlands, heaped confusedly,
And veiled with clematis and ivy, where,
Under their verdurous tufts, the lizard lurks,
And serpents cast their coats, or in the sun
Lie basking in their burnished mail, and roll
Their fascinating eyes. There is a hum
Of settling bees, and the quick swallow darts
Between two columns, sole amid the wreck
Unbroken, with their brief entablature
Telling in scattered characters, half worn
And eaten out by time, here was the temple
Of Pæan and the Muses. But the fountain,
Where wells it? It has gathered in a marsh,
O'ergrown with rustling reeds and water-lilies,
And bordered round with tamarisks and osiers,
The favorite haunt of painted flies and reptiles
That love the midday sun; and here I trace it,
Oozing through tall rank grass and irises
From underneath a falling arch. Here flowed
The gentle fountain, — here they built a shrine
To its peculiar Naiad, where it threw
Its bubbling waters from the opening rocks,
In shade and coolness. Still it gushes over,
Through tangled leaves, and still it gives a murmur,
That soothes and yet inspires. Methinks I see,
Peeping from bosky dells, the nymphs who loved
This sylvan hollow. Grecian girls are they,
With braided locks twined gracefully around
Their ivory foreheads, and their arching brows
Pencilled above such eyes, gems, living gems,
Dark as deep night, and wild, yet winning quick
And darting like a flame; and now and then,
Less timidly, they lean from their retreats;
And then such lips, cheeks, dimples, necks like swans,
And polished arms, colors so bright and clear,
Still dripping from their fountains, glancing still
With water-drops, — they seem to beckon me,

Only to smile and vanish. Happy days,
When ye were seen as real, worshipped too
With dance and song, — worshipped by youths and maidens
Only less bright and fair than deities,
Full of high health and buoyant happiness,
Creatures of poetry and love. Ye ages!
Why have ye borne us downward, till the blood
Flows stagnant, like this fountain from its well,
'Mid weeds and thorns? Or has it ever been
Thus with the dreamer, Man, — ever in love
With an imagined joy?
But what is here,
Perched on the hill-side? Here a chapel stands,
Built of the fragments of the Muses' shrine,
And with its humble cross and rude stone altar
Telling of other faith and lowlier worship
Than that of old. Here are no genial banquets,
No songs nor dances. Here the lonely hermit
Utters his feeble orisons, and chants
His one unvaried hymn. A shadowy elm
O'erhangs his cell; and here, upon the turf,
Half slumbering, half awake, I muse away
The hours of noon. The mountain tops around
Sparkle and glow, — a quivering vapor floats
Above them, and with strange, mysterious power
Lifts them to loftier regions, where they hang
Like hot and fiery clouds. How still the air!
How motionless the leaves! The only sound
Is the perpetual hum of water-flies
Above the reedy pool. My brain feels dim,
And slumber steals apace, and silently
I sink in deep oblivion. Still my fancy
Plays with the shapes before my half-shut eyes,
And tunes the falling murmur in my ears
To music. So I pass away in dreams
The sultry hours; and now, the sun descending
Behind the loftier summits, I awake,
And feel the breezy coolness steal around me,

And give me life and joy. I turn myself
To the fresh evening air, and let it dry
My feverish brow and dripping locks, and twine
them
In artless curls, — then to my pleasant task,
And onward to the summit.
Now my way
Is by a gentler stream, that tinkles down
Over the smooth-worn marbles, hollowed out
In semblances of urns, and bowls, and lavers;
And then in open pipes lapsing away,
Clear as a gush of flowing pearls, and tinged
With shifting colors, as it catches hues
From the stained rock it kisses, purple, green,
And golden, — hues that emulate the dove's
Or trembling opal's, — soft and velvet hues
Due to the water mosses, silent growth
Of centuries, o'er which the hurrying wave
Slides with a stiller murmur. Now the mountain,
Lifted above the forest region, glows
With flowering shrubs, that scatter odorous airs,
Sweet as from Eden, — purple heath and balm,
And lurking beds of thyme, and bright laburnum,
And arbute hung with snowy flowers and fruits
Red as a flammant's wing, and spiry grass,
Breathing of early May, and calling up
Memories of pastoral days, of shepherds lulled
By whispering elms, and nymphs with flowing hair,
Tressing it in the fountains, bleating flocks
Calling their truant lambs, and browsing goats
Pendant from bushy rocks, and harmonies
Of pipes and flutes and voices, warbling out
Unstudied songs, and with alternate verse
Singing the sun to setting, while cool airs
Came from the west, as if Favonius loved
Their minstrelsy, and with the tuneful leaves
Went dallying, and woke the slumbering pool
To music faint but sweet. Such thoughts are wakened
By the low whispering of the evening wind,

Through tufts of flowering grass and withered halm,
The golden harvest of an earlier year,
Still in this happy climate undecayed,
Still nodding with its ears. And as I move
Thoughtfully on, how populous these flowers
With honey-bees! how still their humming sounds
O'er all the voiceless mountain, while they gather
Nectar from golden cups, and urns of pearl,
And homelier vases hidden in their beds
Of heath and thyme, vases that breathe perfume,
And lurking yet reveal their hiding-place,
As if by clouds of incense. There they dart
From bloom to bloom, and till the lengthening shadows
Fall from the mountain peaks, and stretch away
O'er vale and plain, and distant cottages
Tell of their evening fires, they ply their task,
And then go murmuring to their sheltered hives
In cave, or hollow trunk, or straw-roofed shed,
O'er which the ivy climbs. Thus whiled away,
Time flies apace, till suddenly I pause,
And greet the higher fountain, whence uprose
The flying steed, that bore to loftier heights
The young, aspiring soul. It gushes forth,
Sparkling and bright and clear, from out the clefts
Of living rocks, and throws at once a stream
Full and o'erflowing. How the setting light
Tinges it with its hues,—rich, golden hues,
As if the God of Song still loved the spring,
And smiled as he withdrew! No broken arch
Chokes up its way, but from its natural caves
At once it bursts to light, and hurrying takes
Its journey to the plain. Here all is left
Simple and void of art, but where the rock
Is graved with moss-grown characters, that tell
Of earlier pilgrims, when they came and paid
Vows from the heart. Above me swells a throne
Of broad, bare rock, and there Apollo sat,
With all his train of Muses, and indulged

The charm of thought. Here many a poet dreamed,
When night was full of stars, that heavenly voices
Came from that shadowy summit, and they told
The bliss of song. They kindly led him on,
Spite of a scornful world, and filled his heart
With self-approving joy. Now, as the sun
Bends to his ocean couch, and well has neared
The far blue mountains, round his holiest shrine
In Delphi, upward to that pinnacle
My foot must hasten. Let no wandering look
Turn from the one bright goal. Even as the pilgrim
Goes with his eye fixed on his prophet's tomb,
Or where his god is laid, so let me on,
Bent to that summit, where retiring day
Kindles its latest fires.
I now have conquered,
And heaven is all above me. Earth below
Spreads infinite, and rolls its mountain waves
Tumultuously around me. Breathless awe
Broods o'er my spirit, and I stand awhile
Rapt and absorbed. The magic vision floats
Dimly before me, and uncertain lights
Flash on my troubled eye, and then a calm,
High and uplifted, like the peace of heaven,
Steals on my heart, and instantly my thoughts
Are fixed and daring. 'T is the land of song, —
The home of heroes. O, ye boundless plains,
Ye snowy peaks, ye dusky mountains, heaped
Like ocean billows, far retiring vales,
Blue seas, and gleaming bays, and islands set
Like gems in gold! to you I kneel with awe
Deep and unfeigned. If I have ever felt
The stirring energies of warlike virtue,
The sternness of unbending right, the bliss
Of high and holy dreams, the charm of beauty,
The power of verse and song, only to you
Be all the praise. And now ye are before me,
Rich with the tints of evening. What an arch
Of golden light swells, from the point of setting,

Over the Delphian hills! and how it rolls,
In dazzling waves, round all the mingled heights
That rise between! Yonder my eye can catch
Glimpses from out the far Achaian gulf,
Waving with flame, and seeming through the depths,
That dimly open to them, fiery portals
To brighter worlds. But now to calmer scenes,
And shadier skies. I trace the silver stream
Threading its way, now hidden, now revealed,
To the round vale, half up the mountain-side,
Then lost in woods, and then in distant windings
Stealing along the plain. Yon lower ridge
Lies dark in shade; and hidden half in trees,
The whitewashed convent, with its gilded cross
And humble tower, sends upward through the hushed
And vacant air its vesper knoll, by distance
Mellowed to music. This is all the sound
That tells of life. Down through a gloomy gorge,
Walled in by rifted rocks, the vale of Ascra
Lies, like a nook withdrawn beyond the reach
Of violence; and yet the crescent crowns
A minaret, and tells a startling tale
Of woe and fear. Beyond, the Theban plain
Stretches to airy distance, till it seems
Lifted in air, — green corn-fields, olive groves
Blue as their heaven, and lakes, and winding rivers,
And towns whose white walls catch the amber light,
That burns, then dies away, and leaves them pale
And glimmering, while a floating vapor spreads
From marsh and stream, till all is like a sea,
Rolling to Œta, and the Eubœan chain,
Stretching, in purple dimness, on the verge
Of this unclouded heaven. Far in the east
The Ægean twinkles, and its thousand isles
Hover in mist, and round the dun horizon
Are many floating visions, clouds, or peaks,
Tinted with rose. Before me lies a land
Hallowed with a peculiar sanctity,
The eye of Greece, — a wild of rocks and hills,

Lifted in shadowy cones, and deep between
Mysterious hollows, once the proud abodes
Of Genius and of Power. Now twilight throws
Around her softest veil, a purple haze
Investing all at hand, and farther on
Skyey and faint and dim. Methinks I catch,
Through the far opening heights, the Parthenon,
And all its circling glories. Salamis
Lies on its dusky wave; and farther out
Islands and capes, and many a flitting sail
White as a sea-bird's wing. The stars are out,
And all beneath is dark. The lower hills
Float in obscurity, and plain and sea
Are blended in one haze. Cyllene still
Bears on her snowy crown the rosy blush
Of twilight; and thy loftier head, Parnassus,
Has not yet lost the glory and the blaze
That suit the heaven of song. There let me pause;
There fix my latest look. How beautiful,
Sublimely beautiful, thou hoverest
High in the vacant air! Thou seemest uplifted
From all of earth, and like an island floating
Away in heaven. How pure the eternal snows
That crown thee! yet how rich the golden blaze
That flashes from thy peak! how like the rose,
The virgin rose, the tints that fade below,
Till all is sweetly pale! Are there not harps
Warbling above thee? voices, too, attuned
To an unearthly song? Methinks I hear them
Breathing around me, with a charm and spell,
That melt my heart to weeping. It is sad,
That song of heaven, — the funeral symphony
Of ancient worthies, for the murdered peace
And glory of their land. They greet the heroes,
Who rise to meet them in these iron times,
And hail them as their sons; and yet they weep
Their unavailing toil. Is there no hand
To grasp the avenging sword, and tear the knife
From the assassin? Must these generous hearts

Pour out their blood like water, till the flood
Of rage and power has swept them from the earth,
And buried all their bright and hallowed land
In death and darkness? O, forbid it, nations
Who bear the name of Christian, and are proud
Of light and truth and mercy. Arm ye; take
The cross and sword; move to the war of death
Stern and devoted; pause not, till the Turk
Has lost the power to harm; then give to Greece
Her ancient liberty, and ye shall live
Immortal, in your fame.

THE PARTHENON.

THIS rock was once the seat of pomp and power;
Here rest the chiefs of olden time,
And here the orator sublime
Shed on their willing ears his golden shower.

Here stood their temple in its beauty's blaze,
When like a thing of light it rose,
And proudly on their dazzled foes
So brightly beamed, it quelled their daring gaze.

Here stood Minerva with her guardian shield,
And from her threatening lance
Shot such a lightning glance,
None dared to try the heaven-protected field.

Here Genius, Glory, Piety were shrined,
And hence that Spirit flew,
Whose wing has hurried through
The darkened world, and fired the inglorious mind.

THE SUNIAN PALLAS.

By Sunium's rock I took my way
  Along the blue Ægean sea,
That bright in golden sunset lay
  Round the fair islands of the free:
A form of more than mortal mould
  On the high rock sublimely rose;
The bosses of her buckler rolled
  Like eyes of lightning on her foes:
I looked, — the blue-eyed goddess there
Stood glorious in the evening air.

She stood and raised her brazen lance,
  That glittered like a meteor's beam;
Its light below in quivering dance
  Flashed gayly on the ocean stream:
Round her tall casque her plumy crest
  Shook with a terrible sign of power,
And the grim Ægis on her breast
  Told to the Turk his destined hour:
She spake, — and like the rush of flame
Her voice in awful murmurs came.

" Sons, worthy of your warrior sires!
  Yours is the cause of earth and heaven:
Shame to the heart that faints or tires,
  Till the last sacrifice is given!
Go fearlessly along your path, —
  It mounts to liberty and fame;
Go, with an unrelenting wrath,
  And conquer till the Turk is tame:
When the red fires of battle glare,
Remember — I am with ye there.

" These rocks that rise so rudely round
  Were consecrate to me of old;

Here the Athenian sternly bound,
   For rapid fight, his mantle's fold:
He saw the Persian tents below;
   They filled and blackened all the plain:
He rushed, — and, like a torrent's flow,
   Swept them, and hurled them to the main:
This was the wrath that made him free,
The fearless wrath of Liberty.

"What if a cold and coward world
   Leave ye to work your way alone;
Be the new banner never furled
   Till Liberty is all our own.
Tell them we ask no other aid
   Than our own hearts in such a cause;
No, none but Freemen's hands were made
   To fight and win for equal laws.
Go, with a firm, confiding breast, —
Go, fight, and win the conqueror's rest."

THE GREEK MOUNTAINEERS.

Now bind in myrtle wreaths the avenging sword,
Like him who, at the Panathenian games,
With the bold heart no tyrant quells nor tames,
The bosom of the proud usurper gored.
We have a sterner foe to wake our wrath, —
Centuries of darkness have not dimmed us quite, —
We have the heart to feel, the hand to smite.
Wo to the wretch who dares to cross our path!
Our souls are gathered to the effort, — free
We have been, and we will be, and our sires
Shall look from heaven, and see us light the fires
On thy eternal altars, Liberty!
Though the proud fanes of ancient glory lie
Crushed by the hand of havoc and of time,
Still tower, with front as lofty and sublime,
Yon hoary peaks, the pillars of the sky.

There lived the Suliote free, when all below
Bowed to the Ottoman, — the Mainote there
Wandered as wildly as his mountain air,
And dealt at will his vengeance on his foe.
These are thy temples, Liberty! — these heights
Nursed the first hardy Dorian in his cave;
And there, when Sparta sank, the free and brave
Hung on the unconquered rocks their beacon lights.
There stood thy altars, and the eternal flame
Burns round the cloudy summits, with a glow
As bright as when it cheered the plains below,
And lit the sacred band to death and fame.
We too will have our glory, — we will light
Our torches in the fire that never dies;
And with a terrible and solemn rite
Devote us to our country's liberties.
We bind our swords in myrtle, and we go
To meet the proud oppressor on his way:
Let but the tyrant sink beneath the blow,
Gladly we die, — our foes can only slay.
They cannot rob us of that wreath of fame,
The glorious chiefs of ancient Athens bear:
O, how they come to meet us in the air,
Borne on their chariots and steeds of flame!
We hasten to our vengeance and we die, —
Wide to the winds our blood, our lives, are given:
In the mid-joy of fight they hurry by,
Seize us, and bear us to the Patriot's Heaven.

THE LAST SONG OF THE GREEK PATRIOT.

One last, best effort now!
  They shall not call us slaves, —
These iron necks shall never bow
To barter for a hated life,
But we will tell, in mortal strife,

What wrath a freeman braves:
A few short years, and we have known
The pride and joy — to live alone.

Our ancient land was free;
We washed its stains in blood:
Again the hymn of Liberty
Rose from the high Athenian shrine,
And virgin hands did often twine,
In the dark olive wood,
Their garlands for the youthful brow
Who taught the heathen Turk to bow.

These have been glorious days:
Let come what will, our fame
Is like the sun's eternal blaze,
And when they tell of Marathon,
And all the fields our fathers won,
They too shall name
Bozzaris, and the few who died,
Victims of glory, by his side.

The world has told our doom, —
'T is liberty or death!
The tree we planted must not bloom,
For Turk and Christian — all unite,
And royal hands our sentence write,
And yet our breath,
When trampled by the ruffian herd,
Shall never breathe one recreant word.

If we must die, then die!
And let the foul disgrace
Cling to their names eternally,
Who, when they had the power to save,
Doomed to a dark and bloody grave
A high, devoted race.
Awhile the sweets of life to know,
O God, and then to perish so!

But freedom has one shore:
  Would we could shelter there
The tender ones we value more
Than life or fame! O generous men!
Be with us, as ye long have been,
  And we will share
All the poor fruit of toils and pains, —
Our hearts, our lives, perhaps our chains.

Come, at this fatal hour,
  Ye last of high-born souls;
Come, when the crushing weight of power
Has all but bent our necks to earth;
We will not shame our glorious birth;
  Nor Turk nor Hun controls
The heart that holds the Spartan fire,
The sacred relic of his sire.

We know ye cannot fear,
  We know that ye are brave, —
To us, your very name is dear:
O, by that name, and all its light,
We bid ye join the murderous fight,
  To win and save!
O, come, if it be only time
To fall with us, in death sublime!

GRECIAN LIBERTY.

Glorious Vision! who art thou,
With thy starry crown of light,
Like the diadem of night
On the Æthiop monarch's brow?
And why art thou descending
From thy bright Olympian throne,
And thy lavish glory lending,
Like the ever-rolling sun,

To the self-devoted band
On the threshold of their land?
Few, but hardy, are their ranks,
And they never will retire,
Though ten thousand on their flanks
Hurl a storm of steel and fire,—
Though an iron tempest rain
Death and darkness, till the day
Pass in dim eclipse away,—
Though the thunderbolts of war
Plough their furrows in the plain,
And the echoing mountains bay
To the tumult from afar.

O, bright and glorious creature,
Winged and mailed and armed for fight!
Though beautiful in feature,
Like a spirit of delight,
Yet the arching of thy brow,
And thy proud and gallant form,
Tell of one who rides the storm,
When the sternest warriors bow
And the bravest yield their breath
At the summoning of death.
There thou standest on the mountains,
And the sparkle of thy spear,
Like a sunbeam on the fountains
To the gallant few below,
Is a sign of wrath and fear
To the blind and brutal foe:
Like a beacon, let it blaze
Broad and flaring, till it daze
All who come with foot profane
To this consecrated plain,
Where thy pure and perfect shrine
Youths and maidens loved to twine
With the laurel and the myrtle,
And the shadow of thy grove,
Haunt of innocence and love,
Heard the winged arrows hurtle

From the flowery-wreathen bow,
With a whisper like the flow
Of a brook, that winds afar
Underneath the evening star.

O, they were happy days,
When, reposing in the shade,
Elms and vines and poplars made,
It was all thy joy to gaze
On the races and the dances,
Twining hands and burning glances,
Where Passion went and came,
Like an arrow tipped with flame.
Though thou didst often lie
With a pleased and placid eye,
As thy children took their pleasure,
And the merry flute and viol
Told, in light and airy measure,
All the joys and sports of leisure;
Not the less, to meet the trial,
Thou wouldst gird thy warlike arms,
And with bare and eager blade,
On, through dangers and alarms,
To the wreath of Victory wade.
Thou couldst leave thy pleasant woods,
And the harvest of the plain,
And along the torrent floods
To the frozen mountains climb,
Where they reared their fronts sublime;
Or, scorning Slavery's chain,
Make thy dwelling on the main.
From the Dorian rocks and caves,
When the gorged and glutted foe
Lay in careless ease below,
Like an Alpine stream that raves
When the autumn rains are pouring,
And the pines in mist are towering, —
So thou didst rush and sweep
To the dark, remorseless deep,

With thy fury and thy force,
Shield and chariot, man and horse,
And thy sword wrought far and wide,
Till the land was purified.

And now thou dost awake,
And thy dream of ages break.
From the halls of ice and snow,
Whence thy classic rivers flow;
From thy palace in the clouds,
Where the light of evening runs
On the rolling wreath that shrouds
The last refuge of thy sons, —
Peaks, that never Turk has trod,
Where the armed and ardent Klepht
Found his shelter, when he left,
For a prey to wasting fires,
All the temples of his God,
And the dwellings of his sires;
From thy caverns in the rock,
From thy dark and hidden hold,
Thou hast nerved thee to the shock,
And thy warning shout has rolled, —
Height from height has caught the sound,
And thy foes in haste retire;
Now the tumult rises higher, —
'T is a nation's cry of joy, —
"None to ravage and destroy, —
Not a foreign foot is found
On our consecrated ground."

HELLAS.

LAND of bards and heroes, hail!
  Land of gods and godlike men,
Thine were hearts that could not quail, —
  Earth was glorious then;
Thine were souls that dared be free,
Power, and Fame, and Liberty.

In thy best and brightest hour,
  Thou wert like the sun in heaven;
Like the bow that spans the shower,
  Thou to earth wert given:
Nations turned to thee and prayed
Thou wouldst fold them in thy shade.

Like the infant Hercules,
  Thou didst spring at once to power,
With the energy that frees
  Millions in an hour:
From the wave, the rock, the glen,
Freedom called her chosen then.

What though thousands fought with one, —
  Did thy sons draw back in fear?
No, — with Ægis like a sun,
  Pallas hovered near:
Wisdom with her diamond shield
Guarded well the fatal field.

Fair and bright her temple shone,
  Meet for such divine abode;
There in majesty alone,
  Loftily she trode:
Time in vain his bolt has hurled;
Still it stands, to awe the world.

Thine were all that rouse the spirit
  From its dim and deathly dreams:

O, shall man again inherit
  Such undying beams?
Lend thy kindling breath awhile;
Earth shall then in glory smile.

Land where every vale and mountain
  Echoes to immortal strains,
Light is round the stream and fountain,
  Light on all thy plains.
Never shall thy glory set;
Thou shalt be our beacon yet.

Yes, — for now thy sons are calling
  To the tombs that hold their sires, —
One by one their chains are falling, —
  They have lit their fires:
See! from peak to peak they run,
Bearing Freedom's signal on.

On, from peak to peak, they rush;
  Wide and far the glory flows;
Streams of light unearthly gush
  From their crown of snows.
Hear ye not the warning call?
"Shall a nation rise and fall!"

No! forbid it, gracious Heaven!
  Though a world look coldly on;
Be the unyielding spirit given, —
  Be the battle won;
Or if hope desert the brave,
Be their land their common grave!

If they lose the glorious prize,
  Be thy rocks a nation's tomb, —
Man shall sink, no more to rise,
  If they meet that doom!
Come, ye slaves! and read, and fear, —
Freedom's *last*, *best* hope is here!

ODE.

FOR THE CELEBRATION AT BUNKER HILL, JUNE 17, 1825.

WHEN our patriot fathers met
  In the dark and trying hour,
While the hand of Britain yet
  Pressed us with its weight of power,
Still they dared to tell the foe
  They were never made for slaves,—
Still they bade the nations know
  They were free as ocean's waves.

Yonder is the glorious hill
  Where their blood was nobly shed,—
Never with a firmer will
  Hearts of freemen beat and bled:
Shall the son forget his sire?
  No,—the admiring world shall see
High a pillared tomb aspire,
  Like a tower of Liberty.

Now the arch of empire swells
  Proud and daring, fixed and strong:
While the hand of ruin fells
  Nations that have flourished long;
Loftier the temple springs,
  Telling on its front sublime,
How it scorns the rage of kings,
  And the wasting tooth of time.

From its high and lifted brow,
  See, it sends a wakening light,
Where a world is slumbering now
  In the shades of eastern night;
They shall feel the quickening fire,
  Rise and run to meet the day,

And their hearts shall never tire,
  Till their chains are rent away.

None shall ever rashly dare
  Lift his hand against this shrine,
While its pediment shall bear
  Names so honored and divine:
High above the sacred band,
  There in light unfading set,
Like twin stars of glory, stand
  WASHINGTON and LAFAYETTE.

ODE.

FOR THE FIFTIETH ANNIVERSARY OF INDEPENDENCE, JULY 4, 1826.

BRING to this high and holy rite
  A spirit worthy of our sires:
Still may their zeal, a guiding light,
  Inform us with its noblest fires!
    This the day that saw them rise
    Bright, in glory, to the skies.

Then came they forth, a nation new,
  To kindle and to warn a world;
Then high to heaven their eagle flew;
  Defiance on their foe they hurled.
    Britons dared not call them slaves, —
    Freedom flourished on their graves.

Be round us now, a sacred band;
  Assist us, at the shrine ye raised;
Go forth to animate our land,
  Bright as at first your valor blazed.
    Fathers, heroes, you we call;
    May your spirit grace us all.

Look down from that sublime abode,
  Where now ye sit in high repose;
Fair are the battle-fields ye trod;
  No more the tide of slaughter flows.
    Welcome, Peace! the boon is due,
    Full and glorious, all to you.

A few, an aged few remain,
  Your brethren in the war of death;
Their presence — be it not in vain —
  It stirs us with a quickening breath.
    Let us emulate our sires, —
    Let us cherish long their fires.

O, gladly beats the veteran's heart
  To hail this holiest Jubilee;
Theirs was the noblest, proudest part,
  The toils that set a nation free.
    Now those generous toils are done;
    Liberty and peace are won.

The flame that warmed and waked their souls,
  Burns like a beacon on our hills;
Through all our favored land it rolls;
  Bright is the heart it fires and fills.
    Still the watch-word sounds, — be free:
    Still 't is Death or Liberty.

Then close this high and holy rite
  With honor to the wise and brave;
The men who dared the field of fight
  Their homes to bless, their land to save.
    Now to those who fought and fell,
    Bid the lofty chorus swell.

SEA PICTURES.

I.

Wide to the wind the canvas throw;
  The moment calls, — away, away!
And let the full libation flow
  To the bright sentinel of day;
Fill high the beaker to its brim,
  And freely pour it in the sparkling sea,
That the blue-cinctured galley swim
  Light as a bird who feels its liberty,
And, gladdening in the sun's reviving smile,
Floats o'er the water to its osier isle.

Now let the sails be widely spread
  To catch the welcome breath of heaven;
The light clouds hurry overhead,
  By the free mountain breezes driven.
We catch it now, — the enlivening air
  Sounds cheerily amid the crackling sails;
Away, away! the wind is fair:
  Haste on to meet the ever-blowing gales,
Where, softly breathing o'er the marble main,
They smooth its billows to a liquid plain.

II.

Spread every sail before the wind;
  Catch all the breathings of a gale so fair;
It steals upon us from behind,
  Like an invisible spirit through the air:
Wide laughs the quickly heaving sea, —
  Its foam-wreaths twinkle in the sun;
Onward the galley hurries, steadily,
  Like the front horse who knows the victory won,
And with his balanced limbs and waving mane
Skims, lightly as a dove, the even plain.

Yonder the mountains bluely rise,
  Their foreheads whitened by the smile of heaven;
They hang like summer clouds around the skies
  Soft slumbering in the golden light of even:
Yon peaks mount upward from the Elysian vales,
  Where an eternal spring unfolds
Flowers never fading to her quickening gales,
  And the same tree in blended beauty holds
Bud, bloom, and fruitage in its early down,
Or brightly peering forth amid its leafy crown.

There live the blessed, — a gentle air
  Steals round them laden with the breath of flowers;
All tells of an eternal beauty there;
  One glorious sunshine gilds the amaranth bowers:
No rolling cloud, no gusty rain,
  No light-winged snow, come rushing from the sky,
But shining dews bedrop the spiky plain,
  Oft twinkling as the sea-wind flutters by;
There hangs in middle air the princely palm,
  Swaying its broad leaves to the whispering gale,
Its flower-tufts drooping low, as in a calm
  Floats the gay pennon round the uncertain sail;
There springing from the ocean's breast,
  Silent and cool, Hesperian breezes rove;
They only fan the happy to their rest,
  And give a pleasing murmur to the grove.

III.

Steadily breathes the ever-blowing gale;
  The ship rides proudly on the silent sea;
There 's music in the bosom of the sail,
  Like the soft night-wind in a cypress-tree:
Spread smoothly as a temple's marble floor,
  Heaves onward to the sky the long, long swell;
Nothing is heard but the far-uttered roar,
Stealing in undulations from the shore,
  Like the low murmur in a twisted shell.

Steadily moves the ship along its way,
 Sporting its streamers in the tropic sun,
While overhead glows a redoubled day,
 And the still hours in higher circles run,
Till evening, in a wreath of glory drest,
Comes blushing from the rosy kindling west.

There is no visible motion in the air;
 'T is one eternal tide for ever going
On with the glorious orb that guides it there,
 Like rivers down to ocean's hollow flowing:
The gull wheels round them on his balanced wing
 Light as a snow-flake calmly floating by,
Watching with fixed eye, where with sudden spring
 The blue-fin leaps to catch the painted fly:
So deep a calm broods over all, the crew
 Slumber at midday on the shaded deck,
While the lone pilot safely steers them through
 Seas that have rarely borne the shattered wreck;
Where the ship glides upon the pointed rock
So gently, not a sleeper feels the shock,
Then, slowly rocking, dips its plunging prow,
And rushes headlong to the abyss below.

The glory and the beauty of a calm;
 The sun throned proudly in a deep blue sky;
 No mist, no stain to dim its Tyrian dye;
The air all living with a breathing balm
Sent from the scarlet flower-tufts of the palm
 On the lone rocky islet lifted high;
There the flamingo, like a thing of fire,
 Shoots in a meteor flight, and grandly there
 Sits the sea-eagle poised in middle air,
Rolling his red eye with a monarch's ire.
The ocean, as it moves along below,
 Just strikes the rock, and heaves one foaming wave,
 Or sends a hollow murmur through the cave,
Then softly steals away in silent flow.

How high, and yet how soothing, thus to sail
  Steadily o'er a sheet of glassy green,
Curved to its centre like a verdant vale,
Where, all her canvas spread to catch the gale,
  The vessel walks her way like ocean's queen,—
Seeming at distance through the crystalline air,
  Her bright sails fringed with each aerial hue,
  An iris floating on its ground of blue,
Or white-winged spirit calmly hovering there.

A FRAGMENT.

He long had wound his solitary way
  Beneath the branches of a forest old,
And by his tangled path, in murmuring play,
  A little river down its waters rolled;
Now in a deep and darkling pool it lay;
  Then from the sun it caught a touch of gold,
As through the lightly opening leaves it passed,
And gave a cheerful glance that could not last.

And so in long and silent wandering
  He walked beneath the thick inwoven roof
Of the long boughs, and leaves low whispering;
  And nothing sounded near him, but the hoof
Of the scared deer, that with a sudden spring
  Fled his approach, and slyly kept aloof,
Watching him with a dark and eager eye,
Till he had passed the timid creature by.

And so he travelled on till low the sun
  Had sank, and now looked through the ancient
      wood,
And bronzed the mossy trunks, as one by one
  They met the flowing of that airy flood,

Which seemed on the cool evening wind to run,
  Till it flowed o'er the thicket where he stood,
And gave to every shivering leaf and spray
A flush as of the merry morn in May.

And now he saw that he had well-nigh passed
  The weary length of wilderness, for soon,
Between two poplars slender as a mast,
  The sun shone broad, as when he holds at noon
The middle sky, and from behind them cast
  A flash of light, till all the roof was strewn
With brightness, like a multitude of stars,
As the leaves shifted with the shifting airs.

And forth he went, and all before him lay
  A meadow covered thick with summer flowers,
And through that glade the river took its way,
  Now open, then beneath high-arching bowers,
Where the vine hung its clusters, and the bay
  Shot through their purpling tufts its leafy towers;
The wind blew fresher there, and all the grass
Bent low its heavy head to let it pass.

And all that meadow kindled by the flush
  Of the red sun, who now behind a hill
Dipped his broad circle, and with deepening blush
  Each moment clipped his rosy fulness, till
He vanished quite, and then with sudden rush
  Wide flashing streams of glory seemed to fill
The sky above him, and then mounted higher,
'Till half the heaven was like a sea of fire.

And gradually this glow of light grew pale,
  And only hung on the low-lying cloud;
And then a long, dark shadow hid the vale,
  And covered up its beauty, like a shroud;
Then all was dark, but the outspreading sail
  Of the lone eagle, where he circled proud,
Seeming as if he could not bid adieu
To his loved sun, and so to meet him flew.

And then from out the forest boughs was heard,
  As if it faintly mourned the dying day,
The soft complaining of a twilight bird;
  And as the visible world all silent lay,
So that a bush or thicket hardly stirred,
  It floated through the darkness far away;
Then sinking to a faint and fainter tone,
It left the wearied wanderer alone.

THE MYTHOLOGY OF GREECE.

There was a time, when the o'erhanging sky
And the fair earth with its variety,
Mountain and valley, continent and sea,
Were not alone the unmoving things that lie
Slumbering beneath the sun's unclouded eye;
But every fountain had its spirit then,
That held communion oft with holy men,
And frequent from the heavenward mountain came
Bright creatures, hovering round on wings of flame,
And some mysterious sibyl darkly gave
Responses from the dim and hidden cave:
Voices were heard waking the silent air,
A solemn music echoed from the wood,
And often from the bosom of the flood
Came forth a sportive Naiad passing fair,
The clear drops twinkling in her braided hair;
And as the hunter through the forest strayed,
Quick-glancing Beauty shot across the glade,
Her polished arrow levelled on her bow,
Ready to meet the fawn or bounding roe;
And often on the mountain-tops the horn
Rang round the rocky pinnacles, and played,
In lighter echoes, from the checkered shade,
Where through the silvery leaves at early morn
Stole the slant sunbeams, shedding on the grass
Brightness, that quivered with the quivering mass

Of thickly arching foliage; — often there
Dian and all her troop of girls were seen
Dancing by moonlight on the dewy green,
When the cool night-wind through the forest blew,
And every leaf in tremulous glances flew;
And in the cloudless fields of upper air,
With coldly pale and melancholy smile
The moon looked down on that bright spot, the while,
Which in the depth of darkness shone as fair,
As in lone southern seas a palmy isle;
And when a hunter-boy, who far away
Had wandered through the wild-wood from his home,
Led by the eagerness of youth to roam,
Buried in deep unbroken slumber lay, —
Then as the full moon poured her mellow light
Full on the mossy pillow where he slept,
One more than nymph, in sylvan armor dight,
Bent fondly over him, and smiled, and wept.
Each lonely spot was hallowed then; — the oak
That o'er the village altar hung, would tell
Strange hidden things, — the old remembered well,
How from its gloom a spirit often spoke.
There was not then a fountain or a cave,
But had its reverend oracle, and gave
Responses to the fearful crowd, who came
And called the indwelling deity by name.
Then every snowy peak, that lifted high
Its shadowy cone to meet the bending sky,
Stood like a heaven of loveliness and light;
And as the gilt cloud rolled its glory by,
Chariots and steeds of flame stood harnessed there,
And gods came forth and seized the golden reins,
Shook the bright scourge, and through the boundless air
Rode over starry fields and azure plains.
It was a beautiful and glorious dream,
Such as would kindle high the soul of song;
The bard who struck his harp to such a theme
Gathered new beauty as he moved along:

His way was now through wilds and beds of flowers,
Rough mountains met him now, and then again
Gay valleys hung with vines in woven bowers
Led to the bright waves of the purple main.
All seemed one bright enchantment then;—but now,
Since the long sought for goal of truth is won,
Nature stands forth unveiled with cloudless brow,
On earth ONE SPIRIT OF LIFE, in heaven ONE SUN.

PAINTING.

A PERSONIFICATION.

ONE bright sunshiny autumn day,
When the leaves were just beginning to fade,
I saw a gay and laughing maid
Stand by the side of a public way.

There she stood erect and tall;
Her flowery cheek had caught the dyes
Of the earliest dawn, and oh! her eyes,
Not a star that shoots or flies,
But those dark eyes outshine them all.

She stood with a long and slender wand,
With a tassel of hair at its pointed tip;
And fast as the dews from a forest drip,
When a summer shower has bathed the land,
So quick a thousand colors came,
Darting along like shapes of flame,
At every turn of her gliding hand.
She gave a form to the bodiless air,
And clear as a mirrored sheet it lay;
And phantoms would come and pass away,
As her magical rod was pointed there.

First the shape of a budding rose,
Just unfolding its tender leaf;

Then, all unbound its virgin zone,
Full in its pride and beauty blown,
It heavily hangs like a nodding sheaf;
And a cloud of perfume around it flows.

Then a mingling of vale and hill,
Hung around with a woody screen,—
O, how alive its quivering green!
And there a babbling brook is seen
To turn the wheel of a moss-grown mill:
There is a clear and glassy pool,
And a boy lies idly along its brink,
And he drops a pebble to see it sink
Down in that depth, so calm and cool;
And out from behind a bowering tree
There peeps a maiden crowned with flowers;
The two are innocent paramours;—
At her delicate laugh he turns to see,
And then she darts like a frighted fawn
That springs away from the turfy lawn,
And far in the tangled thicket cowers:
So she flies in her haste to hide
The blush that mantles her cheek and brow;
Then he languidly turns his eye aside
To the quiet brook's eternal flow.

There you may see a warrior horse,
All his trappings are dropped with gold;
How his eye sparkles! and oh! how bold,
As he springs away in his pride and force.
There a dark and keen-eyed Moor
Hangs and pulls at his bridle-rein,
But all his skill and might are vain;
He prances and tosses,—and, hark! away,
Bright as the flashing steeds of day,
He has broke from his keeper, and flings his mane,
Like a streaming meteor, over the plain.
Can you not see the creature neigh,
In his vapory nostrils panting wide,
In his tossing head and his arch of pride,

And his rapid glance from side to side,
As he stands and beats the echoing ground
With a quivering tramp, and sudden bound?
Then with a tremble in every limb,
And an angry snort, he darts away,
And round in a circle he seems to swim,
Or bends and turns like a lamb at play.

What is that comes from a golden cloud,
Floating along in thinnest air?
Was there ever a shape so fine and fair?
And oh! what wealth of sunny hair
Clings around like a glittering shroud.
See! she raises a snowy arm,
Pure as a flake, ere it leaves the sky.
She waves it around with a grace and a charm,
And, putting her glossy ringlets by,
Shows to the sight a lip and eye.
Is it a shape of light and air,
A vermeil cloud, and a midnight star,
That meet and mingle in glory there,
Or one of the winged spirits that fly
Like the prophet who rose in his fiery car?
No, 't is a being of human mould,
Changing with blush, and tear, and smile,
Such as the bard in his lonely isle
Close to his heart would love to fold.
Back she throws her tossing curls,
Cheek and brow and neck are bare,
Tenderly crimson and purely fair,
Like a damask-rose when it first unfurls
Its feathery bosom to light and air.
Now that world of grace is calm,
Sweeter and dearer, but not so bright,—
Like a flower when it sends the dew of night
Back from its breast in a cloud of balm.
See on her lids the gathering tear,
Clear as a star in the midnight main,
Such she might drop on her mother's bier,
Or shed for the youth who has long been dear,

When she parts and never may meet again.
O, what flashes of glory break
From that crystalline fount of love and joy!
All her smiles and glances wake,
And those opening lips such music make,
As rings from the heart of the hunter boy,
When he springs through the forest, fleet and proud,
And the startled echoes are many and loud,
Loud as the burst of a nation's joy,
In the rocks that girdle the mountain lake.

Now for the touch of a master-hand!
See! how she poises and waves her wand,
As if in a dream of busy thought
She sought for visions and found them not.
Now it rises, — and look, — what power
Springs to life, as she lifts her rod!
Is it a hero, or visible god,
Or bard in his rapt and gifted hour?
What a lofty and glorious brow,
Bent like a temple's towering arch,
As if that a wondering world might march
To the altar of mind, and kneel and bow;
And then what a deep and spirited eye,
Quick as a quivering orb of fire,
Changing and shifting from love to ire,
Like the lights in a summer-evening sky;
Then the living and breathing grace
Sent from the whole of that magic face,
The eloquent play of his lips, the smile
Sporting in sunbeams there awhile,
Then with the throb of passion pressed
Like a shivering leaf that cannot rest, —
And still as a lake when it waits a storm,
That wraps the mountain's giant form,
When they lie in the shade of his awful frown,
And his gathered brows are wrinkled down.

Such the visions that breathe and live,
The playful touch of her wand can give.

MUSINGS.

My spirit was o'er-wearied with the toil
At which the heart revolts; and dark and chill
The world was hushed around me, and all life
Lay in a deathlike slumber. I alone
Was wakeful, and I looked upon the night
Beautiful in its cloudless firmament,
And in its canopy of myriad stars,
With such a sense of sorrow, as when one
Deeply enamored gazes on a form
Shaped to celestial beauty, with the keen
And bitter thought that he can only gaze,
And love and worship, but can never be
Loved with an equal passion. It was dark,
And all the light that looked upon the earth
Was in those glorious creatures which afar
Shone in their awful grandeur. No sweet moon
Lent to the twilight hills a softer day,
And threw upon the waving folds of mist,
Then curling from the valley, such a tint
Of purity, the far-off mountain snow
Is dim and faint beside it. It was still;
The winds were silent, and the forest boughs
Stood hushed without a motion, and their leaves
Sent out no more that harmony of sounds
By which the unseen ministers of air
Utter their low-tuned voices. All was mute,
Solemnly mute, but the faint-falling chime
Of a small rivulet, that stole away,
Buried in tufts of roses, through a grove,
That rose high-arching o'er it. This would come
At times upon my ear with such sweet sounds
Of clear, yet broken melody, my soul
Drank in the quiet rapture, and was filled
Awhile with a like sweetness, and I seemed
A portion of the pure and motionless air,
And that the voices of invisible forms,

All young and lovely, were enshrined within
The compass of my being, and myself
Was living with their music. Then it sank
Slowly away, and down the flowery bank,
That still sent up its offerings of balm,
And filled the night with odors wafted far
On the calm breathings of the western gale,
Which now seemed waking, and at times would wave
In a wide fold the drapery of my couch,
And shake the wild vine, where it clustered o'er
My half-raised casement, — down the flowery bank
Reflecting, in its beads of dropping dew
Hung on the bending grass, the many eyes
That calmly watched in heaven, and looked on earth,
As mothers on their infants, when the night
Draws near to its meridian, and the pale
Fast-dying taper throws its trembling light
Full on the innocent slumberer, whose repose
Is happiness; whose dreams, if it has dreams,
Are all in smiles; and as the day flits by
Light-winged, and without tears that are not pure,
So is its slumber full of deep delight,
And unembittered by the keen regret
Of past repented follies, or the fear
That darkens in the future, — down the bank
The tinkling of the water-fall would glide,
And stealing through its canopy of flowers,
It then would seem all silent; — yet my ear
Followed it, and I hung upon its sounds
Still warbling near in fancy, as we gaze
Intently on the lips that lately breathed
With a most tender music, and still seem
To listen to that deep, mysterious flow
Of spirit-touching melodies; and when
They tremble with her breath, as the full leaves
Shake on the rose when the still air awakes,
And comes to kiss their dews, — O, then we hear,
Though all is silent, such a strain, the heart
Beats quickly, and dissolves in tears away.

Thus were my feelings softened by the night,
Its silence, and its darkness, and the sounds
That made that silence deeper, as they came
Low-whispering through my window, like the voice
Of one who sighs in love, or as the breath
Of a pure spirit on its ministry
Of comfort to the wretched, or of hope
And courage to the failing. Then my thoughts,
Now freed from their dark burden, took a flight
Into a fonder region, and they went
Back to remembered days, when summer smiled,
Not only in the blue sky, and the fields
Ripe for the harvest, but more sweetly smiled
In my young heart, and in its livery dressed
All forms that moved around me, and endowed
The lovely with a spirit's loveliness,
And made them so divinely beautiful,
I lived in beauty, and it was the sum
Of all my thoughts and feelings, and it threw
Its mantle o'er all creatures, and it gave
An all-pervading color to my life,
And happiness alone was centred in
The contemplation of the fairest things;
And whether it were forms, or hues, or sounds,
Or looks that speak the heart, and shadow out
The workings of the faculty within
Which images all nature, and anew
Shapes it to fresh creations of a port
More lofty, and an attitude and air
More kindred to its tastes and tendencies, —
Whether it was in things that have no life,
The sports of Nature's handiwork, or those
Eternal statues where the soul of man
Stands fixed in immortality, — in flowers
Or leaves light-dancing, or in waving woods
Poised in luxuriant majesty aloft
On the uplifted mountain, — in the wing,
That glided through the yielding element
In every curve of gracefulness, and swept

Proudly the deepest bosom of the air,
And rode in light triumphant, — in the forms,
That bounding scoured the meadow, tense with life,
And nerved to trembling buoyancy, — or those
Who are like us in shape, in look and soul,
Only more beautiful, and nicely tuned
To a far softer harmony : — where'er
Nature was in its being, there my eye
Drank nothing in but BEAUTY, and my thoughts
Were hidden in a tide of loveliness,
And with the delicate motion of young life
My senses were one ecstasy, one thrill,
Which was not hushed, but heightened in my dreams.

I had gone back through darkly-shadowed years,
One round of fears and sorrows, and its long
And stagnant hours, which seemed for ever fixed
In one blank, joyless moment, as if time
Had grown eternity, and life could ne'er
Reach its long wished-for ending, — those dark years
Were passed like waves, when on the broken sea
Before the steady wind the vessel glides
Swift as a darting eagle, and my thoughts
Soon centred in those happy summer days,
And they were as realities, and seemed
Fairer than any I had seen before ;
And in the deep intensity of soul,
Drawn from all outward things, and poised and bound
In this one pure enchantment, — then I formed
Visions of paradise, which to have known
And felt one fleeting moment, in their full
O'erpowering presence, it is more, ah ! more
Than a whole age of cold and heartless years
Spent in one round of animal wants and toils,
With far less innocence and true delight
Than the keen feelings of the mother-bird
Who watches in the thicket o'er her young.

SHE faded, but in beauty; — not a charm
Of feature or expression left her calm
And all-enduring look, that meekly bore
Smiles, as in happier years of infancy,
Before her roses withered; not a sigh
Escaped her, but she seemed to live in hope,
That kindled by deferring. She had fed
So long upon the higher sympathies,
And had so purified her heart's desires,
That all to her was spirit; and a veil
Of an ethereal tenderness was thrown
O'er all that once seemed beautiful; and thus
She saw no other world than such as faith
Had promised to her second life. No dark
And bigot frown o'ershadowed her fair brow,
That every day grew purer, till it seemed
Wrought of an angel's essence, and it rose
Calm as the cloudless canopy of heaven;
And through it came a light, that gave to all,
On whom it sweetly shone, her peacefulness
And silent hope. Her feelings ever grew
Softer, and everything that had a sense
Of suffering was pitied, if the winds
Blew chillier; and even the falling flowers
Were tenderly lamented. She had been
A devotee to Nature, and she felt
Intensely all its loveliness, and hung
Delighted on its wonders, not with dumb
And thoughtless ecstasy, but with an eye
That read a soul within them, and a voice
That hymned the song of gratitude. Her eye
Yet stole abroad at evening, when the wind
Is silent and the landscape all is still,
And flowers are folding up their dewy leaves,
And birds are going to their unfledged young
Hid in the clustered foliage; when the air
Just stirs enough to rock them to repose,
And crisp the surface of a silent stream,

That flashes in the last departing ray,
And circles with its sheet of flowing gold
The islet tufted with an iris crown,
And the bright purple of the floating leaves,
That wave along its current, as the wind
Sways them in graceful curves, and slowly turns
Their ever-changing mirrors to the sun,
Till the pool glitters with their glancing light.

She chose this hour of worship, and she knelt,
Not to the beautiful creatures she beheld,
But to their COMMON PARENT; — though the world
Might claim a spirit's awe, it spread so fair,
So awful, and so wonderful around,
And had such magic hues upon its clouds,
And such a tint of love upon its sky,
And such a blended harmony of light
And shadow, such a host of fairy forms
All mellowed by the misty evening air,
And lovelier in their softness, that a soul
Fresh from its fountain might have worshipped there
Such rare and countless beauty. There she bent,
Herself the fairest; and she first took in,
With an intensest pleasure, all the fair
And wondrous forms around her, and then raised
Her eyes in adoration. Then her brow
Met the clear sky, that was alone as pure,
And her keen eyes, that gathered, as her life
Grew weaker, more of spirit, till they flashed
With her soul's inward movings, — those keen eyes
Looked on the stars, that now came faintly forth
On their night watching, and they seemed to find,
In those ethereal messengers, their home;
And there was such an ecstasy, her form
Seemed changed to something heavenly, and to rise
As a dove rises on a quiet wing,
And float into her kindred purity.

She was the first I loved; but years had gone
Since we had parted. Still the very look,
That lent me such enchantment, that I seemed
Raised to a higher being, when she sat
Sweet in her mildness by me, or with light
And flying footstep hastened to my call,
And hung upon my words with such a fond
And all-confiding earnestness, — that look
Still lived in all its light before me, fair
As the fresh dress of nature in the calm,
Unclouded beauty of an April eve,
When the gay twilight ends, and in her full
The white-robed planet overtops the hill,
And now is far in heaven, and rolls her way
In majesty and love, shedding a wave
Of soothing influences on them who sit
Or walk beneath her all-embracing smile,
To the wood-cinctured mountains in their groves
Wrapped as in a dark mantle, to the hills
Swelled to a sphere of fresh-grown turf, the vales
More darkly greened and fairer-flowered, the lakes
Sheeted in crystal purity, and all
The winding brooks and thread-like rills, that lace
The soft and oozy meadows, one calm look,
Silent and yet expressive, one far glance
Of peace and beauty lending. Thus she seemed,
And fairer in my fancy; and where'er
My eye roved in its wandering through dark shades,
Down close embowered dells, where brooklets steal
Their steps o'er glossy pebbles and bright sands, —
Where'er my quick eye wandered, she was still
The spirit of the beauty it beheld,
The living thing that animates the wild,
The nymph of the still waters, and the woods
Uttering unnumbered whisperings of joy
In their soft-rustling leaves, the Deity
That consecrates the valley and the lake
To her peculiar worship, — so her fair

And tranquil features, and her sylph-like form
Wrought in a purer world, and o'er-informed
With the quick life of feeling, — so she filled
Nature with her dear presence, and alone
Adorned the rudest landscape, and embraced
The desert with an atmosphere of love,
And lent my hours of utter solitude
A fellowship of fondest thoughts, too bright
To be aught else than momentary gleams
Of unsubstantial pleasure. So she lived,
Still loved and lovely, in my head and heart,
The image of my fancy, and the charm
That mastered my affections; and the spot
Where I had first beheld her innocent,
And soft, and spotless features, where I heard
The liquid music of her tender voice, —
That home of all my wishes still commands
My spirit to its centre, and I turn,
Wearied and sated, from all other things,
To that, and there find quietness. The charm,
That hangs around the moment and the place
Of our first sudden meeting, lives for ever,
And grows in strength and freshness as in years.
It cannot die, although thy love is gone,
And thou, too, hast forgotten such a thing
As I am has a being. Though thine eye
Lights on another, dearer one, thy lip
Smiles welcome to him, and thy voice is heard
Inviting him to happiness, — though I
Know this, and even have seen thee hand in hand
With one whom I have scorned, as far beneath
The scope of my high musings, as a toy
Fit to be breathed on by the scented breath
Of childish female flattery, as a thing
Thy pure and lifted spirit would have deemed
Unworthy of communion, — though I see
Thy fond eye resting on him, and thy arm
Locked tenderly in his, I will not curse,
Nor wish thee aught of evil. Those dear hours

Shall be thy safety, and the thoughts that dwell
With a redeeming fondness there shall throw
A veil o'er all thy weaker deeds, and quell
All darker feelings, which might rise within
My crushed and wounded bosom. I have lived
Too long for such a heart as mine, and life
Must henceforth be an unprized gift, resigned
When Nature shall recall it, as a load
That I have long cast from me with a wish
To be from earth all free; for if a wórld
Purer and brighter follows, I would know
How it is pure and beautiful, and be
One of its high inhabitants, and fly
On a quick pinion through its cloudless skies,
And with the gladness of life's newest spring
Would breathe its balm, and wanton round its flowers!

He had a twofold nature, and the one
Was of a higher order, with the souls
Who shine along the path of centuries
In full and perfect brightness, standing forth
In their own loftiness, the beacon-lights
By which the world is guided and upborne
From its forever downward tendency, —
By which it gathers beauty and is formed
To the one true refinement, that of thought
And chastened feeling, — with such better souls
Communing in an equal fellowship,
As clear in intellect, as brightly clear
In every high conception, and as warm
In all emotions, where the heart of man
Ascends and widens, and with outspread wings
Shadows all human hearts in kindness, lending
Its inspiration unto all who feel
The glow of its benignity, and dwell

Blessed in its steady sunshine. As a rock
Lifts its blue forehead from a mountain ridge,
And heaves a cloudless summit into heaven,
For ever smiling in the softened beam
Of an eternal noonday; — to the world
Of living things, who watch it far below
With a mute look of wonder, as a throne
On which the gods are dwelling, — to that world,
Soaring in unstained purity, it seems
The centre of devotion, and the fane
Where the heart bows in awe, and offers up
Its deepest adoration: — so these souls
Are to the humbler spirits, who go on
Mincing along the track they draw, upreared
To a commanding loftiness, and set
As idols on their pedestals to fill
The crowd with wonder. Men are made to bend
Before the mighty, and to follow on
Submissive where the great may lead, — the great
Whose might is not in crowns and palaces,
In parchment rolls or blazoned heraldry,
But in the power of thought, the energy
Of unsupported mind, whose steady will
No force can daunt, no tangled path divert
From its right-onward purpose. Few are they,
And well that they are few, who in the blaze
Of genius kindled, like a baleful star,
To such a flame as terrifies, and bears
Ruin when rushing onward, — who in wrath
Are launched along the path where nations go,
The highway of the battle, and the field
Where power is won, and thrones are emptied. Few
The spirits who originate and bend
All meaner hearts to wonder and obey,
As if their look were death, their word were fate;
As if they held the balance and the sword
To measure out their happiness, and give
To each his stated portion, and avenge
All such as dare to murmur. Few are they,

And if they were not, earth would be the list
Of an eternal conflict, the abode
Of ever-warring fiends, who in the train
Of a controlling spirit, in the march
Of a high conqueror's madness, still athirst
For a new field of bloodshed, never tired
Of the hot harvest of a passionate war,
Where the deep feelings of a nation's rage,
And the awakened thoughts of long revenge,
Are blended with those passions which arise
From the uprooted evils of an age
Of ever-growing tyranny, the sense
That chains are broken, prison-gates unbarred,
And the more galling servitude of mind,
The bowing of the spirit to the weight
Of a corrupted priesthood, and a court,
Which robs to show unto their famished eyes
Their earnings, with a splendid mockery
Of pageants, and false justice, and the pomp
Of a bedizened soldiery, the tools
Who forge and link their fetters, — the glad sense
That this deep charm is scattered, that this weigh
Is from their long-bowed shoulders shoved away,
And, like the waking from a painful dream,
Has left them in the wonder and the joy
Of lightness and deliverance, — who go on,
As tigers in bloodthirstiness, to slake
Their longing in the plunder and the waste
Of those who dare not, like themselves, be free,
At least who dare not cast the spell aside
That binds them to the altar and the throne,
And palsies all their vigor, and subdues
All their due might of soul; for men know not
The force that sleeps within them, till the sound
Of a loud warning wakes them from the sleep
Of a long night of darkness, — they know no
How they may rush upon the coward foe,
Whose power was in delusion, and the maze
Of falsehoods sanctified by time, and made
Sacred by being hallowed to the use

Of an unmeaning worship, feared the more,
The more it is unmeaning: they know not
How they have only to come forth, and say,
"Ye shall not be our masters, ye shall not
Riot, as ye were wont, in our best blood,
And feed upon our toil, and in our sweat
Bathe as in perfumed waters"; how at once
By firm resolve, and union, and the act
That lingers not one moment, they are free,
And lords of those who were their lords. O slaves!
How long will ye be silent, and await
The task-word of a master, and bow down
To his unfeeling ministers, and bear
His manacles and stripes, and see your loves
And little ones torn from you with a dumb
And quivering terror, and with fruitless tears
Water the bitter bread of toil, and fill
The cup of want and sorrow? Ye are strong,
And Nature has been kind to you; — your hands
Might work an awful vengeance, could your minds
Throw off the sottishness of servitude,
And concentrate their energies, and feel
Intensely their just power and rights. The heart
Sinks when want presses on it, and the world
Turns from the claims it urges, and will hear
None of the earnest words by which it pleads
For right and justice only, — then he feels
Lost in that darkest wilderness, the crowd,
Who know not, care not, when or how he die,
Who pass him by as if he were a thing
Fit only for the grave, and if he beg
One single act of mercy, he has then
Resigned all nobler feelings, and come down
To such a sense of wretchedness, it weighs
Like a cold rock upon him, and the strength
And light and action of his soul are gone,
And he can only linger on his way,
The scorn of those who prosper, and the hate
Of his own better spirit, which will seek
Death or forgetfulness, its only cure.

INSCRIPTION.

THE NAIAD OF THE FOUNTAIN.

THOU who art wearied with the idle world,
Come to my hospitable shade. No sound
Shall here disturb thee, but the gentle gush
Of a clear-flowing fountain, poured away
From a rude, rocky hollow. Overhead
My branches weaved with ivy and spring flowers,
Moss-rose and woodbine, intercept the day,
And make perpetual twilight. Dark below
Gushes the ever-spouting spring, and spreads
Light dew upon the moss that beds it in,
As with a velvet margin. There it lies
Clear to its lowest depth, for ever circling
With the undulation of the wave below,
And with the faint, uninterrupted dash
Of the bright crystal curve, that from the rocks
Darts with a never-wearied leap away.

Enter beneath my hospitable shade,
And thou mayest hold communion with the world
Of beautiful and pure imaginings,
Egerias and Dianas, such as came
On the soft moonlight to Endymion,
Or such as to the thoughtful Roman king
Were all apparent at the silent hour
When the sun sank beneath the Iberian wave,
And gayly on the Alban mountain's cone
Glittered the last departing beam of day.

Here thou mayest sit, and, making of the moss
A pillow for thee, ponder silently
On thy most inward feelings, and control
Thy passions to a calm. 'T is wisdom oft
To leave the bustle of resort, and seek
Silence wherein to meditate and hold

Communion with the spirits of better men,
And better times, — for so we always deem,
When we are over-wearied with the push
And jostling of life, — of better times,
When our gray ancestors grew purely old,
And in the last declining hour of life
Had all the innocence of childhood. Fond
And soothing is the dream: it quickens us
To emulate them, so that we may look
Upon their monuments without the blush
Of shame to mantle o'er our brows. One hour
Of thoughtful solitude may nerve the heart
For days of conflict, — girding up its armor
To meet the most insidious foe, and lending
The courage sprung alone from innocence
And good intent.
The sun glows overhead
Intensely, and the hot and sultry blue,
Unclouded and unstained, burns with the blaze
That fills the orb of noon: the panting hart
Looks for a shelter, and a cool, fresh spring
To slake his thirst; the cattle in the brook
Lave their hot sides, and underneath the elm,
Arching its hanging branches till they dip
And kiss the scarcely gliding water, mute
And patiently await the coming on
Of evening, to go out around the beds
Of tufted grass and wild-flowers, there to crop
The tender herbage. Wearied as thou art,
Come to my woodland hall, and thou wilt find
Beneath my canopy of leaf and vine,
And on my beds of moss, so soft, they seem
Instinct with a quick spirit swelling them
To meet thy gentle pressure, — thou wilt find
In these, and in the clear and glassy depth
Of the round basin, strewed with sands, like snow
Drifting and heaving, as the waters gush
From their unknown and hidden cave, — the fall
Of molten crystal lapsing from the rocks

Amid an intertangled mass of fern
And cresses, where the sifted fountain flies
Away in a light vapory cloud, that fills
Freshly my secret bower, — ah! thou wilt find
The coolness thou dost long for, and the peace,
The silent peace, thy over-wearied heart
So long has sought and found not.

A FRAGMENT.

It is the noon of night, — the stars look faint
With their long watching, and the slumbering earth
Heaves not a breath, — the very air is still, —
The waters hush their voices, and the leaf
Hangs silent in the woods. No living thing
Looks on the sleep of nature; — I alone
Sit like a sentinel, and feel how calm
And beautiful is night.

I have thus often sat, and deep in thought
Outwatched the stars; have seen their fires grow dim,
Till the young morning stood upon the hills
Wreathed with her dewy roses. I the while
Have fed my spirit on the inspiring dreams
Of the olden time, and with inquisitive eye
Pried in the depths of nature. I have gained
Much doubt and little certainty; have lost
Youth and its innocent joys, and blanched my hairs,
Even in my newest prime.

But I have gained a mastery o'er spirits,
And can evoke them from their secret caves,
Or from the viewless regions of the air,
And call them at my bidding. It is so.
I have seen glorious creatures throng around me,
All loveliness and light. They were not dreams,
But were substantial essences, pure forms,

That had a look and voice. I spake to them,
And they did answer, and their tones were music,
Such as they say the harmony of spheres,
When the seven orbs move round the golden sun,
Hymning too deep and ravishing melodies
For mortal ear to listen to, and live.
They spake, or rather chanted, and their song
Revealed a mystery so high, methought
The fountains of all knowledge opened up
To meet my gaze, and from their hidden caves
Came forth the darkest elements of things,
And stood before my presence.
I will try
Once more the potency of muttered charms,
And they shall come in their particular forms,
And do as I shall bid them.

Spirits! if ye are such, I do command ye,
From your most secret hiding-place come forth,
And be apparent to me. Spirit of light!
From the clear concave of the southern sky,
The world of elemental flame; and thou
Whose dwelling is the abyss of rolling waters;
And thou who lurkest deep in central caves;
And thou, light-footed messenger of Heaven,
Whose way is in the thin and empty air;
I challenge your obedience.
Hear ye not?
There is no sound to interrupt my voice,
And yet I have no answer. Comes there not
New brightness from the south? The very air
Burns with the living glory. Haste, thou spirit
Of most celestial beauty! I have loved thee,
And worshipped thee, when thou didst come at morning,
Scattering thy light on earth, and kindling heaven,
And wakening all to life. Dost thou not come;
Or is it only that the moon looks out,
In her unstained and virgin loveliness,

From the white cloud that dimmed her like a veil?
'T is so. I have dreamed myself to the belief
Of my own crowding fancies, and have made
The visions of my brain realities.
But no! there is a sound on the far waters;
A form is rising from their depths, and shedding
Brightness on the blue waves. It fades, — and now
There is no other light shed on the waters,
Than that beneath the moon, or some lone star
Deep sunk amid their darkness. Ye have vanished,
Dreams of delight and power! Ye gave to me
All I have known of joy; for in the sense
Of power I dwelt delighted: and though dreams,
Baseless and empty dreams, ye had to me
The force of strong reality, and made me,
In the chill winter of untimely age,
Even too happy. O, there was a spell
In the belief that some unearthly spirit
Held high communion with me, and informed
My heart to higher deeds, and gave revealings
Of a sublime futurity, and fed
Those hopes that lend even to the grave a charm.

But I have tried them, and have found them vain.
I have sought wisdom, and for this have pored
Over the blind imaginings of man,
And racked unwilling nature to reveal
A few half-hidden laws. In the vain search,
Age has come on me, and the proper joys
Of youth are lost for ever. O, how gladly
Would I resign all I have ever gained,
Or hoped to gain, of knowledge or of power,
For a few moments of the innocent gladness
A young heart feels, when the pure bloom of health
Runs o'er the cheek, and all things look of love.

THE DEATH OF A CHILD.

I SAT beside the pillow of a child, —
His dying pillow, — and I watched the ebb
Of his last fluttering breath. All tranquilly
He passed away, and not a murmur came
From his white lips. A film crept o'er his eye,
But did not all conceal it, and at times
The darkness stole away, and he looked out
Serenely, with an innocent smile, as if
Pleased with an infant's toy; and there was then
A very delicate flush upon his cheek,
Like the new edging of a damask-rose,
When first the bud uncloses. As I watched,
I caught at these awakenings better hope,
And, yielding to the longing of my heart,
Fancied I saw him opening from a trance,
And with a gentle effort shaking off
The oppression of a dream. A moment more,
And the film mantled o'er his eye again,
And the faint redness left his faltering lips,
And backward to its centre in the heart
The crimson current rallied, leaving him
Like a chill statue, icy cold and pale.
He was my only one, and I had long
Loved him for all his innocent playfulness,
And his endearing fondness. He would hang
Whole days around me, watching all I did,
And questioning each particular act, as if
He could not rest till he had known the why
Of every word and motion. I indulged him,
And in that kind indulgence found his love
Grow every hour, till I was as his life,
And he was more than mine. Well pleased I saw
His opening faculties, and well I knew
His curious bent betokened better things
In a maturer age; but when he seemed
Rosy, and full of health, and o'er-informed

With life's young buoyancy, a hidden blight
Nipped him, and he decayed. He sank away
With scarce a visible token, like a breath
Of summer wind, when it has spent itself,
And blows so faintly, that the feathery leaves
Of the mimosa only tell of it,
All others resting as if nothing stirred
In the wide air. I watched him eagerly,
And I could only see that he decayed,
And soon must die. With a consenting stillness
My heart grew calm, and while his dying breath
Stole from his lips so faintly, not a murmur
Met the deep listening ear; I felt a power,
Too peaceful for an earthly emanation,
Come with a tranquillizing influence o'er me
And soothe me to the trial. As I looked,
The quivering of his lids, that lay like leaves
Of alabaster on his darkened eyes,
And the small trembling of his parted lips,
Curled outward like the margent of a lily,
Suddenly died away, and all was still.
Life was no more. I knew it, and at once
The utter loneliness of sorrow sank
Deep, deep within me, and awhile I sat
Without a tear. The stream was frozen up
And would not flow; but soon relenting nature
Gave way, and a full burst of passionate weeping
Flowed with a sudden gush, that quite unmanned me,
Then ebbing silently, it left me calm.

CLOUDS.

Ye Clouds, who are the ornament of heaven;
Who give to it its gayest shadowings,
And its most awful glories; ye who roll
In the dark tempest, or at dewy evening
Hang low in tenderest beauty; ye who, ever

Changing your Protean aspects, now are gathered
Like fleecy piles, when the mid-sun is brightest,
Even in the height of heaven, and there repose,
Solemnly calm, without a visible motion,
Hour after hour, looking upon the earth
With a serenest smile : — or ye who, rather,
Heaped in those sulphury masses, heavily
Jutting above their bases, like the smoke
Poured from a furnace or a roused volcano,
Stand on the dun horizon, threatening
Lightning and storm, — who, lifted from the hills,
March onward to the zenith, ever darkening,
And heaving into more gigantic towers
And mountainous piles of blackness, — who then roar
With the collected winds within your womb,
Or the far uttered thunders, — who ascend
Swifter and swifter, till wide overhead
Your vanguards curl and toss upon the tempest
Like the stirred ocean on a reef of rocks
Just topping o'er its waves, while deep below
The pregnant mass of vapor and of flame
Rolls with an awful pomp, and grimly lowers,
Seeming to the struck eye of fear the car
Of an offended spirit, whose swart features
Glare through the sooty darkness, fired with vengeance,
And ready with uplifted hand to smite
And scourge a guilty nation ; ye who lie,
After the storm is over, far away,
Crowning the dripping forests with the arch
Of beauty, such as lives alone in heaven,
Bright daughter of the sun, bending around
From mountain unto mountain like the wreath
Of victory, or like a banner telling
Of joy and gladness ; ye who round the moon
Assemble, when she sits in the mid-sky
In perfect brightness, and encircle her
With a fair wreath of all aerial dyes ;

Ye who, thus hovering round her, shine like mountains
Whose tops are never darkened, but remain,
Centuries and countless ages, reared for temples
Of purity and light; or ye who crowd
To hail the new-born day, and hang for him,
Above his ocean couch, a canopy
Of all inimitable hues and colors,
Such as are only pencilled by the hands
Of the unseen ministers of earth and air,
Seen only in the tinting of the clouds,
And the soft shadowing of plumes and flowers;
Or ye who, following in his funeral train,
Light up your torches at his sepulchre,
And open on us through the clefted hills
Far glances into glittering worlds beyond
The twilight of the grave, where all is light,
Golden and glorious light, too full and high
For mortal eye to gaze on, stretching out
Brighter and ever brighter, till it spread,
Like one wide, radiant ocean without bounds,
One infinite sea of glory: — Thus, ye clouds,
And in innumerable other shapes
Of greatness or of beauty, ye attend us,
To give to the wide arch above us Life
And all its changes. Thus it is to us
A volume full of wisdom, but without ye
One awful uniformity had ever
With too severe a majesty oppressed us.

THE GRAVES OF THE PATRIOTS.

Here rest the great and good. Here they repose
After their generous toil. A sacred band,
They take their sleep together, while the year
Comes with its early flowers to deck their graves,
And gathers them again, as Winter frowns.

Theirs is no vulgar sepulchre, — green sods
Are all their monument, and yet it tells
A nobler history than pillared piles,
Or the eternal pyramids. They need
No statue nor inscription to reveal
Their greatness. It is round them; and the joy
With which their children tread the hallowed ground
That holds their venerated bones, the peace
That smiles on all they fought for, and the wealth
That clothes the land they rescued, — these, though mute,
As feeling ever is when deepest, — these
Are monuments more lasting than the fanes
Reared to the kings and demigods of old.

Touch not the ancient elms, that bend their shade
Over their lowly graves; beneath their boughs
There is a solemn darkness, even at noon,
Suited to such as visit at the shrine
Of serious liberty. No factious voice
Called them unto the field of generous fame,
But the pure consecrated love of home.
No deeper feeling sways us, when it wakes
In all its greatness. It has told itself
To the astonished gaze of awestruck kings,
At Marathon, at Bannockburn, and here,
Where first our patriots sent the invader back
Broken and cowed. Let these green elms be all
To tell us where they fought and where they lie.
Their feelings were all nature, and they need
No art to make them known. They live in us,
While we are like them, simple, hardy, bold,
Worshipping nothing but our own pure hearts,
And the one universal Lord. They need
No column pointing to the heaven they sought,
To tell us of their home. The heart itself,
Left to its own free purpose, hastens there,
And there alone reposes. Let these elms
Bend their protecting shadow o'er their graves,

And build with their green roof the only fane,
Where we may gather on the hallowed day
That rose to them in blood, and set in glory.
Here let us meet, and while our motionless lips
Give not a sound, and all around is mute
In the deep sabbath of a heart too full
For words or tears, here let us strew the sod
With the first flowers of spring, and make to them
An offering of the plenty Nature gives,
And they have rendered ours — perpetually.

THE DESOLATE CITY.

I had a vision. —
A city lay before me, desolate,
And yet not all decayed. A summer sun
Shone on it from a most ethereal sky,
And the soft winds threw o'er it such a balm,
One would have thought it was a sepulchre,
And this the incense offered to the manes
Of the departed.
In the light it lay
Peacefully, as if all its thousands took
Their afternoon's repose, and soon would wake
To the loud joy of evening. There it lay,
A city of magnificent palaces,
And churches towering more like things of Heaven,
The glorious fabrics fancy builds in clouds,
And shapes on loftiest mountains; — bright their domes
Threw back the living ray, and proudly stood
Many a statue, looking like the forms
Of spirits hovering in mid-air. Tall trees,
Cypress and plane, waved over many a hill
Cumbered with ancient ruins, — broken arches,
And tottering columns, — vaults, where never came
The blessed beam of day, but only lamps

Shedding a funeral light, were kindled there,
And gave to the bright frescoes on the walls,
And the pale statues in their far recesses,
A dim religious awe. Rudely they lay,
Scarce marking out to the inquisitive eye
Their earliest outline. But as desolate
Slumbered the newer city, though its walls
Were yet unbroken, and its towering domes
Had never stooped to ruin. All was still;
Hardly the faintest sound of living thing
Moved through the mighty solitude; — and yet
All wore the face of beauty. Not a cloud
Hung in the lofty sky, that seemed to rise
In twofold majesty, so bright and pure,
It seemed indeed a crystalline sphere; — and there
The sun rode onward in his conquering march
Serenely glorious. From the mountain heights,
Tinged with the blue of heaven, to the wide sea,
Glassed with as pure a blue, one desolate plain
Spread out, and over it the fairest sky
Bent round and blessed it. Life was teeming there
In all its lower forms, a wilderness
Of rank luxuriance; flowers, and purpling vines
Matted with deepest foliage, hid the ruins,
And gave the semblance of a tangled wood
To piles, that once were loudly eloquent
With the glad cry of thousands. There were gardens
Round stateliest villas, full of graceful statues
And temples reared to woodland deities;
And they were overcrowded with the excess
Of beauty. All that most is coveted
Beneath a colder sky grew wantonly
And richly there. Myrtles and citrons filled
The air with fragrance. From the tufted elm,
Bent with its own too massy foliage, hung
Clusters of sunny grapes in frosted purple,
Drinking in spirit from the glowing air,
And dropping generous dews. The very wind
Seemed there a lover, and his easy wings

Fanned the gay bowers, as if in fond delay
He bent o'er loveliest things, too beautiful
Ever to know decay. The silent air,
Floating as softly as a cloud of roses
Dropped from Idalia in a dewy shower, —
The air itself seemed like the breath of heaven
Filling the groves of Eden. Yet these walls
Are desolate, — not a trace of living man
Is found amid these glorious works of man,
And nature's fairer glories. Why should he
Be absent from the festival of life,
The holiday of nature? Why not come
To add to the sweet sounds of winds and waters, —
Of winds uttering Æolian melodies
To the bright, listening flowers, and waters falling
Most musical from marble fountains wreathed
With clustering ivy, like a poet's brow, —
Why comes he not to add his higher strains,
And be the interpreter of lower things,
In intellectual worship, at the throne
Of the beneficent Power that gave to them
Their pride and beauty? — "In these palaces,
These awful temples, these religious caves,
These hoary ruins, and these twilight groves
Teeming with life and love, a secret plague
Dwells, and the unwary foot that ventures here
Returns not. — Fly! To linger here is death."

MORNING AMONG THE HILLS.

A NIGHT had passed away among the hills,
And now the first faint tokens of the dawn
Showed in the east. The bright and dewy star,
Whose mission is to usher in the morn,
Looked through the cool air, like a blessed thing
In a far purer world. Below there lay,
Wrapped round a woody mountain tranquilly,

A misty cloud. Its edges caught the light,
That now came up from out the unseen depth
Of the full fount of day, and they were laced
With colors ever brightening. I had waked
From a long sleep of many-changing dreams,
And now in the fresh forest air I stood
Nerved to another day of wandering.
Before me rose a pinnacle of rock,
Lifted above the wood that hemmed it in,
And now already glowing. There the beams
Came from the far horizon, and they wrapped it
In light and glory. Round its vapory cone
A crown of far-diverging rays shot out,
And gave to it the semblance of an altar
Lit for the worship of the undying flame,
That centred in the circle of the sun,
Now coming from the ocean's fathomless caves,
Anon would stand in solitary pomp
Above the loftiest peaks, and cover them
With splendor as a garment. Thitherward
I bent my eager steps; and through the grove,
Now dark as deepest night, and thickets hung
With a rich harvest of unnumbered gems,
Waiting the clearer dawn to catch the hues
Shed from the starry fringes of its veil
On cloud and mist and dew, and backward thrown
In infinite reflections, on I went,
Mounting with hasty foot, and thence emerging,
I scaled that rocky steep, and there awaited
Silent the full appearing of the sun.

Below there lay a far-extended sea,
Rolling in feathery waves. The wind blew o'er it
And tossed it round the high ascending rocks,
And swept it through the half-hidden forest tops,
Till, like an ocean waking into storm,
It heaved and weltered. Gloriously the light
Crested its billows, and those craggy islands
Shone on it like to palaces of spar

Built on a sea of pearl. Far overhead,
The sky, without a vapor or a stain,
Intensely blue, even deepened into purple,
Where, nearer the horizon, it received
A tincture from the mist, that there dissolved
Into the viewless air, — the sky bent round,
The awful dome of a most mighty temple,
Built by omnipotent hands for nothing less
Than infinite worship. There I stood in silence; —
I had no words to tell the mingled thoughts
Of wonder and of joy that then came o'er me,
Even with a whirlwind's rush. So beautiful,
So bright, so glorious! Such a majesty
In yon pure vault! So many dazzling tints
In yonder waste of waves, — so like the ocean
With its unnumbered islands there encircled
By foaming surges, that the mounting eagle,
Lifting his fearless pinion through the clouds
To bathe in purest sunbeams, seemed an ospray
Hovering above his prey, and yon tall pines,
Their tops half mantled in a snowy veil,
A frigate with full canvas, bearing on
To conquest and to glory. But even these
Had round them something of the lofty air
In which they moved; not like to things of earth,
But heightened, and made glorious, as became
Such pomp and splendor.
Who can tell the brightness,
That every moment caught a newer glow,
That circle, with its centre like the heart
Of elemental fire, and spreading out
In floods of liquid gold on the blue sky
And on the opaline waves, crowned with a rainbow
Bright as the arch that bent above the throne
Seen in a vision by the holy man
In Patmos! who can tell how it ascended,
And flowed more widely o'er that lifted ocean,
Till instantly the unobstructed sun
Rolled up his sphere of fire, floating away, —

Away in a pure ether, far from earth,
And all its clouds, — and pouring forth unbounded
His arrowy brightness! From that burning centre
At once there ran along the level line
Of that imagined sea, a stream of gold, —
Liquid and flowing gold, that seemed to tremble
Even with a furnace heat, — on to the point
Whereon I stood. At once that sea of vapor
Parted away, and, melting into air,
Rose round me, and I stood involved in light,
As if a flame had kindled up, and wrapped me
In its innocuous blaze. Away it rolled,
Wave after wave. They climbed the highest rocks,
Poured over them in surges, and then rushed
Down glens and valleys, like a wintry torrent
Dashed instant to the plain. It seemed a moment,
And they were gone, as if the touch of fire
At once dissolved them. Then I found myself
Midway in air; ridge after ridge below
Descended, with their opulence of woods,
Even to the dim-seen level, where a lake
Flashed in the sun, and from it wound a line,
Now silvery bright, even to the farthest verge
Of the encircling hills. A waste of rocks
Was round me, — but below how beautiful,
How rich the plain! a wilderness of groves
And ripening harvests; while the sky of June,
The soft blue sky of June, and the cool air,
That makes it then a luxury to live,
Only to breathe it, and the busy echo
Of cascades, and the voice of mountain brooks,
Stole with such gentle meanings to my heart,
That where I stood seemed heaven.

THE PERPETUAL YOUTH OF NATURE.

A SOLILOQUY.

WITH what a hollow voice these broken ruins
Tell of the vanished past. Here they are thrown
Too rudely for the most inquiring eye
To read one legend of the men who reared them,
Or even form a guess of those who made
These walls their home. It is a beautiful clime,
And all the year is lovely on these shores;
For there is neither winter here to blight,
Nor the hot sun to dry the fountains up,
And make the plains a desert. Nature here
Has built her bower of evergreens: and flowers
Are never wanting for her festivals,
And these are every day, and there is in them
Such a perpetual variety
Of bright and fair, the heart is never weary
Of the soft revelry; — and yet no trace
Of human footsteps on the bordering sands
Of the calm ocean gives a sign that man
Has found his way before me to this haunt
Of silence and repose. Well, be it so,
And I will hold myself the rightful lord
Of all this fair domain, by the strong claim
Of first discovery. No inheritance
Of gilded palaces, or loaded fields
Bent with a thousand harvests, could so fill
My spirit with the stirring health of joy,
As thus to hold myself the sole possessor
Of such a solitude, — so full of life,
And yet so mute, — so bright and beautiful,
And yet so darkly shadowed with the pall
Of buried ages. How the merry vines
Go gadding in the brisk and spirited air,
That even calls from out the barren rocks
A welcoming smile. The wind is very low, —

It hardly wags the shrinking violet,
Or sends a quiver to the aspen-leaf,
Or curls the green wave on the pebbled shore,
Or gives a wrinkle to the quiet sea,
That, like a giant resting from his toil,
Sleeps in the morning sun. That flowery palm
Has a most glorious aspect as he bows
In silent worship to his rising god;
And from his station on the tallest pile
Of these mysterious ruins, once the shrine,
It may be, of the living Sun himself,
How like a most majestic sovereign
He keeps his lofty seat, and yet adores
The Lord that made him! It is wonderful
That man should hold himself so haughtily,
And talk of an immortal name, and feed
His proud ambition with such daring hopes
As creatures of a more eternal nature
Alone should form. Why, 't is a mockery
Too poor for tears, and yet too sad for smiles,
To think how much of glitter and of pride
Has flaunted in the sun, and sent him back
His fullest beams. These rude, disjointed heaps,
That seem the chaos of a broken world,
And hardly give us signs enough to show
They were not thrown from out the central earth
By an upheaving earthquake, — these were bright
With such barbaric pomp, as made the sun
Muffle his head, and hide himself at noon
To shun the poor encounter. So they sung,
The sycophants, who told the gorgeous tyrant
Of these once peopled shores, he was a god,
And with the port and bearing of a god
Sat on his throne, or in his chariot
Went sounding on his long triumphal way.
Fools! and where are they? Not a mark to tell
The shadows of their names. The tooth of Time
Has ground the marble sculptures to rude forms,
Such as the falling waters eat from rocks

In the deep gloom of caves! — and yet, as if
They meant to show their scorn of him who calls
Himself their lord, the beasts and creeping things
Have come from out their deserts and their holes,
And made their dens in the crushed palaces,
And round the buried altars hollowed out
Their lurking-places. O, how fresh and fair
Grows the young grass, and how the wild vines clasp
The rifted columns, with as bright a foliage
As when from out the bosom of the earth
First rose the rampant Spring, and the glad Sun
Laughed from his azure throne to see the buds
Put out their tender leaves, and the soft green
Spread like a carpet to the tented sky.

ITALY.

A CONFERENCE.

A. WHY hast thou such a downward look of care,
As if thine eye refused the sweet communion
Of these enchanted skies? I cannot weary
In gazing on them, there is such a clearness
In the mid-noon; and then the calmer hours
Have such a glory round them, that I grow
Enamored of their clouds. O, they have caught
Their hues in heaven, and they come stealing to us
Like messengers of love, to kindle up
This volatile air. How light and thin it floats!
Methinks I now can pass into the depths
Of yon wide firmament, it lies so open
And shows so fair. The stars are hung below it,
And they are moving in a vacancy,
Like the poised eagle. How the studded moon,
All dropped with glittering points, rolls on its way
Between the pillowy clouds, and that which seems
A crystalline arch, — a dome that rests on air,

Buoyed by its lightness! Can thy heavy eyes
Still pore on the discolored earth, and choose
Their home in darkness? Something weighs upon thee
With no light burden, if thou hast no heart
To mingle with the beautiful world around thee.

B. Thou talk'st of clouds and skies. Has the sweet face
Of Spring a power to charm away the fiends
That riot on the soul? Will the foul spirit
Go, when the cock crows, like a muttering ghost,
To find his kindred shades, and leave the heart
To gladden through the day? and dares he not
To fill it with his terrors when the sun
Is out in heaven? Is there a sovereign balm
In cloudless skies, and bright and glowing noons,
To make the spirit light, and drive from it
The moody madness and the listless sorrow?
I feel there is not. Something tells me, here,
There may be such a grief, that nothing earthly
Hath power to stay it. I too have a feeling,
How beautiful this clime! and though the native
Looks on it with a blank indifference,
To us who had our birth in clouded skies,
And reckoned it a bright and fortunate day
If the sun gave us but an hour at noon,
It is indeed a luxury to see
Whole days without a cloud, but these light shapes,
That float around us more like heavenly spirits,
They are so bright and wear such glorious hues,
Or hang so quietly, and look so pure,
When all is still at noon. O, I have felt
This luxury of sense, but yet it comes not
So far as here. The heart knows nothing of it;
And now that I have seen so many days,
All of an equal brightness, like the calm
That reigns, they say, perpetually in heaven,

Why, I grow weary of them, and my thoughts
Are on the past. Thou need'st no other answer.

A. 'T is not the barren luxury of sense
That makes me love these skies; but there is in them
A living spirit. I can feel it stealing
Even to my heart of hearts, and waking there
Feelings that never yet have stirred within me,
So blessed, that I almost weep to think
How poor my life without them. I now walk
In a glad company of happy visions,
And all the air seems like a dwelling-place
For glorious creatures. Like the shifting waves,
That toss on the white shore when evening breezes
Steal to the land in summer, they are floating
In airy trains around me. Now they come
Laughing on yonder mountain-side, a troop
Of jovial nymphs; and now they flit away
Round the far islands of the golden sea,
Islands of light that seem to hang in air,
Midway in heaven. No wonder they so love
The song and dance, and walk with such a look
Of thoughtless gayety, — the merry beggars,
Who breed like insects on these sunny shores,
And live as idly. There are glorious faces
Among them, — there are Roman spirits here,
And Grecian eyes that tell a thousand fancies,
Like those that shaped their deities, and wrought
Perfection. True, they have no stirring hopes
To lift them; yet at times they will give vent
To the o'erburdened soul, and then they speak
In oracles, or, like the harp of Memnon,
They utter poetry, as the bright skies
And wandering winds awake it. Who can wonder,
That every voice is bursting out in music,
And every peasant tunes his mandolin
To the delicious airs, that creep so softly

Into the slumbering ear! O, 't is a land
Where life is doubled, and a brighter world
Rolls over this, and there the spirit lives
In a gay paradise, and here we breathe
An atmosphere of roses!

B. Yes, — but this
Is nothing to the heart. They never felt,
These summer flies, who buzz so gayly round us,
They never felt, one moment, what we feel
With such a silent tenderness, and keep
So closely round our hearts. We do not wake
The echoes with our loud and thoughtless carols,
Nor sit whole days beneath a bowering vine,
Singing its amber juice, and telling too
Of starry eyes, and soft and languishing looks,
And talking of our agonies with smiles,
Making a sport of sorrow. No, our year,
With its long time of gloom, and hurried days
Of warmth, that call for more of toil than pleasure, —
Our pensive year forbids the wandering spirit
To make itself a song-bird. We must keep
Our sorrows and our hopes close cherished by us,
Till the heart softens, and by often musing
Takes a deep, serious tone, and has a feeling
For all that suffer. So we often bear
A grief that is the burden of a life,
And will not leave us. Something that would seem
Too trifling to be laughed at here will weigh
And weigh upon us, till we cannot lift it,
And then we pine and die. Her heart is broken,
And the worm feeds upon her early roses,
And now her lily fades, and all its brightness
Turns to a green and sallow melancholy,
And then we strew her grave; but here the passion
Breaks out in wildness, then is sung away
With a complaining air, and so is ended.

I have no sympathy with such light spirits,
But I can see my sober countrymen
Gather around their winter's hearth, and read
Of no unreal suffering, and then weep
Big tears that ease the heart, and need no words
To make their meaning known. One silent hour
Of deep and thoughtful feeling stands me more
Than a whole age of such a heartless mirth,
As a bright summer wakens.

THE FAIR ITALIAN.

SHE looked how lovely. Not the face of heaven
In its serenest calm, nor earth in all
Its garniture of flowers, nor all that live
In the bright world of dreams, nor all the eye
Of a creative spirit meets in air,
Could, in the smile and sunshine of her charms,
Not feel itself o'ermastered by such rare
And perfect beauty. Grace was over all;
Her form, her face, her attitudes, her motions,
Each had peculiar charms. Like gliding swans,
Sailing upon a smoothly mirrored lake
Before the breeze of evening, when the waves
Curl rippling round their bosoms, so she moved
Through all the mazy dance. She bore herself
So gently, that the lily on its stalk
Bends not so easily its dewy head,
As with a gliding step she wound her way
To the soft echoes of the light guitar,
The dreamy music of her sunny clime,
Where all is languishing. There was a brightness,
How high, and yet how soothing, in her smile!
O, I could look on her a summer's day,
Delighted, — every moment more delighted,
With the soft sense that hovers over me
When on a slope of moss I lay me down

In the warm sun of April. I could kneel
In worship to her, as a radiant vision
Sent from a purer world, without a stain
Of earth breathed over her, but all entire
In infant loveliness, yet ripe and full
In her meridian elegance, a flower
With all its leaves expanded, and its hues
Mellowed by kindly sunbeams.
It was evening;
The sun looked through the wood of chestnut-trees,
And bronzed their rugged trunks, and lit their leaves,
Till, as they rustled on the bending boughs,
Each seemed a flake of gold; and far beyond them
My eye caught glimpses of a quiet bay,
A nook of sleeping waters, where the light
Shone with a flashing blaze. It was so still!
The wind had stolen into the mountain valleys,
And left the plains and hillocks to the calm
That sinks upon the world when night steals on,
And the day takes its farewell, like the words
Of a departing friend, or the last tone
Of hallowed music in a minster's aisles,
Heard, when it floats along the shade of elms,
In the still place of graves. A wood of palms
Rose on a far hill, where the amber light
Was rich and dazzling, with their pointed leaves
So nicely balanced, that the faintest breathing
Of the wide air swayed them in graceful curves,
While all below seemed in the still repose
Of sleep, the twin of death, that infant slumber
Where life is only visible in the play
Of blushes, which for ever come and go
On the soft cheek's transparency, as pure
As the clear rime that masks the untimely rose,
Mellowing its purple to the hues of heaven,
The tremulous tints of air.
I lay abroad
In careless dreaming, by the twisted roots

Of an outspreading beech-tree, and methought
The swains of Enna and Parthenope
Were dancing round me to the sound of viols
And oaten pipes. As the light sank away,
The rose and jasmine thickets, and the shades
O'erhung with vines, in the full scent of flowers,
Seemed populous with the sylvan family
Of nymphs and fauns. I listened to the sounds
Of Grecian melody and song, and lay
Reclining on a couch of new-plucked leaves,
Attentive to the many quiet voices,
That fill a summer's night, — the drowsy hum
Of beetles, and the shrill cicada's song,
And the complaining of the nightingale,
That in a bush of brambles passed away
The silent hours in answering to the echoes
Herself had made. As thus I sank away
In pleasant thoughts of the dear times of old,
I saw a group of dancers, on a lawn
Not distant, to the music of a lute
Cross the yet rosy twilight. She was there,
Lovelier for the witching time they chose
To be their hour of joy. Her full, dark curls
Were clustered on a brow of ivory,
And fell in lavish wealth, shading a neck
Clear as an alabaster shrine concealing
A ruby, that with soft suffusion fills it,
As with a living glow. Her face was kindled
By the quick glances of her large black eyes,
That flashed from underneath her arching brows,
Like gems in caves; and yet there was a softness
At times, when shades of thought stole over her;
But in the happy consciousness of beauty
Her heart was all so joyous, that her smiles
Gave a perpetual sunlight to that face,
So beautiful, to see it was to love.
I could not choose but watch with earnest gaze
One of so perfect form, and finished grace,
That those who moved around her were but foils

Heightening the one sole diamond. When I look
On one so fair, I must believe that Heaven
Sent her in kindness, that our hearts might waken
To its own loveliness, and lift themselves,
By such an adoration, from a dark
And grovelling world. Such beauty should be worshipped,
And not a thought of weakness or decay
Should mingle with the pure and hallowed dreams
In which it dwells before us. It should live
Eternal; or, if it must pass away,
And lose one tint of its now perfect brightness,
Let it be hidden from me, for the sense
That all this glow must fade falls on my heart
Like the cold weight of death.

INSCRIPTION.

STRANGER, if thou hast ever blessed the shade
That lent thee shelter from the sun and rain,
Thou wilt not rest thee underneath this elm
Without a sense of gratitude. The boughs
That overshadow thee have borne the brunt
Of centuries, and have records of the past
In all their whispering leaves. We cannot hear them
Telling their tales, through the long summer day,
To the cool west-wind, and have other thoughts
Than of the generations who have sat,
In long succession, on the mossy turf
That beds these twisted roots. Sunshine and calm,
Darkness and storm, have been around these boughs,
And they have smiled to the unclouded sky,
And rocked in the rude tempest, but have stood
Unbroken, while the stream of human life
Has ebbed and flowed like the perpetual tide,
And hardly left a trace upon its shores
To tell us where it came. Then rest thee, stranger,

And think thou hearest in the ancient wood
A monitor, that warns thee of thy end
With a low, earnest voice, a voice of kindness,
That, like a silent fountain running over,
Refreshes where it flows, and, like its waters,
Gives life to the sere heart it passes by.

A VISION.

I HAVE been haunted by an awful dream, —
A vision of my childhood, — one that grew
From an o'erheated fancy, nursed to fear
In a dark, visionary creed. A star,
Of a malign aspect, had been to me,
For a few weeks of dread uncertainty,
The prophet of evil; and I saw in it
The minister of judgments, such as oft
Had been denounced before me, and had grown
To an undoubting faith.
Methought that star,
As in a vision of the night I lay,
Stood with its train directed to the earth;
And every moment it did spread itself,
And grew a deeper crimson. Where I was,
I could not tell; but I stood gazing on it
With unaverted eye, and I could watch it
Taking ten thousand fiery shapes, and changing
To every terrible hue and form, and still
Widening and widening out its burning orb,
Till a whole quarter of the heavens was red
And glowing like a furnace. Then, methought,
A form stood visible within it, vast
And indistinct, as a far mountain seen
Through a dense vapor, when the morning strikes it,
And makes it such a thing as the mind frames,
When it goes wandering through the infinite,
And builds on dreams. I gazed upon it, charmed

And fascinated by its terrible glory,
And with it such a sense of fear, the drops
Stood thick upon my forehead, and my heart
Was near to bursting. 'Twas an agony
Of wonder and of death; for I beheld
Already come the day of doom, and earth
Seemed parched and burnt by the intensity
Of that approaching flame. The sky above
Was like a vaulted furnace, and it quivered
And sparkled in the heat, and at the centre,
Transparent in the fierceness of its fire,
Still that illimitable form did frown
Blacker than tenfold night. His quick approach
Left me no time to scan him, but he seemed
To gather in himself all I had heard
Or dreamed of horrible. A muttering sound,
Like that of far-off winds, or smothered flame
Roaring in caves, — a sound that fell like fate
On my stunned ear, — came as a warning voice,
That earth was now within the wasting sphere
Of that consuming plague. At once the wind
Seemed to blow over me, with hot, thick breath,
Wafting such clouds of smoke and sheets of fire,
That all around me seemed one conflagration;
And even the firm foundations of the hills
Cracked and fell inward, and one long, long peal
Gave warning, that this ponderous globe was rent
And shivered. Suddenly a burst of flame,
So clear and strong no thought can image it,
Filled the whole visible space; and still it flashed,
And flashed, till in an instant utter darkness
Closed heavily around me, and I woke:
I woke, and yet the horrors of that dream
Would visit me at times, even when I grew
To know its causes, and could reason of it;
And though the mind moved in its own pure light,
And stood aloof from fear, yet there were moments,
When the dark memory of this dream would quell me
Well-nigh to trembling.

DREAMS.

"Aut quæ sopitos deludunt Somnia sensus."

I.

METHOUGHT 't was night; and my unquiet spirit
Stood in the silent presence of a Power
Invisible, though felt. There was no voice,
And yet unutterable thoughts came o'er me,
Accompanied by feelings such as grow
From some unearthly music. There were words
Spoken as in the fever of a dream,
Breathless and indistinct, yet full of awe
High and mysterious. The air was full
Of sights, that scarce were seen, dim images,
Crowding from out the depth of darkness, wild
And terrible, though calm. They looked upon me
Intensely, and they seemed to beckon me
Thoughtful and sad. No utterance meanwhile
Told me their wishes, but they made themselves
Visible to me in their gathering brows
And lowering glances. Then they waved me on
To follow them, and, like a vanishing troop
Of shadows, mingled in the thicker shades,
And all were lost. A deeper darkness hung
Around me, like a burden, and it seemed
To close me in a prison, like the grave,
Narrow and cold. A damp and deathly chill
Ran through me, and methought the earth beneath
Sunk, and the utter night that circled me
Grew thicker, till all thoughts were objectless,
And memory vanished. All the little light
That centred in my brain seemed like a taper
Amid the vapors of a charnel-house,
Quivering and pale; a blue, unearthly flame
Hovers awhile above it, and it falls
Beneath the dank oppression, and then dies.

So thought, and life, and all their energies
Trembled awhile, and hung upon their close,
And then went out. I lay entranced, I know not
If hours or ages, — not a sleep of dreams,
Busy and full of forms and fantasies,
But blank and desolate, without a motion,
Even in the spirit's core, — an utter death,
That leaves no memory of itself, and makes
Myriads of years a moment. So I lay,
Forgotten and alone. Methought a stir
Came to my heart and brain, and some dim feelings
Were moving there, faint as the light of shadows,
When night is deepest, and the waning moon
Hurries behind a cloud. They grew upon me,
And there was light and joy, — a happy dream,
Confused and shapeless, but a dream of days
That are to us our heaven ; the early days
Of wonder and of hope, the blissful days
Of buoyancy and love, unspeakable
And holy love, stainless and bright and pure, —
The heart's devotion. They were in my dreams
Struggling to life, and taking, every moment,
A fairer being. I was on the hills,
Methought; and it was spring; and one sweet bird
Settled beside me, on a flowering thorn,
And sang how softly ! Then the morning came,
And there was brightness, and the kindling clouds
Were pearl and gold and flame ; and then the sun
Rolled up, and all was day. An avenue
Of ancient elms bent over me their boughs,
And the slant light came underneath the arch,
And tinted all the leaves, the quivering leaves,
With rainbows, till a vault of liquid fire
Seemed lifted round me, and I walked unhurt
Amid the glorious furnace. There was magic
And wonder in the hour ; and then I looked
On the calm ocean, like a burnished sheet
Of emerald, and all its long, long waves
Were ridged with flame ; and by me flowed a brook,

Prattling its merry tale to the cool winds,
That shook the grass and flowers, that stood around it
To gaze upon its mirror, and behold,
Narcissus-like, their beauty; and it wound
Its way unto a meadow, all one bed
Of glancing diamonds. 'T was a dream of light,
And soon as full of love. Methought a voice,
A well-known voice, a voice of very sweetness,
So tender that I felt the first fresh tears
Flow at its touch of music, and dissolve me
In the young happiness, once known, and then
For ever gone, — methought that tender voice
Came from a wood hard by; and it was singing
Catches of old familiar tunes, the treasures
Of infant memory, that warble on
In the bright stream of innocent joys, through all
Our darker years, and hold their unchecked way
Even to the old man's grave. I heard that voice, —
And then awoke within me such a flow
Of passionate thoughts, blended of bright and dark,
Gentle and wild, — a flood that long had swelled
And borne me on its crest, till it became
A sea of cloud and storm, — that, in the grasp
And agony of passion, and the last,
Fixed struggle of despair, again the light
Faded around me, and I sank once more
In night and horror.

II.

Darkness was thick around me, as of old,
In Egypt, it was felt. No glimmering lamp,
Nor solitary starlight, found its way
Through the dim shadows that encompassed me,
But all was waste and void, — a desolation
Without a form or voice, — a deathlike silence,
Where even the waters had forgot to flow,
And winds to whisper, — such a total silence,
My breathing startled me, although I held it

In fear and awe. The heavens had vanished then,
And earth was gone, only the foothold where
I stood and dared not move, — in like suspense
As when, upon a mountain crag, a mist
Sweeps suddenly around the hunter's path,
And hides the precipice and dread descent,
Where all is death, — he pauses, and awaits
The passing of the vapor, till it rolls
Its heavy wreaths around the glacier heights,
And all at once reveals the dark abyss
Below him, where he hung close on the verge,
And knew not of his danger; such a fear
And wild suspense held me, and then I stood
Waiting for morning, while the laggard hours
Seemed lengthened out to ages. Who has felt
The sickening doubt, the cold uncertainty,
The dying of all hope, when we have seen
Day after day pass on, and yet no sight,
No tidings of the expected happiness,
On which our being rested, we had fixed it
So deeply in our hearts, — he only knows
How much I suffered in those long, dull hours,
That heavily dragged on, and brought no dawn,
No token of it; still the same blank void
Closed me, and narrowed to a sepulchre's
Scant compass all the universe to me,
And left me nothing but to count my pulses,
And tell my hours by throbs. The air seemed thick
And deathly, aud a sense of suffocation
Pressed on me, like a mountain's weight, and bore
me
Seemingly down a gulf, from which I struggled
To lift me; but the ever-backward plunge
Hurried me, like the rushing of a torrent,
Farther and farther from all hope of light
Or the sweet face of heaven. O, had a star,
A single lonely star, one of the smallest,
That scarcely twinkles when the winter's night
Is clearest, and there is no moon to shade

The lesser lights, and the bright evening planet
Has set, and Jove not mounted yet his throne,
And made his vassals dim, — had such a star
Broke out a moment, from the thick obscure,
To tell me where to look upon the sky,
And, in that utter void, forget not where
To wait the dawning, I had then had hope,
And not been wholly desolate; and yet
None greeted me, but all was like a chaos,
After its waves have settled to a calm,
And even the swell, that follows on the storm,
Subsided into stillness.
                                Then, methought,
I heard a sound, like the far roar of winds
Amid the forest oaks, when the whole sea
Of branches tosses, as the coming tempest
Stoops from its car of clouds, and scourges them,
Till the wide wilderness bows to the dust
Before its anger. Such a hollow sound
Rolled onward, and, yet louder every moment,
Seemed like the rush of myriad wings, or sweep
Of mailed horsemen, when the beaten plain
Trembles, and, in the mid-encounter, wide
Their armor shocks and rings. A breathless fear,
A terror that had winged my flying feet,
Had not the deeper dread of what I knew not
Beyond the point I stood on held me fixed
And rooted to the ground, and with it, too,
A mingled feeling of desire and hope,
Wakened me from my trance, and turned me whence
The rushing came. Methought the darkness seemed
To fade, and from its womb a glimmering rose,
Pale and uncertain, as the flitting glance
Of moonlight through a storm. Anon it took
More fixedness, and then it reared itself
Into a dreamy shape, a wavering form,
Hovering in mist far on the sleeping waves,
When night is deep, and all the light in heaven

Just gives a visible outline, so that earth
Seems like a land of shadows. Then it stood
Before me, and a chill and spectral glare
Invested it, and as it onward drew,
With ominous bearing, I could dimly catch
Traces of human likeness, yet it seemed
More like a moon-struck ghost than living thing;
For there was not a motion in its limbs,
Gesture, or step, but it seemed borne along
On the swift tide of air, — its glaring eyeballs
Rolled not, and had no meaning, but they stared,
Like a blind statue's, with everted lids,
Glassy and cold, — and from its bloodless lips
There seemed to come no voice, for they were still,
And yet stood open, like the last fixed gasp
Of dissolution. Soon the vision neared me,
And then I heard a low and muttering sound,
Like the faint utterance of forbidden charms,
When, even herself in fear, the sorceress
Evokes the shades of hell, or calls the spirits
Whose dwelling is in air. Then, as I heard it,
I started and looked round me; for no breath
Quivered upon those ashy lips, and yet
I knew the voice came from them, and it sounded
Hollow, as from the tomb: "Creature of earth,
Child of despair and fear, of doubt and madness,
I bid thee follow me; the spell is on thee,
And where I go, thou must perforce attend me;
And I will show thee such unearthly things
As will not leave thee to thy dying day,
But haunt thee like the secret consciousness
Of undiscovered crime." He said; and then
Turned from me, and went moving through the darkness,
Lofty and proud. At once I felt myself
Lifted, as by the sweeping of a tempest,
And borne along so rapidly, my breath
And sense were lost. Awhile I knew of nothing,
But that my flight was onward; then my brain

Grew wonted to the change, and fined itself,
So that all objects took a startling clearness,
Though seen in deepest shade. A magic world
Seemed bursting into being, wondrous, wild,
Majestic, beautiful, obscure, and dark,
Then bright to dazzling. Countless images
Crowded before me, till the eye was weary
In looking onward through the living sea,
That rolled upon me, like the toppling waves
Heaved from the womb of ocean, surge on surge,
To burst upon the shore. I hurried by them,
And back they rushed behind me, like the hills
And groves and towns and spires, when borne along
The bosom of some mighty stream by winds
That send the vessel through the frothy waves,
Like a shaft winged with fate. It were a tale
Too high for mortal utterance, to tell
The shapes that met me, and they ravished me
With such unearthly joy, the vision melted
In its own fervor, and I found myself
Alone in darkness.

III.

I HAD a dream of music and of song.
Methought one thrill of general harmony
Pervaded all the region, and the winds
Were all attuned, each to its several part,
As if some master spirit had controlled
Their sounds to one accord. Fast-flowing waves
Seemed rolling from an ocean, whose deep heart
Fed them and never failed; and they came onward,
Each with its crown of foam; and as they struck
The shaken shore, their burst was like the echo
Of organ notes in heaven, — majestic sounds,
Awful and terrible, yet far and sweet
As the last pause of thunder, when it sinks
In the embrace of silence. So my ear
Seemed full to overflowing with these strains

Of modulated sound, — loud, airy swells,
And solemn pauses, — touches, as if made
By a most gentle hand; then lingering peals,
That died away in echoes; and again
Soft-stealing symphonies, that wound their way
Into my heart, like Zephyr, when he haunts
The first-blown field of spring, in fond delay
Pausing at every flower, and loading thence
His wings with balm.
As yet there was no vision,
But deep and utter night, — the night of Hades,
Through which the bodiless spirits make their way,
Unheard, unseen, and one impervious veil
Of darkness covers all. The music paused,
And all was one deep hush, — so deep and still,
The beating of my heart was audible,
And my own breathing mingled in my dreams
Like the far rush of waters. Then there came
A solemn march of melody, a flow
Of faint, unearthly warblings, like the sighs
Of sorrowing ghosts; and these stole through my brain
Like lapsing fountains; and anon there rushed
One tide of sound, that poured its airy surges
Into my inmost soul. And as the curtain
Rolls up its shadowy folds, and slowly opens
The glories of the scene, far back retiring
In avenues of pomp, and fading off
In the blue tint of mountains, where some rock
Catches the coming dawn, all else below
Cradled in slumbering shade, so, it meseemed,
The vision opened on me. Faint and chill
It rose before me; and its floating forms
Drew their dim outlines on a cold, wan heaven,
Where neither moon, nor star, nor even dawn
Gave light and hope, — one rayless blank, embracing
Within its leaden cope shapes indistinct,
Confused, and void, — a chaos, like the dreams

That haunt a sick man's couch, — a waste of shadows,
Like mountains in a storm, swelling and heaving,
Broader and higher still, their giant peaks,
Till the eye shrinks from gazing. So it rose,
That visionary pomp, and stood awhile
In terrible obscure; but then it seemed
As if the opening eyelids of the dawn
Unveiled their kindly beams, and sent abroad
The charm of early day. Soft lights and shadows
Now parted from each other, till they took
Distinct and certain shapes; and then a world
Of beauty lay before me. O, how calm
And still it lay! — an infant world, reposing
In its fresh, dewy cradle, hung with flowers,
And rocked by summer winds, such as in June
Crisp the smoothed ocean, till it smiles and kisses
The green, embracing shore.
Methought I stood
Somewhere above it, and it stretched beneath me
In beautiful stillness, for no living sound
Stole upward on the motionless atmosphere,
That circled it as with a brooding wing,
And hushed it all to peace. Far off it lay,
Too far to give the fainter lineaments,
But the broad outline, that was broad and clear, —
Clear as, at noon, the ridges and the vales
On the blue mountain sloping to the sun
Its walls, a nation's bulwarks; liker still
That mountain, when it comes in the dense air
That with a crystalline brightness ushers in
The invisible storm, — when it comes drawing near us,
Till the eye looks into its closest dells,
And sees the fountain flowing so at hand,
That fancy hears it murmur. Thus it lay
In the new dawn; — but soon a cone of flame
Rose up behind a circling ridge that closed
The bosom of a vale, and poured abroad

Rich golden waves, wherewith the mountain peaks
And lowest hollows kindled up, and shone
In more than dazzling brightness, — burnished gold,
And liquid, trembling silver, so the rocks
And winding rivers shone; and far away
Lay the wide sweep of ocean, like a sheet
Of molten glass, and all its islands burnt
Cerulean, like the many hues that play
On the hot gush of steel.
Such was the pomp
That ushered in the day; but when the sun
Had come abroad, and now in the wide heaven
Held on his lordly way, these glorious hues
Were faded, and a clear and steady light
Settled on all below. Methought I sank
Slowly to earth, as through the summer air
Floats the light plume, or from his heavenward seat
An angel stoops to be the messenger
Of love and joy. So gently I descended
Into a flowery plain. Then rose around me
A spacious theatre of wood and mountain,
Stage over stage, from the low shrub that blooms
Beside the hunter's path, up to the rocks
With forehead bald and bare. Not long I stood,
Before a strain of music flowed from out
The forest, as if harps and voices joined
In one unearthly song. It had the power
Of magic, for at once my eyes were closed
On all the beauty, that with near embrace
Threw round its circling arms. The waving woods,
Fresh flowers, and gurgling brooks, and rustling winds
Had vanished, and my spirit, at the sound
Transported, saw another world, and heard
That music all alone.
There lay before me
A broad, bright river, glancing to the morn
In silent motion; waving to and fro,
Not in the wind, for the tall palm-tops stood

Still, as if pillared marble, and the canes
Shook not their spiry blades. Not even a ripple
Gurgled along the shore; but to and fro
Slowly it waved, and from its sloping mirror
Sent back the coming day. Masses of shade
Lay on the sleeping water, and between
Opened its depths, how clear! — far down, the heavens
Were vaulted, and the bands of lazy clouds,
All in their gorgeous trim, went moving by
With scarce perceptible motion, and their trains
Waved, like the heavy banner of a ship
Down-rolling from the top-mast, when the calm
Has only breath enough to bend its folds
In slow meanderings, and its stars shine out
A momentary glance, and then retire,
And twinkle then again, even as at night
The stars dance on a fountain. Smooth it spread,
That river, and the lotus leaves and flowers
Covered its quiet bays with broidery
Of blue and scarlet, on a ground of purple
And virgin green; and with the long, slow swell
They turned their mirrors sunward, one short flash,
And then fell back in shade. A tall pagoda
Rose opposite, and stretched its frowning walls,
And lifted high its pyramids, o'erfretted
With a wild waste of dreams; and high above
Glittered the golden trident, for the sun
Had risen there, in all that burst of power
Had risen, with which he rushes on the heaven
In equatorial climes. This was the hour
Of prayer, and many white-robed devotees
Came to the river's brink, to sip its wave
And bathe them in its waters. Then I saw
One like a nymph in shape, yet darkly tinted,
Sit on the shady shore. She wove a crown
Of starry flowers, and twined it gracefully
Over her locks of jet; then to the east
She turned, and sung her hymn.

"Forth from thy mountain throne
Advance along thy starry-vaulted way,
Thou burning Lord of day!
Thou holdest on alone,
And all the gods of darkness steal away.
Before thy luminous ray
Night and her shades are flown.

"Forth from the Swerga's bowers
Thou issuest in thy robe of flame;
And over heaven's blue lotus-flowers
Rush the wild steeds no other hand can tame.
They champ, they snort, they blow;
They heave their winnowing manes;
And round thy wheels, in sparkling showers,
Perpetual streams of lightning flow,
And fill yon azure plains.

"Thy beamy car descends,
And, gliding o'er the forest-trees,
To the still river bends,
Up-curling with the newly wakened breeze.
Over its bright expanse
Thy bounding coursers dance,
And sweep the rolling foam before thy path.
They hurry, hurry by;
I hear the chariot's thunder nigh,
I see the radiant God;
He lifts his golden rod, —
How terrible the flashing of his eye!
SURYA, Lord of day, retain thy wrath, —
Send forth thy light to bless, and not to scath."

Her song had ceased,
Its magic ended; but another spell
At once was on me. Then, methought, a garden
Spread out its avenues, o'erarched with planes,
And filled with citron-flowers. One ancient tree
Towered over me, and threw its shadow broad

And deep below. Beneath it flowed a fountain
Hewn from a natural rock, and by it rose
A tomb, plain wrought in marble, turban-crowned,
And on it carved, "GULGHESHTI MUSELLARA."
This was the tomb of Hafiz, — these the walks
Of roses, by the fountain Mosellay,
Dearer to him than bowers of Paradise,
The Eastern heaven of love. Far around me lay
One harvest of ripe roses, sending out
The vaporous dews in one invisible cloud
Of odorous bliss. The silence and the calm,
The coolness and the shade, the sweet, low sound
Of the still-flowing fountain, and the breath
Of a faint wind that panted through the thickets,
Were beautiful. They sank upon my soul,
Like dews on withering flowers. They quickened me,
And freshened all my thoughts. And then a voice
Came from the garden, silver-toned and clear,
But melancholy sweet, and often choked
By stifling sobs, as if the bulbul wooed
And languished for his rose, or as the dove
Gurgles around his mate, or sadly mourns
His widowed nest, and makes the twilight wood
Responsive to his sighs. Slowly it came
On through the vaulted alleys, till a group
Of maidens, veiled and fearful, from the bowers
Stepped cautious forth. On to the poet's tomb
They glided, and, low bowed, their offerings gave
Of garlands silken-twined, and with them dressed
Their favorite shrine; then, throwing back their veils,
Revealed their sunny locks, and full black eyes,
Soft as the dove's, and rich in starry light
As the gazelle's. So to the fountain bending,
They dipped their pictured vases, and then rose
And sprinkled all their wreaths, and bade them hang
Fresh till the coming dawn, — then round the tomb
They linked their hands, and, slowly moving, sang
Their pious hymn.

"O, weave the poet's tomb with flowers,
And bring it water from the spring;
And ever with the dawning day,
O, let us haunt these lonely bowers,
And on our withering garlands fling
The freshening dew of Mosellay.

"He best deserves a maiden's heart,
Who teaches best her heart to love.
O, how can she so well repay
The bard who taught the gentle art?
O, can she give him aught above
The freshening dew of Mosellay?

"He loved this calm and cool retreat,
And with his friend and mistress oft
In music passed the summer day.
In vain the noonbeam fiercely beat, —
He only felt it murmuring soft,
The gushing dew of Mosellay.

"And then he crowned his bowl with wine,
And pressed it to his maiden's lip, —
She smiled, and moved the gift away.
A maiden, who would seem divine,
Had better fill her bowl, and sip
The freshening dew of Mosellay.

"O gentle bard of joy and love!
A gentle heart can only feel
Thy sweetness, and alone repay.
O, may we, like the trembling dove,
From care and tumult often steal
Beneath the bowers of Mosellay."

Another change: — The desert,
Wide as an ocean, indistinct and dim
Beneath the moon, now full, but hanging low
In the pale west. A well, — its clustered palms,

Tall columns, throwing far upon the sands
Their shadows, and the stars between their leaves
Coming and going. All beneath in sleep, —
A wandering tribe, stretched round the stifled glow
Of a half-covered fire, and quietly
Behind them in a circle, deep reposing,
Their only friends, their camels and their steeds,
Harnessed and ready. Not unguarded rest
The wanderers, but a sentinel apart,
With spear uplifted, watches through the night,
With the keen tiger's instinct, and afar
Catches the faintest sound, and quick espies
The smallest creature, on the very verge
Of the encircling waste. There on his watch,
I hear him cheat his weary hours, with tales
Slow chanted, and with songs of love and sorrow,
The treasures of his tribe, from age to age
Transmitted even with awe. A mournful air.
Well suited to his utter loneliness,
Is now his pastime; sung so faint and low,
It rather seems but sighs, — some captive's song,
In a far distant land.

"My father's tent is far away,
And they are weeping there;
And often, often do they say,
'Where is our Kaled, where?'

"My master tells me to forget
My home, my own dear home: —
'Why wouldst thou close thy heart, nor let
Another fondness come?'

"And Leila, then, his dark-eyed girl,
Sits blushing by her sire, —
I know that sire is not a churl;
Can love be pointed higher?

"But Leila, fair and sweet and young,
And gentle as a fawn, —

Though fairer poet never sung,
Though fresh as early dawn, —

"O Leila, think not of my heart, —
I left my heart at home;
O, from my home it could not part, —
My spirit could not roam.

"A fairer and a sweeter one
Has all my fondness there, —
And, 'Oh!' she often sighs alone,
'Where is my Kaled, where?'"

Another change: —
A valley, freshly green, and girdled round
With white rocks, tufted o'er with feathery ferns
And rambling vines, and at their foot a cave,
The issue of a spring, clear bubbling out
In a perennial flow. Religious hands
Have arched it over, for a fount, a well,
In such a thirsty land, is loved and cherished,
As a choice gift of Heaven. A date-tree bends
Its clustered fruit, and nard and cassia scent
The ever dewy air. The bibulous turf
Catches the rolling moisture, as it glances
O'er the bright pebbles, down the winding dell,
Till one intensest verdure tapestries
The level lawn. Between the parting hills,
Off-stretching into dimness, opens out
A sweep of plain, spotted with clumps of palms,
White cottages and dove-cotes, avenues
Of sycamores, and woods of olives blue
With their autumnal load, and vineyards hung
On the slope mountains; in the midst, the walls,
And towers, and temple-tops, and pinnacles
Of a wide city, sitting like a queen
Amid her beautiful fields, and shining bright
In the low evening sun. Around it flows
A wandering river, hidden now beneath

Its willows, now outflashing like a gush
From the tapped furnace, now its course revealing,
By wilderness and garden, ever fed
From out its quickening wave,—still further winding,
Like a gilt serpent, through a naked plain,
On to a lake, now bright, but dimly fading
Into a boundless blue. Up in that cove,
On whose encircling battlements the cedar
Nods to the evening wind, and the set sun
Gilds with a fringe of gold the tall, gray rocks,
Now glittering, though beneath them all is dim
And shadowy cool, — up in that cove, a tent
Is planted for the night, and round it throng
A shepherd's train, — his children and his dogs
Busy at play, his ruminant sheep reposing
Under the shelving walls, with here and there
A lordly ram, gazing upon his likeness
In the deep, mirrored pool, and seeming half
Intent on war, — a patriarchal scene,
Like that of old, when Abraham fed his flocks
In Mamre. 'T is the hour of evening prayer.
A reverent pause, — and then the loud, clear voice
Comes up amid those rocks, to Him who rules
Alone in heaven, and after it a hymn
Low sung by gentle voices. From the tent
Flows the soft melody, more touching sweet
For the veiled mystery within whose shade
So much of beauty breathes.
With that low hymn
Came darkness to my dream; and all the pomp
Of mountain, forest, vale, and ocean faded
Slowly and solemnly away, and vanished
In utter gloom. As after many a train
Of bright illusions, cities, camps, and caves,
Dark robbers, helmed hosts, and monarchs seated
Proud on their thrones,—after gay sights and sounds,
The measured march, the merry dance, the rush
And clash of battle, — when the eye is fixed
Intensely on the full catastrophe,

Glad for relief, yet lingering o'er the scene
Of false but real woe, — slowly descend
The curtain's massy folds, and, to the sound
Of distant music, one by one withdraws
Each glittering pomp, till dark before us hangs
A funeral pall, as if in mockery
Of this poor world; — so from my spirit's eye
My dream withdrew, and to the still repose
Of midnight left me.

SONNETS.

I.

If on the clustering curls of thy dark hair,
And the pure arching of thy polished brow,
We only gaze, we fondly dream that thou
Art one of those bright ministers who bear,
Along the cloudless bosom of the air,
Sweet, solemn words, to which our spirits bow,
With such a holy smile thou lookest now,
And art so soft and delicately fair.
  A veil of tender light is mantling o'er thee;
Around thy opening lips young loves are playing;
And crowds of youths, in passionate thought delaying,
Pause, as thou movest by them, to adore thee;
By many a sudden blush and tear betraying
How the heart trembles, when it bends before thee.

II.

Oh! I could wish I sat upon yon cloud,
Moving with such a silent flight away,
And pure, as if it were an angel's shroud,
And bright, as if it were the veil of day.
Silently on the wind it passes by,
And o'er the mountain glides, and comes no more;
So, when a few short days are gone, shall I
Glide to a dim and undiscovered shore.

O, thou art pure and beautiful, sweet form!
Who softly movest by me in the light
Of thy young beauty, as upon the storm
Falls, with a fainter tint, the bow of night:
Thy way is to a better world, and there
Thou lookest as a cloud that smiles at even.
O, be to me that cloud, and kindly bear
My spirit with thee to thy own pure heaven.

III.

Thy form may fade, but thou wilt not all die,
For love with thee is deathless. Thou wilt be
Dear, as thou ever hast been, unto me,
For thou wilt ever have the speaking eye;
And that alone is beauty, and it tells
How many fond affections burn within;
And it too hath a magic power to win,
By the enchantment of its living spells.
Only with that fond heart, and that dark eye,
Thy love will ever guide me, and control
My spirit to thy gentle sympathy;
And as the needle trembles to the pole,
So shall my heart for ever to thee fly,
The centre and attraction of my soul.

IV.

If, when I look on thee, and hear thy voice
In a low-whispered melody alone,
When it is breathing in its softest tone,
All the deep feelings of my heart rejoice, —
O, what were it to sit beside thee long,
And gaze on thy bright looks and thy dark eyes,
And hear thy tender words and thy sweet song,
As sweet as if it floated from the skies!
O, what were it to know that thou art mine,
Indissolubly mine! — that thou wilt be
For ever as an angel unto me,

Whether the day be dark, or fortune shine,
Giving me, in the bliss of loving thee,
A portion of the bliss they call divine.

V.

Calm look of gentleness! — I see thee now,
Even in the dead of night I see thee. Fair
Thou movest like a spirit through the air,
And there is light unearthly on thy brow, —
Yes, by that smile, it can be only thou;
For as the fresh dew trembling on the rose,
When first the silken leaves their red unclose,
Or as the jewel on the frosted bough,
So bright and pure thy tender look of love;
And as thou hoverest over me, my heart
Beats gentler, and I feel my spirit play
Light as a linnet on his airy way;
And as thy blue eyes look on me, they dart
The soft and winning glances of the dove.

VI.

Green herbs and flowers new opening, ye have known
The soft hand that once gathered you, and made
Of your bright leaves and tender stalks a braid,
To crown those angel looks, which long have flown.
Ere the warm wind from off the sea had blown,
And waked the sleeping buds among the bowers,
She loved to pluck the pale and soft-eyed flowers
Of tint so purely fading, like her own.
These were her chosen woodlands, where she paid
The tribute of her spirit to the Power
Whose voice is heard in every wind that blows,
Whose tears descend in every vernal shower,
And as they trickle through the mantling shade,
A stream of life and love and beauty flows.

VII.

O Love! thou art a pure and holy thing,
And none should ever dare to breathe thy name
Whose hearts are lit not with as bright a flame
As sunward burns around the eagle's wing:
O, let me not unworthy offerings bring
To one, whose all-commanding power can tame
Each vagrant wish, and stamp the brand of shame,
Where the least stains of earthly passion cling:
Then let me gather from my inmost heart
Pure feelings, that from infancy have slept,
Silent as waters in a hidden well;
And to the gentle offering then impart
The fire and tears that Sappho breathed and wept,
When her faint cithern gave its dying swell.

When the woodlands are covered with leaves and
flowers,
In the loveliest time of the year;
When the sky is now clear, and now checkered with
showers,
And life rambles on through the warm sunny hours,
Undimmed with a shade or a tear;
O, sweet are the feelings that kindle and burn
As we gaze on the flowers and the sky;
But to higher and purer devotion they turn,
As water takes tint from the hue of its urn,
When they burn in the light of thine eye

And when, in the calm of a moonshiny night,
A serenade steals o'er the bay,
As it curls in the smile of her mellowest light,
Or lies in its beauty, as silent and bright
As it slept in the sunshine of day, —
O, sweet is the clear and silvery tone,

As it softly comes over my ear;
But sweet as it breathes when I hear it alone,
It breathes like a flute by a wind-spirit blown,
When I know thou art listening near.

O, the music and beauty of life lose their worth,
When one heart only joys in their smile;
But the union of hearts gives that pleasure its birth,
Which beams on the darkest and coldest of earth,
Like the sun on his own chosen isle;
It gives to the fireside of winter the light,
The glow, and the glitter of spring.
O, sweet are the hours when two fond hearts unite,
And softly they glide, in their innocent flight,
Away on a motionless wing.

SPRING.

AGAIN the infant flowers of Spring
Call thee to sport on thy rainbow wing.
Spirit of beauty! the air is bright
With the boundless flow of thy mellow light;
The woods are ready to bud and bloom,
And are weaving for Summer their quiet gloom;
The tufted brook reflects, as it flows,
The tips of the half-unopened rose,
And the early bird, as he carols free,
Sings to his little love and thee.

See how the clouds, as they fleetly pass,
Throw their shadowy veil on the darkening grass;
And the pattering showers and stealing dews,
With their starry gems and skyey hues,
From the oozy meadow, that drinks the tide,
To the sheltered vale on the mountain side,
Wake to a new and fresher birth
The tenderest tribes of teeming earth,

And scatter with light and dallying play
Their earliest flowers on the Zephyr's way.

He comes from the mountain's piny steep,
For the long boughs bend with a silent sweep;
And his rapid steps have hurried o'er
The grassy hills to the pebbly shore;
And now, on the breast of the lonely lake,
The waves in silvery glances break,
Like a short and quickly-rolling sea,
When the gale first feels its liberty,
And the flakes of foam, like coursers, run,
Rejoicing beneath the vertical sun.

He has crossed the lake, and the forest heaves,
To the sway of his wings, its billowy leaves,
And the downy tufts of the meadow fly
In snowy clouds, as he passes by,
And softly beneath his noiseless tread
The odorous spring-grass bends its head;
And now he reaches the woven bower,
Where he meets his own beloved flower,
And gladly his wearied limbs repose
In the shade of the newly-opening rose.

THE REIGN OF MAY.

I FEEL a newer life in every gale;
  The winds that fan the flowers,
And with their welcome breathings fill the sail,
  Tell of serener hours, —
 Of hours that glide unfelt away
 Beneath the sky of May.

The spirit of the gentle south-wind calls
  From his blue throne of air,
And where his whispering voice in music falls,
  Beauty is budding there;

The bright ones of the valley break
Their slumbers and awake.

The waving verdure rolls along the plain,
And the wide forest weaves,
To welcome back its playful mates again,
A canopy of leaves;
And from its darkening shadow floats
A gush of trembling notes.

Fairer and brighter spreads the reign of May;
The tresses of the woods
With the light dallying of the west-wind play,
And the full-brimming floods,
As gladly to their goal they run,
Hail the returning sun.

TRUE GREATNESS.

There is a fire, that has its birth
Above the proudest hills of earth;
And higher than the eternal snows,
The fountain whence it rose.

It came to man in ancient days,
And fell upon his ardent gaze,
A god descending in his car,
The spirit of a star.

And as the glorious vision broke
Full on his eye, at once he woke,
And with the rush of battling steeds
He sprang to generous deeds.

Then first he stood erect and free,
And in the might of destiny

A stern, unconquerable fate
    Compelled him to be great.

He strove not for the wreath of fame;
From Heaven the power that moved him came,
And welcome as the mountain air
    The voice that bade him dare.

Onward he bore, and battled still
With a most firm, enduring will;
His only hope, to win and rise,
    His only aim, the skies.

He saw their glories blaze afar;
A soul looked down from every star;
And from its eye of lightning flew
    A glance, that thrilled him through.

Full in the front of war he stood;
His home, his country, claimed his blood:
Without one sigh that blood was given;
    He only thought — of heaven.

THERE is nothing can equal the tender hours,
  When life is first in bloom;
When the heart, like a bee in a wild of flowers,
  Finds everywhere perfume;
When the present is all, and it questions not
  If those flowers shall pass away,
But, pleased with its own delightful lot,
  Dreams never of decay.

O, it dreams not the hue that freshly glows
  On the cheek shall ever flee,
And fade away like the summer rose,
  Or the crimson on the sea,

When far in the west the setting sun
  Goes down in the kindled main,
And the colors vanish one by one,
  But never revive again.

O, life in its springtime dances on
  In smiles and innocent tears;
It casts not a look to the moments gone,
  But hails the coming years;
They shine before its fancy's eye,
  Like eastern visions bright,
Gay as the hues in the western sky
  At the coming on of night.

Thus happy in all their bosoms feel,
  And in all their fancy dreams,
Their quiet moments onward steal
  Like the silent flow of streams,
Gliding through tufted flowers away
  To the far and unknown sea;
So on with a flight that cannot stay
  Their days of innocence flee.

But soon, too soon their hearts shall know,
  The future was falsely bright,
And its gay and far-deluding glow
  Shall change to the gloom of night;
O, then with a fond and lingering eye
  They shall turn to the early hours,
When life, as their moments hurried by,
  Was a wild of sweets and flowers.

DEAR moments of childhood! how sweetly ye smile,
As I gaze on the vista of years that are gone!
Ye smile in your innocent loveliness, while
In the downhill of life we are hastening on.

O, could I return to your beautiful prime,
When ye shone like the morn of a clear summer day,
And my spirit ne'er thought how the footsteps of time,
Like the flight of an eagle, were hastening away;

O, could I return to those innocent hours,
When my heart knew no sorrow, that fled not as soon
As the soft drops of April that fall upon flowers,
And vanish at once in the bright air of noon;—

O, then I might taste of the silent delight
That beams in the eye of an infant, and flows
As peacefully on as the dove in her flight,
Or the dew stealing out of the cup of a rose;

O, then I might lay all my sorrows at rest,
And be calm as the first whispered zephyr of spring,
When it comes on its pinions of down from the west,
And shakes the soft fragrance of May from its wing;

O, then I might know what it is to be free
From a burden that presses a heart to the grave,
Might charm back the feeling of lightness and glee,
The first look of love and of gentleness gave.

But no,—I have passed from the fresh blooming shore,
Where life gathers round it its verdure and flowers;
I can fondly look backward,—but ah! never more
Can I taste of your sweetness, ye innocent hours!

Then whither—ah, whither escape from the night,
Which darkens more deeply, the farther I go!
Look out from the gloom, some benevolent light!
Like a star on the traveller who wanders below.

A light now is breaking,—it comes from above,—
Still clearer and purer than life's early dawn;
It descends with the motionless flight of a dove,
And guides me in safety and cheerfulness on.

Then let me not turn to the innocent hours
Of childhood, when brighter hours wait me before;
There are thorns in life's earliest and tenderest flowers,
But yonder are flowers that shall sting me no more.

Come from thy home in the far blue sky,
Spirit of beauty and love and song!
Hang on thy airy pinions nigh,
When the dreams of my wayward fancy throng;
Give them a brighter and gayer hue,
Shape them to forms of finer mould,
Fairer than ever painter drew,
Brighter than all the gods of old.

Lead me to that delicious clime,
Where the anana swells and glows;
Lay me beneath the flowering lime,
Where the dew in drops of nectar flows:
There let the visions of beauty rise,
And float in fairy trains away,
Bright as their own unclouded skies,
And rich as the parting light of day.

Bring to my heart the melting tone,
Once so sweet to my lingering ear;
Though the days of youth have flown,
Still that tone to my heart is dear.
Now it seems to murmur by,
Soft as the wind in a bed of flowers;
Now the falling whispers die,—
Gone is the dream of my fairest hours.

Dimly the visions of beauty fade,
Like the cloud that melts in the evening air,
When its colors vanish shade by shade,
Till the blue of the sky alone is there;

Ere they have wholly faded, throw,
  Spirit of beauty! one glance to me,
Bright as the last and fullest glow
  Of the setting sun on the golden sea.

THOU hast come from thy home in the far blue sky,
  To dwell in the bosom of flowery dells;
Thou hast laid thy mantle of glory by,
  With its heavenly hues and magic spells;
Thou hast wrapped thee in weeds of sober gray,
  And simply braided thy flowing hair,
And thy locks in fond and amorous play
  Sport with the soft and balmy air.

From thy wintry hall in the evening cloud,
  Where gathered thy pomp of airy hues,
And thine eye, from the folds of thy golden shroud,
  Looked down on the glistening of frozen dews,
Where each drop, like a bright, particular star,
  Caught the iris colors around thy throne,
And the moon, as she mounted the hills afar,
  On a world of seeded silver shone, —

From thy glittering hall in the lonely sky,
  Thou hast come to dwell in the tangled bower,
Where a stealing brook is murmuring by,
  And bathing the roots of herb and flower.
Here thy beneficent hand shall throw
  Its thousand hues o'er the budding plain,
Till we dream the clouds, in their sunset glow,
  Have melted in showers of golden rain.

  SOUL of the lyre and song!
Who comest from the blue and boundless air,
  And bearest me along
To read the starry glories gathered there, —

Who callest from the deep
The spirits of the long departed dead,
To move in gallant sweep,
And proud array, above their honored bed:

Whether from air or sea
Thy voice is uttered, or from mountain heights,
Where the hawk hovers free,
And morn and evening hang their thousand lights, —

Whether from cove or stream
Bosomed in shady forests, where of old
To the rapt prophet's dream
A tale of visionary pomp was told, —

'T is the one stirring breath
That moves through every creature, urging on
The warrior to death,
The bard to give to fame the victory won.

I LOOKED on the broad setting sun,
When his flight through the wide heaven was done,
And the waves glowing bright with his fire
Rose around like a funeral pyre.

I watched the red twilight decay,
When its tints melted slowly away,
Till the light of the soft evening-star
Looked out on the blue sea afar.

I saw it hang low in the west,
Till it sank on the ocean's calm breast,
And it seemed, as its brightness grew dim,
In the mirror of waters to swim.

I turned and beheld a new day
From the low-lying clouds burst away,

And its light on their wreathed volumes throw,
Till they rolled like a deluge of snow.

I followed the round, ruddy moon,
Till she stood at the height of her noon,
And watched her deep blushes expire,
As she rose on the blue heaven higher.

I saw the far ocean grow bright
With the flow of her mellowest light,
And the waves, in their long-rolling swell,
Caught her smile as they mounted and fell.

I marked, as her pale-tinted ray
In the first flush of dawn died away,
Broad pillars of fire dart again
From the breast of the kindling main.

Then the sea flashed, like gold, in its flow,
And the clouds caught the beautiful glow,
Till the sun from the wide ocean came,
Like a god in his chariot of flame.

THOU glorious spirit of life and love!
  There is not a leaf or flower,
That spreads to the sun, when meadow and grove
  Awake with the April shower, —
There is not a creature that walks the earth,
  And is glad in his liberty,
But feels and knows, from his earliest birth,
  How his being is full of thee.

The waters, that fall from the mountain's brow,
  Or in verdurous valleys flow;
The waves, that around the gallant prow
  In the noon-light flash and glow;

The sea, as it heaves from the line to the pole,
In calm or in tempest — free,
Feels deep in its heart the enlivening soul, —
The ocean is full of thee.

The clouds that hang in the evening sky,
And burn with the setting sun;
The glorious beings who meet on high
When the light of day is done;
The brightness that fills the boundless blue,
When the shades of twilight flee, —
O, the quickening air with its rain and dew, —
The air is full of thee.

"Where hast thou been on thy rainbow wing,
Soul of the light and festive song?"
"I have been where around the magic spring
The spirits of love and beauty throng;
There, to the sound of languishing airs,
They wheel their dance on the moon-lit well,
And every breath of the night-wind bears
Through wilds of roses the warbled spell;
Then it silently steals away,
Like a floating bird, when the sea is calm,
And the lingering breeze, with a fond delay,
Hovers around those bowers of balm:
Thence on my rainbow wing I flew,
To bear this bud of a rose to thee;
Never a fairer blossom blew,
Than this when it opens its leaves shall be."

"Whither is now thy airy flight?"
"Over the blue and boundless ocean,
Where it lifts, to embrace the setting light,
Its golden waves with a softest motion:

Far to the pictured west I fly,
  Where the wings of the spirits of fire are glancing,
And their radiant forms on the kindled sky,
  Like sparks in a stormy sea, are dancing:
Thither I go, and I soon return,
  When my torch is lit in the fount of glory,
That thy pen with a hallowed glow may burn,
  When thou givest the names of the good to story.

" Then I will bring, from the coral cave,
  Flowers of a brighter and purer hue
Than ever Hesperian gardens gave,
  Or drank from the sky its tender blue;
Down in the fathomless deep they lie,
  Tufted with leaves of glassy green,
And their pearly tints, like the opening sky
  Through the rift of a cloud, look out between;
Some shall mimic the setting sun,
  Or the reddening glow of a distant fire,
And in some every tint shall blend and run,
  Like the mingling sounds on a trembling wire;
These I will pluck from the coral cave,
  In the silent depths of the tropic sea;
Then the treasures of earth and sky and wave
  Shall be borne on my rainbow wing to thee.

" Then I will bend my airy flight,
  From my wanderings, back to the magic well,
Where the gentle spirits, who love the light
  Of the moon, in its fullest beauty, dwell;
There, when the fountain bubbles over,
  Shedding a soft and vapory dew,
Their glistening wings, as around they hover
  In the silvery cloud, shall quiver through;
Whether I fly to the setting sun,
  Or down in the depths of ocean roam,
Still I seek, when my flight is done,
  In the wild of flowers, my cherished home."

THE SPIRIT OF LIFE.

FROM the flowery isles of the southern sea,
  Where the fulness of life for ever flows,
Where the waters are ever gliding free,
  And the ripened fruit by its blossom glows:
From the region of light and wooing gales,
  Where the plumed wanderer loves to roam,
And glad, as the fair wind fills his sails,
  Bounds over the wave to his unseen home:

From the flowery isles of the southern sea,
  Where life seems one long and glad repose,
And the savage beneath his sheltering tree
  No fairer and happier being knows;
Where he wakes to a clear and cloudless day
  With the notes of the earliest matin-song,
And silently dreams the hours away,
  Or hurries to join the sportive throng:

From those flowery and happy Elysian isles,
  Where the ocean kisses the coral shore,
And, spread like a silvery mirror, smiles,
  Nor ever awakes to the whirlwind's roar;
Where the halcyon ever might fold its wing,
  And float on the calm and silent sea,
And wide the joyous mariner fling
  His sails to the wind's full mastery:

I come from those blest Elysian isles,
  With the dews of life in my brimming urn;
Young Spring at my bidding wakes and smiles,
  And the infant blushes of Beauty burn;
A thousand busy and joyous wings
  O'er meadow and forest my treasures bear,
And Health, in her innocent gladness, flings
  New-braided wreaths from her flowing hair:

All waken and brighten where'er I go,
  Like the hearts that welcome a festive day,
And happy creatures around me flow,
  Like the crowds that greet a conqueror's way.

SPIRIT of high and mighty souls!
  Thine is the darkly hovering cloud,
Deep in whose heart the thunder rolls,
  With a murmuring echo long and loud;
Thine the gulf where the cataract pours
  With a sudden rush its emerald tide;
Thine the height where the eagle soars,
  And the winds in their stormy chariots ride:

Thine the unbounded world of waves,
  Bursting aloft with fiery foam;
Thine the fearless bark, that braves
  Danger and death on its ocean home;
Thine the mountains that gird the pole,
  Wreathed like a starry crown of light, —
These are the haunts of the mighty soul, —
  Thither it bends its daring flight.

But by the side of the hidden spring
  Shaded with newly-budding flowers,
Where the butterfly floats on its filmy wing,
  And the rose breathes sweetlier after showers;
But in the cool, sequestered shade,
  At the lonely foot of a wooded hill,
Where a low and pleasing din is made
  By the dash of the brook at the village mill;

But in the colored sky at even,
  When the glorious tints are fading away,
And shapes like the missioned spirits of heaven
  Round the top of the gilded forest play;

But by the sweep of the silent river,
Where its waters in gentle stillness roll,
Like the tides of eternity, ruffled never ; —
O, these are the haunts of the tender soul.

Had I the pinions of an eagle's wing,
In the pure mountain air,
Poised like a glorious and celestial thing,
My soul afar should fling
Its glances there.

Above the midway haunt of clouds and storms,
In the bright summer sun,
Whose tempered influence kindles, as it warms,
O'er beauty's fairest forms
My eye should run.

There all that dims and darkens fades away ;
One flow of mellow light,
Fresh as the newly-risen beam of day,
In ever-varying play,
Makes all things bright.

The woods that wave below in tufted green,
The meadows pranked with flowers,
The pebbly brooks that wind in light between,
Glad as their blushing queen
Descends in showers, —

From the clear height of that aerial throne,
Heaved like a prop of heaven,
Towering in solitary pride alone,
Where never storms have blown,
Nor clouds were driven, —

Seen from that airy tower, so far below,
They swim in waving gold,

As when the misty hills at evening glow,
And light in liquid flow
  On earth is rolled.

On the far confines of the bending sky,
  Where ocean melts in air,
Light curls of snowy vapors hover by,
And azure islands lie
  In slumber there.

Like halcyons floating on the silent sea,
  With wings of skyey hue
Shading their weary eyes, — so tranquilly
They take, bright heaven! from thee
  Thy purest blue.

There as I gaze, I feel a gentle power
  Steal through my heart, and lay
Its cares at rest, as when the dewy shower
Freshens at night the flower
  That drooped by day.

ON THE DEATH OF ——.

  I SHED no tear upon thy early grave,
For thy pure soul has found deliverance now,
  And from the eminence that Nature gave
Looks down upon a world that sought to bow,
  With a low burden of consuming cares,
Thy spirit to the reach of theirs.
  Thou wert not fashioned for the menial throng,
Who plod with easy step the common way,
  But thy delight was in the sons of song,
And, sooth, to play
  On the light strings of some unearthly lyre
  Was all thy office, and thy sole desire.

Thy spirit could not brook the common lot.
   Not that it wore the plume and crest of pride,
For the meek tenant of a shepherd's cot
   Went as a loved companion by thy side;
   But all thy thoughts were lent,
   With a perpetual bent,
To meditations of an unknown sphere,
   And therefore life below
   Seemed all too lag and slow,
And every look was cold that met thee here;
   So thou didst keep thy melancholy way,
   With earnest longing for a brighter day.

And it has come, — and now a loftier air
   Encompasses about thy liberal soul:
The welcome winds that blow around thee bear
   Sounds that from fitly-chiming planets roll,
And now thy all-attentive spirit hears
The harmony of spheres;
   Thy path is now through amaranth beds, and lines
Of laurel, such as crown the chosen few,
   Whose tuneful company in glory shines
Bathed with large offerings of Castalian dew,
That from a golden overshadowing cloud
   In full effusion flows,
And, while their harps and voices echo loud,
   Breathes round the living perfume of the rose.

And now, admitted to their willing train,
   Thou standest high upon the starry floor,
And thou shalt walk on that cerulean plain
   Inlaid with burning gems and sparkling ore:
   Thou shalt behold no more
   The clouds that overshade our darker day,
   For they have rolled away.
      Like a bright jewel in a coronet,
   Or, fitter simile, a rolling star,
   Imperial Jove in his eternal car,
      In the full front of Heaven's armada set,

That ride the airy sea,
Spreading without a limit or a shore,
And, stead of rush and roar,
Moving to a most gentle harmony, —
Thus bright, and thus upheld in port and place,
Thou shalt maintain thy station evermore,
And, with such lofty grace
As Theron erst the palmy garland wore,
Bear on thy youthful brow the immortal bay,
And so thy fame shall never pass away.

Then why should we with long and vain lament
Weep o'er thy early fate, as if it were
Inflicted on thee with no good intent,
But dropped unkindly from the infected air?
Rather be glad, for 't is the blessed care
Of some benevolent power,
Whose wont it is with open hand to shower
His liberal gifts, that thou so soon hast given
Thy spirit to the full embrace of Heaven.

THE LAST DAYS OF AUTUMN.

Now the growing year is over,
And the shepherd's tinkling bell
Faintly from its winter cover
Rings a low farewell: —
Now the birds of Autumn shiver,
Where the withered beech-leaves quiver,
O'er the dark and lazy river,
In the rocky dell.

Now the mist is on the mountains,
Reddening in the rising sun;
Now the flowers around the fountains
Perish one by one: —

Not a spire of grass is growing,
But the leaves that late were glowing
Now its blighted green are strowing
With a mantle dun.

Now the torrent brook is stealing
Faintly down the furrowed glade,—
Not as when, in winter pealing,
Such a din it made,
That the sound of cataracts falling
Gave no echo so appalling,
As its hoarse and heavy brawling
In the pine's black shade.

Darkly blue the mist is hovering
Round the clifted rock's bare height,
All the bordering mountains covering
With a dim, uncertain light:—
Now, a fresher wind prevailing,
Wide its heavy burden sailing,
Deepens, as the day is failing,
Fast the gloom of night.

Slow the blood-stained moon is riding
Through the still and hazy air,
Like a sheeted spectre gliding
In a torch's glare:—
Few the hours her light is given,—
Mingling clouds of tempest driven
O'er the mourning face of heaven,
All is blackness there.

THE SOUL OF SONG.

WHERE lives the soul of song?
Dwells it amid the city's festive halls?
Where crowd the eager throng,
Or where the wanderer's silent footstep falls?

Loves it the gay saloon,
Where wine and dances steal away the night,
And bright as summer noon
Burns round the pictured walls a blaze of light?

Seeks it the public square,
When victory hails the people's choson son,
And loud applauses there
From lip to lip in emulous greetings run?

Dwells it amid the host,
Who bear their crimson banners waving high;
Whose first and only boast
Draws tears of anguish from the patriot's eye?

Follows it on the path
Where the proud conqueror marches to his home,
And, wearied of his wrath,
Smiles as he steps beneath the imperial dome?

No, — not in festive halls,
In crowded marts, nor in the gay saloon;
Not in the forum falls,
Nor on the conquering host, the gracious boon;

But where blue mountains rise
Silent and calm amid the upper air,
And pure and cloudless skies
Bend o'er a world, that lies below as fair;

But where uncultured plains
Spread far and wide their beds of grass and flowers,
And heaven's bright pencil stains
Clear gems that roll away in silent showers;

But in the depth of woods,
Where the slant sunbeam gilds the hoary tree
And the soft voice of floods
Glides on the pinions of the evening breeze;

But in the broken dell,
Where the crisped ivy curls its tangled vines,
And the wild blossom's bell
Drops with the dew that in its hollow shines;

But in the gulfy cave,
Where pours the cascade from the glacier's height,
And all its waters wave,
Like rainbows, in their luxury of light; —

There dwells the soul of song:
It flies not to the city's festive halls,
But loves to steal along,
Where the lone wanderer's silent footstep falls.

MORNING TWILIGHT.

The mountains are blue in the morning air,
And the woods are sparkling with dewy light;
The winds, as they wind through the hollows, bear
The breath of the blossoms that wake by night.
Wide o'er the bending meadows roll
The mists, like a lightly moving sea;
The sun is not risen, — and over the whole
There hovers a silent mystery.

The pure blue sky is in calm repose;
The pillowy clouds are sleeping there;
So stilly the brook in its covert flows,
You would think its murmur a breath of air.
The water that floats in the glassy pool,
Half hid by the willows that line its brink,
In its deep recess has a look so cool,
One would worship its nymph, as he bent to drink.

Pure and beautiful thoughts, at this early hour,
Go off to the home of the bright and blest;

They steal on the heart with an unseen power,
And its passionate throbbings are laid at rest;
O, who would not catch, from the quiet sky
And the mountains that soar in the hazy air,
When his harbinger tells that the sun is nigh,
The visions of bliss that are floating there!

"The memory of joys that are past." — OSSIAN.

WHERE are now the flowers that once detained me,
Like a loiterer on my early way?
Where the fragrant wreaths that softly chained me,
When young life was like an infant's play?

Were they but the fancied dreams, that hover
Round the couch where tender hearts repose?
Only pictured veils, that brightly cover
With their skyey tints a world of woes?

They are gone, — but memory loves to cherish
All their sweetness in her deepest core.
Ah! the recollection cannot perish,
Though the eye may never meet them more.

There are hopes, that like enchantment brighten
Gayly in the van of coming years;
They are never met, — and yet they lighten,
When we walk in sorrow and in tears.

When the present only tells of anguish,
Then we know their worth, and only then:
O, the wasted heart will cease to languish,
When it thinks of joys that might have been!

Age and suffering and want may sever
Every link, that bound to life, in twain:
Hope — even hope may vanish, but for ever
Memory with her visions will remain.

INSPIRATION.

Glorious creatures! Shapes of light!
  Where are now those looks of power?
Where the eyes that glistened bright,
  In my visionary hour?

Ye were fair, and ye were high;
  Far, too far away from earth;
Shadowy pinions hovered nigh,
  When my fancy gave you birth.

I was in a trance of heaven;
  Spirits then would come and go:
Where the eternal walls were riven,
  Rushed a dazzling overflow.

I was then, on sounding wings,
  Borne along the living air;
All of bright and beauteous things,
  All of great and good, were there.

Not a sound, but seemed to tell
  Harmony and holy love;
Every echo gently fell,
  Like an answer from above.

Then the soul assumed its reign;
  Then it stood erect and bold;
All it sought so long in vain,
  Then in torrents round it rolled.

With a full and sudden rush,
  Thought and light and knowledge came,
Like an instantaneous gush
  From the purest fount of flame.

Thick as atoms in the sun,
  Dancing on the dusty way,

Thousand sparkles seemed to run,
  Meeting, mingling into day.

'T was the spirit's jubilee;
  Passion sprang, and rent his chain,
Mounting into ecstasy,
  Bright and free from every stain.

Visions, many as the stars,
  Glowing like a summer even,
Proud as victors on their cars,
  Heralded my way to heaven.

REMORSE.

I AM banished from home and from heaven,
Like the rush of a thunderbolt driven;
Ever blacker the night sinks before me,
And louder the storm rages o'er me;
A whirlwind behind me is rushing,
And torrents around me are gushing:
My flight must be onward for ever,
And a rest from my wandering be never.

My proud heart is broken and saddened;
My brain, like a scorpion, maddened,
When a circle of flame has fast bound him,
And death is within and around him;
My hopes are all scattered and flying,
And the last pulse that stirred me is dying:
Of memory no time can bereave me;
It may torture, but never will leave me.

O, where the ambition that hovered,
Till its pinions with glory were covered!
Where the hopes, ever fonder and lighter,
Like the morning sun brighter and brighter!

Where the fancy that colored and painted,
Till the picture was hallowed and sainted,
And the love, a devoted adorer,
That bent in his ecstasy o'er her!

O, these were my forfeited heaven!
But few were the days they were given:
And now, like a wanderer benighted,
Every blossom and bud torn and blighted,
In the regions of darkness and sorrow,
Forbidden the hope of a morrow,
From all that was dear I must sever,
And rush to my ruin for ever.

Now rage, like a hurricane, wings me,
And the goading of memory stings me;
If I look for a moment behind me,
The arrows of thought sear and blind me;
The far-echoed music of gladness
Now stirs me to fury and madness,
And the fame that once wooed me now spurns me,
And its brightness now scorches and burns me.

Then welcome the rush and the roaring,
And the storm that is bursting and pouring,
And the darkness that thickens around me,
As if earth in its centre had bound me;
Better onward through chaos be driven,
Than be scared by the frowning of heaven,
Though a rest from my wandering be never,
And my flight be for ever and ever.

A FANCY-PIECE.

I FOUND thee where the woods were wild,
  And weeds and thorns had round thee grown;
No hunter's foot, no wandering child,
  Had met thee, thou wert all so lone.

Above, the cypress and the yew
  Had wreathed around their funeral shade,
And the still wind, that faintly blew,
  A sound, like that of sorrow, made.

And ever, as it o'er thee swept,
  Low-breathing melodies were heard,
As if a mourner sobbed and wept,
  Or nightly sang the widowed bird.

And now, as fitfully the blast
  Shook the tossed branches overhead,
A voice like that of terror passed,
  And like a midnight vision fled.

And then again a mingled tone
  Of all sweet echoes met my ear,
Sweet as, when storms are over blown,
  The warm south-wind comes stealing near;

Sweet as the closing breath of even,
  When wet with dews her pinions fall,
And, like a messenger of Heaven,
  Night comes, and whispers peace to all.

I took thee from thy sylvan haunt,
  And brought thee to the cultured plain,
And saw thee flourish, like a plant
  Nursed by the dews and kindly rain.

And there was music round thee still,
  And it was sweet — O, sweeter far!
Like voices echoed from the hill,
  When Love has lit his trembling star:

Or like the fluttering airs in May,
  Stealing among the musky flowers,
And bearing mingled sweets away
  From pansied beds and orange bowers:

A sound, that with the fretting stream,
  And feeding flocks, and murmuring bees,
Blent, like the closing of a dream,
  In undistinguished harmonies.

And ever, as the mounting sun
  Shone broader in the summer heaven,
Voices and symphonies would run,
  In hurried chords around thee driven.

And then the melody was high,
  Like organs pealing through a choir,
Or thunders mingling in the sky,
  Or like the distant roar of fire, —

A solemn, tempered tone, that gave
  A shuddering, not unmixed with joy,
  As when the proud, unshrinking boy
Fears, and yet breasts the bursting wave.

And ever as the loftier swell
  Sank from its airy throne, there came
Soft utterings of peace, that fell
  Silently breathing one loved name.

Still loftier grew the master-song,
  And sweeter stole the under-tone,
When suddenly there rolled along
  Rude storms, and every breath had flown.

Silent and cold I saw thee lay
  Thy honors and thy hopes aside,
And slowly, faintly sink away,
  Slow as the long-retiring tide.

The breath of spring to thee was balm,
  And summer gave thee light and love;
Thy leaves were green, when air was calm,
  And heaven dropped blessings from above.

But when the hills are bleak and bare,
  Thou canst not stand the open plain;
But rather thou wouldst wither where
  I found thee, in thy woods, again.

SPIRIT OF MAY.

Welcome, thrice welcome, Spirit of May!
Blessings be round thy airy way;
Come, with thy train of rainbow hues,
Of hovering clouds and falling dews, —
Come to our garden beds and bowers,
And cover them over with leaves and flowers
Already the summer bird is there,
And he sings aloud to the warm, warm air;
There he carols strong and free,
And his song and his joy are all for thee.

Come when the sparkling rivers run,
Full and bright, to the gladdening sun;
Come, when the grass and springing corn
In their newest and tenderest green are born;
When budding woods and tufted hills
Wake to the music of foaming rills,
As they rush from their fountains deep and strong,
And in calm and in sunshine roll along;
Come, when the soft and winning air
Tells us a quickening life is there.

Come to our bosoms, Spirit of May!
We would not be sad when the earth is gay;
Wake, in the heart that is newly strung,
The love that dwells with the fair and young;
Give, to their full and speaking eyes,
Visions that glitter like sunset skies;

Waft them with quick and favoring gales,
Filling with music their glancing sails;
Theirs be a flight o'er a summer sea,
Where nothing of cloud or storm can be.

And give us, who long have bode the storm,
To feel for a moment our spirits warm;
Let the hopes, that once were a world of light,
Look out from our sorrows serene and bright,
Like stars that come forth from the midnight air,
When the cloud has passed and the sky is fair;
Give us awhile to forget our cares,
And be light as thy own enlivening airs;
Let feelings of childhood awake like flowers,
When they open to catch the falling showers.

Come from thy palace, Spirit of May!
Where flowers ever blossom and fountains play;
Bring with thee Plenty's brimming horn,
And the tears of evening and dews of morn;
Build thy throne in the clear, blue air,
And earth shall be bright, and heaven be fair,
And the winds that rushed from the rolling cloud,
And lifted their voices and called aloud,
Shall sink to a softer and mellower tone,
Like gales from a happy island blown.

Then the sea shall glow in its darkest bed,
And life shall revisit the mountain head;
And the valley shall laugh, and the forest ring,
For Joy shall be out on his glittering wing;
And the old shall pause, and the young shall stare,
As they hear his voice in the sunny air;
Glad shall their hearts and their spirits be,
When they know he is sent to tell of thee, —
To tell them, the Queen of Love and May
Is now on her bright, triumphal way.

SHALL I gather the rose of the mountain,
Or the violet low in the vale,
Or the birch bending over the fountain,
Or the flower that wakes up with the gale?
Shall I bring thee the pink-colored blossom,
That closes its leaves on the rain,
Or the petals that open their bosom
To the night, and are lovely in vain?

The violet is sweet in the valley,
And the wind-flower that welcomes the gale;
And the birch, where the bright waters sally,
Tells the night-wind a murmuring tale.
Not the sun-loving flower of the dry land
Do I choose, nor the blossom that blows
In the moon, but I go to the highland,
And pluck from the mountain the rose.

TO A SHIP, ON GOING TO SEA.

THE gallant ship is out at sea,
Proudly o'er the water going;
Along her sides the billows flee,
Back in her wake, a river, flowing:
She dips her stem to meet the wave,
And high the tossed foam curls before it;
As if she felt the cheers we gave,
She takes her flight,
Where the sea looks bright,
And the sun in sparkles flashes o'er it.

Gallantly on she cuts her way,
And now in distance far is fleeting;
There are some on board whose hearts are gay,
And some whose hearts are wildly beating:
Loud was the cheer her seamen gave,
As back they sent our welcome cheering;

Many a hand was seen to wave,
And some did weep,
And fondly keep
Their gaze intent when out of hearing.

They have parted, and now are far at sea, —
Heaven send them fair and gentle weather!
They part not for eternity;
Our hands shall soon be linked together:
The sea was smooth, and the sky was blue,
And the tops of the ruffled waves were glowing,
As proudly on the vessel flew,
Like the feathered king,
On his balanced wing,
To a distant land o'er the ocean going.

APOSTROPHE TO THE ISLAND OF CUBA.

NOVEMBER, 1822.

THERE is blood on thy desolate shore,
Thou island of plunder and slaves!
Thy billows are purpled with gore,
And murder has crimsoned thy waves;
The vengeance of nations will come,
And wrath shall be rained on thy head,
And in terror thy voice shall be dumb,
When they ask for their brothers who bled.
Thy hand was not stirred when their life-blood was spilt;
And therefore that hand must partake in the guilt.

Thou art guilty or weak, — and the rod
Should be wrenched from thy palsied hand;
By the pirate thy green fields are trod,
And his steps have polluted thy land;
Unmoved is thy heart and thine eye,
When our dear ones are tortured and slain;

But their blood, with a terrible cry,
  Calls on vengeance, and calls not in vain;
If Europe regard not, our land shall awake,
And thy walls and thy turrets shall tremble and shake.

The voice of a world shall be heard,
  And thy faith shall be tried by the call;
And that terrible voice shall be feared,
  And obeyed, — or the proud one shall fall.
Enough of our life has been shed,
  In watching and fighting for thee;
If thy foot linger still, on thy head
  The guilt and the vengeance shall be:
We have sworn that the spirit of ALLEN shall lead,
And our wrath shall not rest till we finish the deed.

TO MELANTHE.

I SAW thee, like a lovely dream, —
  I heard thy flowery voice, —
I saw that eye of mildness beam,
And even the air around did seem,
  In brightness, to rejoice.

Thou wert before me, pure and fair,
  A nymph, a saint, a child
Of very loveliness, and there
Was glory, such as angels wear,
  When all that beauty smiled.

Thou wert before me, but my heart
  Was anything but gay, —
There was a quick, a sudden start,
And then my spirit took no part,
  But wandered far away.

It could not rest in that delight,
  So natural to thine, —

It had been darkling long in night,
And it was round thee all too bright,
Too gentle, too divine.

The thoughts of many hopeless years,
Dark, visionary hours,
Wild phantoms of unholy fears,
The woe that wrings, the grief that sears, —
They could not dwell with flowers.

Thou hadst a smile for me, — for me.
O, would that I had known
A friend, a more than friend, like thee,
When my young heart was pure and free,
When love was newly blown!

My life had been a dearer thing, —
I had not then despaired;
And all the many joys, that fling
Their colors round the fleeting wing
Of time, been with thee shared.

O, thou wert all I could have dreamed,
In love's first purple bloom;
I saw thee smile, and then it seemed
As if a blessed vision beamed,
All light and all perfume.

The very air was musical, —
A glory round thee flowed, —
The winds sank to a dying fall,
And melody encircled all
In that serene abode.

It could not last, — it would not stay, —
It was not real, — no.
Yet thou didst speak to me, — they say
Such memories cannot pass away,
And it is with me so.

That smile, — that smile, — it was not mine;
And yet on me it smiled.
Would I had met thee so divine,
When I could dare to call me thine,
A boy, and thou a child!

SONNET.

Behold yon hills. The one is fresh and fair;
The other rudely great. New-springing green
Mantles the one; and on its top the star
Of love, in all its tenderest light, is seen.
Island of joys! how sweet thy gentle rays
Issue from heaven's blue depths in evening's prime!
But round yon bolder height no softness plays,
Nor flower nor bud adorns its front sublime.
Rude, but in majesty, it mounts in air,
And on its summit Jove in glory burns;
'Mid all the stars that pour their radiant urns,
None with that lordly planet may compare.
But see, they move; and, tinged with love's own hue,
Beauty and Power embrace in heaven's serenest blue.

CANZONETS.

I.

Tell me, heart, O tell me where
All my loves and hopes are flown?
Ah! to weep and sigh alone
Withers all that 's fresh and fair.

Hours of tenderest pleasure, where,
  Where have fled your golden dreams?
  Sorrow now in life's warm streams
Mingles cold and wintry care.

Youth, — how proud and light it springs,
  Shouting, "Welcome, flowery May!
See, the turtle sleeks his wings,
  Roses bloom, and fountains play;
Earth is full of joyous things!" —
  Ah! but soon they fade away.

II.

I DIE, my love, my treasure!
  My heart, my soul, I die.
  O, turn that gentle eye!
  My ebbing life shall fly
Back, in one tide of pleasure.
O fairest, sweetest, dearest! —
  O, soft as any dream,
  When by the meadow stream
  Thy loved one's lute thou hearest!
I ask one gift, deny not, —
  Those eyes of living light,
  O, let them glad my sight!
Look hither, love, and fly not.
  My heart, my heart is beating, —
  O, hear its fond entreating!
  O, turn those eyes in kindness, —
  What if the look be blindness!
My prayer, my prayer, deny not.

SONNET.

[*Acrostic* tribute (in 1825) to a Boston lady of surpassing beauty.]

EARTH holds no fairer, lovelier one than thou,
  Maid of the laughing lip, and frolic eye!

Innocence sits upon thy open brow,
  Like a pure spirit in its native sky.
If ever beauty stole the heart away,
  Enchantress, it would fly to meet thy smile;
Moments would seem by thee a summer day,
  And all around thee an Elysian isle.
Roses are nothing to the maiden blush
  Sent o'er thy cheek's soft ivory, and night
  Has naught so dazzling in its world of light,
As the dark rays that from thy lashes gush.
  Love lurks amid thy silken curls, and lies
  Like a keen archer in thy kindling eyes.

THE LANGUAGE OF FLOWERS.

In Eastern lands they talk in flowers,
  And they tell in a garland their loves and cares:
Each blossom that blooms in their garden bowers,
  On its leaves a mystic language bears.

The rose is the sign of joy and love, —
  Young, blushing love in its earliest dawn;
And the mildness that suits the gentle dove
  From the myrtle's snowy flower is drawn.
Innocence shines in the lily's bell,
  Pure as a heart in its native heaven;
Fame's bright star, and glory's swell,
  By the glossy leaf of the bay are given.
The silent, soft, and humble heart
  In the violet's hidden sweetness breathes;
And the tender soul that cannot part,
  A twine of evergreen fondly wreathes.
The cypress, that darkly shades the grave,
  Is sorrow, that mourns her bitter lot;
And faith, that a thousand ills can brave,
  Speaks in thy blue leaves, forget-me-not.

Then gather a wreath from the garden bowers,
And tell the wish of thy heart in flowers.

EVERY day I muse upon thee:
Life and joy thou art to me.
If a faithful heart could win thee,
Soon my own love thou wouldst be.
Ah, how sweet to dwell with thee!

Swift my years would glide away;
All around would laugh with pleasure;
Rich would be the priceless treasure.
Art could find no words to say,
How my bounding thoughts would play.

Let me then be ever nigh thee.
Youth shall be our spring of love;
Mild as any mother dove,
Age shall sit in quiet by thee.
Never may misfortune try thee.

HOME.

MY place is in the quiet vale,
The chosen haunt of simple thought;
I seek not fortune's flattering gale,
I better love the peaceful lot.

I leave the world of noise and show,
To wander by my native brook;
I ask, in life's unruffled flow,
No treasure but my friend and book.

These better suit the tranquil home,
Where the clear water murmurs by;
And if I wish awhile to roam,
I have an ocean in the sky.

Fancy can charm and feeling bless
 With sweeter hours than fashion knows;
There is no calmer quietness,
 Than home around the bosom throws.

THE FLIGHT OF TIME.

Faintly flow, thou falling river,
 Like a dream that dies away;
Down to ocean gliding ever,
 Keep thy calm, unruffled way:
Time with such a silent motion
 Floats along on wings of air,
To eternity's dark ocean,
 Burying all its treasures there.

Roses bloom, and then they wither;
 Cheeks are bright, then fade and die;
Shapes of light are wafted hither, —
 Then, like visions, hurry by:
Quick as clouds at evening driven
 O'er the many-colored west,
Years are bearing us to heaven,
 Home of happiness and rest.

FADING FLOWERS.

Can the rose of summer fade,
 The bright and blooming rose?
Shall winter sweep the glade,
 Where its tender beauty blows?
There is perfume in the air,
 And it steals from the opening flower;
But the winds shall rudely tear
 The treasures of field and bower.

They fade,—how soon they fade,
  The flowers of earth and sky!
Was all that beauty made,
  To smile a moment and die?
O, will not the colors stay,
  That glow in the west at even,
And the hues of the rising day
  Be ever the charm of heaven?

O, let me not think the flowers
  Shall ever be borne away
From the full and loaded bowers,
  Where they welcome the early day.
I would not indulge one thought,
  That a rose or a cheek could wither;
But believe their colors, caught
  From heaven, shall be wafted thither.

MOONLIGHT IN A WOOD

Moonlight is gleaming,
Where the brook, streaming
Over the bright sands,
Winds through the woodlands;
Where the trees, bending
Lowly, are lending
Gloom to the clear flow,
Erst in a full glow
Under the broad light
Of the starred midnight.
But now it darkles,
Save a few sparkles,
Where some stray moonbeam
Falls in a pale stream,
Or a soft shower,
Through the high bower
Which the dark wood weaves
Close with its young leaves.

Then as I view them,
Light trembles through them;
While far above them,
(O, how I love them!)
See the stars twinkle,
Where the clouds crinkle,
And the bright moon sheds
Light on the hill-heads,
With such fair glances,
As when she dances
Where the calm ocean,
With a soft motion
  Hushing its roar,
Rolls its white breakers,
Those wide earth-shakers,
  Slow to the shore.

THE CONTRAST.

I SAW the fair one pass away,
In her earliest beauty's bright array,
In the glow of hope and the flush of pride,
And the innocent joy of a virgin bride,
When her heart, yet pure as the fallen snow,
Gave loose to its feelings' fullest flow,
And her cheek, as rich as the crimson flower
That opens in India's sunny bower,
Was hung with curls that danced and flew,
As the wind of the morning lightly blew,
And swelled the sail of the bark that bore
The bride from that loved and lovely shore.
O, thus in her maiden beauty gay
I saw that fair one pass away!

I saw that faded fair return
With heart as chill as a marble urn,
And cheek of as pale and wan a hue,

As a blossom wet by the poison dew,
That falls from the leaves of the funeral yew;
Her eye had lost its glancing fire,
Her cheek the glow of young desire,
And she gazed on the home of her tender years
With a look too cold for smiles or tears,
But a look that told how her peace had flown,
And how she was left in her grief alone.
Thus pale and still to the shore she drew,
As the wind of the morning lightly blew,
O, how unlike to the joyous day
When she passed in her beauty's pride away!

MY NATIVE LAND.

O, NOT the clear and sunny wave
  That rolls around the Ægean isles;
Nor all that ancient beauty gave
  Of fondest dallyings and smiles;
Nor all the spirit-stirring notes
  That come from high Apollo's shrine,
When the full hymn and song divine
  Round Delphi's golden temple floats; —
O, not the hills that bear the vine,
  And far their breathing odors throw;
Not the bright skies, whose evening twine
  Outvies, in tints, the breded bow;
Not all the luxury of shade
  Beneath the spreading chestnut-tree;
Not all the flowers that never fade,
  Rude land of storms! can equal thee.
In thee my infant being drew
  The first reviving breath of air;
My early years in gladness flew,
  Light as a dream of summer there:
Still round thy rocks my spirit clings, —
  It cannot tear itself away;

And if it had an eagle's wings,
  There it would ever hovering play;
For oh! there is no spot of earth
Dear as the land that gave us birth.

ODE.

JULY 4, 1826.

BRIGHT day! with thee the song
  Of Independence rose;
Then Freedom, bold and strong,
  Defied her mortal foes:
Armed into life and light she sprung,
  Like Pallas born of Jove;
At Britain's feet the gauntlet flung,
  And back her champion drove:
Young, and yet wise, she won her cause,
  And war's red banner furled;
Then fixed the reign of equal laws,
  And awed a wondering world.

Bright day! with thee our sires
  Proclaimed Columbia free:
Light with auspicious fires
  This holiest jubilee!
'Mid clouds of war thy sun arose,
  And danger met thy birth;
Now wide and full thy bounty flows,
  It warms and kindles earth:
The Andes redden in thy blaze;
  Their millions kneel to thee,—
They hail thee, earliest born of days,
  First dawn of Liberty.

Earth owns thy influence now:
  'T is not the few who dared

Refuse to bend and bow
  When Power's right arm was bared —
'T is not that sacred band who tore
  The charter and the chain,
Then on a nation's altar swore
  Their birthright to maintain —
Now hear a continent proclaim
  One vow, one prayer, to Heaven,
For every foreign lord in shame
  Back to his home is driven.

Then, be thy quickening light
  Still brighter as it rolls,
Till all on earth unite,
  One band of kindred souls;
For ever may thy altar burn
  With Freedom's holiest flame,
And ages after ages turn
  To venerate thy name.
O, never may our sons forget
  The men who dared be free,
And on its firm foundations set
  Thy temple, Liberty!

ODE.

CONCORD, APRIL 19, 1825.

When first from the land of the tyrant and slave
  Our forefathers ventured to cross the wide ocean,
They kneeled as they came from the perilous wave,
  And uttered their vows with an earnest devotion:
    Bright Spirit! in thee
    We will ever be free,
      While thy sun gives its light
    To the land and the sea,
  And here on the storm-beaten rock we unite
  To conquer or die for our God and our right.

Then deep in their bosoms they nourished the flame
  That burst from their hearts in the moment of danger,
When proudly the minion of tyranny came,
  Polluting their homes with the foot of the stranger.
    Then they flew to the fight,
    Where Liberty's light
      Called the bold-hearted yeoman
    To rise in his might,
  And the hard hand of labor undauntedly gave
  The welcome of death to the murdering slave.

Here first in the red field of battle they stood,
  And fearlessly gathered the harvest of glory;
Here they first stamped the seal of their union in blood,
  And imprinted their names on the records of story:
    Here proudly again
    We meet on the plain
      Where England first tried
    To enslave us in vain,
  And, firm in their purpose, our fathers unfurled
  Bright Liberty's flag to a wondering world.

Here, flushed with the high hopes of Freedom, we join
  In an act of the purest and deepest devotion.
O, long may our children be drawn to this shrine,
  By an instinct as sure as the tides of the ocean;
    May they never forget
    How their forefathers met,
      And planted the green tree
    That flourishes yet,
  But, warm with the spirit of Liberty, raise
  To the brave hearts who saved us, one chorus of praise.

WASHINGTON'S NAME.

At the heart of our country the tyrant was leaping,
To dye there the point of his dagger in gore,
When Washington sprang from the watch he was keeping,
And drove back that tyrant in shame from our shore:
The cloud that hung o'er us then parted and rolled
Its wreaths far away, deeply tinctured with flame;
And high on its fold
Was a legend that told
The brightness that circled our Washington's name.

Long years have rolled on, and the sun still has brightened
Our mountains and fields with its ruddiest glow;
And the bolt that he wielded so proudly, has lightened,
With a flash as intense, in the face of the foe:
On the land and the sea, the wide banner has rolled
O'er many a chief, on his passage to fame;
And still on its fold
Shine in letters of gold
The glory and worth of our Washington's name.

And so it shall be, while eternity tarries,
And pauses to tread in the footsteps of time;
The bird of the tempest, whose quick pinion carries
Our arrows of vengeance, shall hover sublime:
Wherever that flag on the wind shall be rolled,
All hearts shall be kindled with anger and shame,
If e'er they are told
They are careless and cold,
In the glory that circles our Washington's name.

LIBERTY.

A VOICE is on our hills,
  And it echoes far at sea:
With a quickening power it fills
Every heart, and inly thrills, —
  'T is the voice of Liberty.

A glance darts from yon cloud,
  And it frights thee, tyrant, — thee;
But the freeman rises proud,
And his sire stirs in his shroud, —
  'T is the glance of Liberty.

A warning calls at night:
  "Nations, rouse ye, and be free."
They hear it with delight,
But the monarch looks affright, —
  'T is thy warning, Liberty.

There 's a presence in the air,
  Which we feel, but cannot see;
Every bosom gladdens there,
High to hope, and strong to dare, —
  'T is thy presence, Liberty.

The God our hearts adore,
  Builds his throne on land and sea;
He is in the tempest's roar,
Or when ocean laps the shore, —
  That God is Liberty.

THE GREEK SONG OF VICTORY.

THE red day of slaughter is done;
The rose tint is pale in the west;
The triumph of liberty won,
Joy swells each Athenian breast:
We have buried our foes in the wave
That rolls on our iron-bound shore;
And the foot of the Ottoman slave
Shall dare scale our ramparts no more:
They came in their pride and their pomp to the fight,
But have scattered like dust, in the rush of our might.

They came with the dawning of day;
The sun brightly glanced on their sails,
And their fleet, on its conquering way,
Bore forward with favoring gales:
Like a dark cloud of tempest they came;
Already they uttered their yell, —
When we let loose our arrows of flame,
And the pride of the Mussulman fell:
Then the waves with the fire and the slaughter were red,
And our prows hurried on through the dying and dead.

They are gone, — and the sea rolls again
In peace on our iron-bound shore;
They have left but the wreck and the stain,
Where the green waves heaved purple with gore:
As the last light grows dim in the west,
O God of the brave and the free!
How the fulness that swells in each breast
Is poured forth in blessings to thee!
For we trusted in thee, — and the arm of thy might
Has scattered our foes in the perilous fight.

BIRTHDAY OF LINNÆUS.

In a temple built by God,
The bright and boundless heaven, —
Its pavement the green sod,
With the woods to wave around,
In a harmony of sound,
To his favorites only given, —
Only given to those ears
Who can catch the chiming spheres, —
Only given to those hearts
Who can feel him in the flowers,
Who with high and holy arts
Know to steal away the hours
From the blank of vulgar men, —
We are spirits only then,
And with voices pure and free
Only then can worship thee, —
Then can only at thy throne,
Thou unseen, invisible One!
At thy throne of earth and air,
In the common gladness share
Of a universe that smiles
Underneath thy quickening ray,
As we see at noon of day,
Through wide groups of palmy isles.
The ocean dance its way.

In that temple, wide as earth,
And unlimited as air,
May the mind who called to birth
A creation none may dare
With a reckless hand profane, —
May he look from out his heaven,
And with smiles, like early rain
Falling on the joyous flowers,
Be among us through these hours,

When we meet to weave a crown
For his sacerdotal brow.
Not to this our spirits bow:
A better light came down
With thy teaching, — thou didst ever
Lead us upward to the Giver.
Like the white-robed priest of old,
In a mantle pure as light,
Thou didst lead us on through night
Into nature's deepest fold,
Till we caught the fire divine
Beaming from the inmost shrine, —
Caught the radiance of that sun,
Where the spirit dwells alone.

'T is a pure and holy rite,
One that loves the blessed light.
With a sacrifice of bloom,
Rich in colors and perfume,
Let the altar now be graced;
And that living breath shall rise
Unburnt incense to the skies.
Be our hearts as free from stain,
Thou, invisible One, shalt smile
Kindly on our rites, the while.
With our dear ones at our side,
We are gathered here again,
In thy fairest month of May,
Our grateful debt to pay
To thy servant, and our guide.

HOPE OF FAME.

To live beyond the grave, — to leave a name,
That, like a living sun, shall hold its way
Undimmed through ages, — to be hailed hereafter
As first among the spirits who have gifted

Their land with fame, — to dwell amid the thoughts
Of all sublimer souls, as deities
Are treasured in their shrines, — to load the tongues
Of nations, and be uttered in the songs
And prayers of millions; — he who bears such hope
Fixed in his heart, and holds his lonely way
Cheered by this only, and yet keeps himself
Unwavering in the many shocks that push
His purpose from its path, — he was not cast
In nature's common mould. Such hope itself
Is greatness.

THE VOICE OF LOVE.

"E 'l parlar di dolcezza e di salute." — PETRARCA.

THERE is a voice, and there is only one,
Thrilling my bosom, as if tuned on high
Amid the spheres revolving round the sky,
Whose roll is tempered to the sweetest tone,
Whose blended harmonies are heard at night,
Now falling distant, now ascending nigh,
And with the saffron burst of dawning light
Peal like the long, loud clarion-swell of fight,
When columns in the deadly charge rush by.
As sweet, but fainter, of as a clear a note,
Yet softened into calmness, is that sound
Whose tones in recollection round me float,
Seeming to steal from some enchanted ground,
Giving the present to oblivion, throwing
Lightly around, in all its beauty glowing,
The pictured veil that gave my early days
A coming Eden, whose serene delight
Shone with a pageant more intensely bright
Than all the ever-changing pomp that plays
On Iris, when she waves her wings in flight.
So bright the tints, when first the vision shone,
Rolling its lofty arch o'er all below,

From peak to mountain-peak in glory thrown,
Resting its pillars on their icy zone,
Where myriad streams of liquid amber flow,
When the low sun, emerging from the storm,
Hangs broad and fiery on the gilded wave,
That prouder swells around the godlike form,
Who sinks, a conqueror, setting in his grave.
Such were the dazzling tints, when first they threw
Enchantment on the yet uncheated eye,
Feeding upon the beautiful and new
With all the keen delight of ecstasy;
But such they were not ever; — as the bow
Grows fainter when the setting sun retires,
And clouds and peaks no longer, in his fires,
Lift round the burning west their magic show,
Wherein the waving summit, crowned with gold,
Seems like a flash suspended on its path,
And festooned light around the tempest rolled,
The smile of beauty on the brow of wrath, —
These fade away when night assumes her reign,
Or only sicken in her paler beams,
That mark with silver lines the hill and plain,
Along the still meandering of streams; —
So life, when novelty has gone, and youth
Flitted on silent wings of down away,
When now the clear and steady torch of truth
Shows it, a moment's pride, a long decay, —
So life grows pale and cold, and chillness creeps
Through the crushed heart, elate and full before;
So glory on his broken falchion sleeps,
Nor love can fire, nor beauty madden more.
O, in that night of feeling, still one tone
Comes through the silent watches low and sweet,
And hours of happiness for ever flown
Are thronging round, and youthful pulses beat;
A fountain of deep love the heart uncloses,
And all its purest tides are flowing o'er,
And memory, from the cell where she reposes,
Brings out her fairest and her choicest store.

Fancied or real, still that voice is flinging
Its sweetness on the desert winds, and all
The seraph choirs of heaven are round me singing,
So loud and clear the tones; and now they fall,
And as they die in languishment away,
Stealing to some far-distant world above,
Methinks I hear a well-known accent say,
" Follow me, — 't is the voice of her you love."

'Ο ΚΟΣΜΟΣ.

"Omnia mutantur, nihil interit." — Ovid.

The world is thrown around us as a veil,
To dim the searching of the spirit's eye
Through all the fair variety that lies,
In undiscovered majesty, beyond
The canopy of light and beauty, rolled,
In pure and awful distance, o'er the throne
On which the Universal Being dwells
Alone amid his wonders. Time goes on
In its eternal orbit, and compels,
As with a boundless torrent, all that move
Nearer its consummation. All things change;
As in the tranquil mirror of a lake,
When Day has closed his portals, and his light,
Softly retiring, throws upon the cloud
Its fairest glances, and in pictured pomp
Unrolls a magic curtain round his seat
Of glory on the mountain-tops, and bends
An iris arch above him; — as that cloud
Sailing before the ministers who bear
The message of the Mighty One abroad
O'er continent and ocean, with a voice
Now melting in a whisper, and now loud
As waves that meet around a mid-sea crag,
And lash it in their fury, — as that cloud

Floats o'er the clear, deep water, till the sky,
That swells within its bosom, seems on fire
With quickly-coming flashes of bright hues
Born of the beam of ether, and unstained
With aught of earthly tincture, — all below
In the calm depths of purity, flit by
Like doves along the north-wind, when they seek
The softness and the sweetness, and the light
And warmth of spring unfading, on the shores
Where ever bloom the orange and the lime,
And fruits are ever hanging wreathed in flowers,
And glancing out intensely from the dark,
Full-tufted verdure, whose unwasting shade
Hath ever spread abroad a sacred gloom
Above the temple of the sylvan powers.

So all things change, and yet are all the same:
And He, whose eye looks forth, and measures all,
As we behold the full moon, when she hangs
Mantled in palest tenderness, and weeps
Tears on the sleeping landscape, till the hills
And plains and meadows catch her tender light,
And softly send it on the musing eye
In infinite reflections, — when we dream
Of oceans rolling on her spotted orb,
And islands crowned in beauty, and of fires
Lit on her volcan summits, till we trace,
On a bright map, a world for spirits, where
Live the light forms that fancy oft at night
Sees floating on the moonbeams, or at sail
High on the fleecy vapor, as it rolls
Its foam above the mountains, — whence they come,
As angels came on messages of peace,
To whisper consolation, or convey
The wishes of a pure and humble heart
Unto the Universal ear, where all
May speak, and feel a kind reply descend
In words of gentleness, as evening dews
Melt on the silent landscape, and it smiles: —

So the All-seeing eye, whose viewless seat
Is shrouded in infinitude, beyond
The flaming walls that gird creation in, —
So the All-seeing eye looks forth, and blends
The world of suns and satellites, that sweep
O'er the broad path of ages, in one orb
Hung in the centre of immensity,
And from the solemn void, wherein he dwells,
Contemplates all existence, as a point
Twinkling amid the glory that enshrouds
His throne, as with a mantle of dim shade,
And from the eye of sense conceals the flame
From whose exhaustless fount all being rose.

SONNETS.

I.

Is it not true, as one has proudly sung,
  " A Poet's love is Immortality ? "
Many a time and oft that note has rung
  Echoings of high and heavenly harmony.
Sweet, when the weary day is done, to be
  Greeted by budding lips and kindling eyes,
Pressed to the one true heart in ecstasy, —
  Enchantment only worthy of the skies.
Repose my heart has sought, and all in vain;
  Care, like a demon, hunts me everywhere;
  In vain this faded brow a wreath may wear,—
Vain laurels, colder than the captive's chain:
  A look, a word of fondness, kindly given,
  Love-lit and tender, to that fame were heaven.

II.

O THOU sole-sitting Spirit of Loneliness!
Whose haunt is by the wild and dropping caves,

Thou of the musing eye and scattered tress,
I meet thee with a passionate joy, no less
Than when the mariner, from off his waves,
Catches the glimpses of a far blue shore, —
He thinks the danger of his voyage o'er,
And, pressing all his canvas, steers to land,
With a glad bosom and a ready hand.
So I would hie me to thy desolate shade,
And seat myself in some deep-sheltered nook,
And never breathe a wish again to look
On the tossed world, but rather, listless laid,
Pore on the bubbles of the passing brook.

APPENDIX.

I.

The following Essay was published in the first number of "Clio," in 1822.

[I have here attempted to sketch a picture of the feelings and musings of an imaginative mind. I have adopted a peculiar style, because it seemed to coincide with the nature of the subject, and my own feelings when I wrote it. Writers are allowed to adopt different styles and measures in poetry, — why not different dictions in prose?]

"Ego, apis Matinæ
More modoque."

THAT the minds, the tempers, and the intellectual and moral powers of individuals are as different as their forms, their features, their health, and their vigor, is a truth as evident to me as any truth which does not admit of absolute demonstration. Some men are endowed by nature with great vigor of mind and body, capable of long-continued and gigantic efforts; but moving in all their operations slowly, though surely. These men often show a degree of obtuseness in childhood, which leads the less sagacious to augur nothing good of their maturer years; but strength, exactness, and perseverance become to them the certain means of high and permanent advancement; and although they never can pour around them the lightnings and terrors of genius, yet they render the whole circle of their life one day of warm, bright sunshine. Others, endowed with that fearful and mysterious gift of genius, which the world has so often worshipped for its resistless manifestations, and neglected for its repulsive irregularities; high-toned, irritable, feeling every sense of pleasure and pain with the poignancy of agony or rapture; moving with the rapidity, the eccentricity, and the ominous glare of a comet; never moderate in their desires and endeavors; now springing with the collected energy of an eagle to some high and unattainable glory, and then sinking down exhausted, and brooding, in all the bitterness of despair, over the wrecks of their celestial longings; now giving their intellectual powers, with a lavishing madness, to the instant comprehension of truths which should have required a long and calm investigation, and then exclaiming, in weary listlessness, against the folly and nothingness of every exertion to be wise or great or good; — these men, who, in their stronger and darker deeds, put forth the intellectual might of Milton's Satan, and who, could their efforts be justly directed, would always move on, like the sun in his unclouded summer glories, diffusing life and warmth to all around them, — these men, after an agitated life, in which health and honor, and peace and friendship, have been sacrificed to sudden and impetuous feelings, after every suffering of body and torture of mind have been endured, go down, neglected and unlamented, to an early grave, and leave the world astonished that one being could unite in himself energies which command even awe and admiration, and weaknesses which fill us with pity and contempt.

And that such men should be neglected by the soberer part of the world is nothing wonderful. Men do not like to be dazzled. They can enjoy a warm, soft sunshine, and feel emotions of thankfulness to the dispenser of so comfortable a sensation; but they close their eyes against a brilliancy too strong for their feeble organs, and feel only pain, where intellects keener and more exalted gaze with pleasure. Besides, the mass of the world go through life in search of comfort and present enjoyment; or they spend all their efforts in hedging in themselves and their families with a circumvallation of earthly treasures, and then look out from the loopholes of their strong castles in proud defiance on the crowd who wander unsheltered around them. The far-off blessings, which the etherealized imagination is always dreaming of, and never reaches, have no community with their more fleshly spirits, and they either profess to look with contempt on these insane reveries, or they pour upon them the anathemas of a moody religion, which would cramp the expandings and aspirings of our higher nature within the allowed hopes and prospects of a bigot's creed.

There is a fountain of thought and feeling in those chosen spirits, which is ever springing up fresh and full, and pouring over the richness of its treasures on all things around it, giving them hues which they have not in themselves, and covering them with a luxuriance which another and a colder heart would not find around them, and making of the barrenest spot an Eden, and of the driest desert a land of brooks and watercourses.

They have within them, too, a creative energy, which culls from the stores of memory the choicest and the fairest, and forms them into landscapes of surpassing loveliness, a rich and harmonizing union of mountain and valley, where the sunlit rock lifts its bald forehead from the deep gloom of forests, and the leaves are moving in the wind, and twinkling in the sunbeams; where the full light of heaven descends and rests on the waving meadow, and the brook steals along from rapid to pool, and from overbowering shade to open sunshine; where the living things of earth are asleep in their midday slumber, and nothing is heard but the solitary whistle of the Phebe in the dank hollow, and the chirp of the locust on the oak-top; where the heart goes away to the blue sky, and the white clouds that sleep around it, to meet the spirits of departed pleasures; where it finds its loved ones in their earliest beauty, and lives over the hallowed moments of condensed beatitude, and forgets for a while it is still dwelling on earth, and thinks it has taken a last leave of its grosser encumbrances, and is now a pure and winged spirit in the bright and boundless sea of immortality.

And if ever there are moments which one would wish to live over again, — which leave no stain upon the spirit, and no wounds to fester in the bosom, and are to us as gay islands in the cold and stormy ocean we are sailing over, — it is when the pure nature within us has thrown off the shackles of chilling want and besetting appetite, and has entered into communion with its better feelings and holier aspirations; when it has forgotten itself in its minglings with kindred spirits, and has found absorbing ecstasies in the communication of mutual blessings; when it has given to another and a dear one a new pleasure of taste or tenderness, and has taken back in return the kind look and the delighted accent; when it has felt, as the blended feelings partook deeper and deeper of the same enjoyment, a linking together of two existences, till every thought and glance and motion seemed in unison, and one could not be joyous and the other unhappy, and the tear could not rise on one eyelid and the other's heart not overflow in sympathetic sorrow.

And who would wish to rob the feeling mind of his ideal happiness, and call down his imagination, now revelling in bowers of Eden, and rejoicing with angels and blessed spirits in the undiscovered mansions of a long-wished-for hereafter, — where he has pictured his companions in all the perfectness of form, and charm of feature, that ever poet conceived, or painter embodied, and has taken the flowers and the birds, when the sweetest and the fairest, and the thinking and feeling beings of his paradise, when youngest and gayest, in the glad season of life's spring, when taste is nature, and sensibility the untaught movings of a stainless bosom, — where he has made them sleepless in delight, and ever active in enjoyment, looking on all around them with the keen glance of novelty, catching at once the fitness of groupings, and the harmony of motion and expression with the thoughts within them, and never knowing what it is to have the dull call of unfeeling command breaking in upon their lovely musings, and marring the beauty of a high-wrought fancy-piece with the heavy obtrusion of some homely and spiritless labor?

These minds of fine and ethereal texture are indeed not made for the inevitable toils and crosses of a life like this. They are always connected with a constitution so delicate, and so sensible to every touch, that the slightest breeze of misfortune ruffles them, and a neglect at which heartier spirits would laugh, in their reckless independence, weighs upon them, and bows them, till the air around them is unmingled blackness, and the sickened ear is shocked with the liveliest music, and the heart is ready, in its bitterness, to say, that all on earth that is sweet and fair is a mockery, and existence but an ugly dream.

And if they attempt to throw off the gloom that weighs so heavily upon them, and to mingle in the press and jostle of a busy world, they find their souls grow dead and senseless, unmoved by the fine touch of beauty, and unmelted by the tender; then they grow disgusted with their coarseness, and think they have put away the charm of their better nature, and are ashamed that they can stoop to grosser indulgences, and waste their hours in rude and heartless merriment, that they can look upon another's suffering with dull emotion, and be contented, like the many, to gather wherever a harvest is offered, and ask not whether their own luxuries be purchased by the sparing of a fellow-creature, or even wrenched from the helpless hand that felt in losing them as if its life was plundered, and the fruit of long and patient toiling torn away to gladden the heart of a greedy tyrant.

And when he muses on this, and embraces, in the grasp of his benevolence, the whole world of feeling, and sees how much of evil is endured, and how inevitably it must be suffered, and that if he be set apart in a purer region, it is only at the expense of another's toil and privation, he then begins to feel that there is even a sin in his purer musings; and if he return from the noise of the city to the lonely wood and the secret valley, to hold communion with his own better thoughts, to recall his former intercourse with ancient worthies, and to renew high society with the master spirits who live in their recorded outpourings, he feels that he is taking from the accumulated stores of beings who might equally relish these high enjoyments, but who, to give him a quiet and a shelter, toil on through the weary day of life, bringing down their souls from their native quarry, and mixing them with grosser things, till the fine spirit is evaporated, and nothing but bitter dregs is left to be drank in the hopeless years of age and exhaustion.

Then a new feeling rises within him, and he wishes to betake himself to the solitary desert, or to live on an island in the lonely ocean, there to be fed by the toil of his own hands and the bounties of nature; and as he had before fled from the society of living men, because all could not be equal, so he would now abandon his books, because they take from him the power of independence, and steal from him that time which should be spent in more gainful labors, and that strength which should supply his own physical necessities; and he would then wish to divest himself of every thought he had borrowed from others, to return to the simple ignorance of childhood, and be the pupil of none but nature, and, while his hand ministered to his unavoidable wants, wander with his eye over the glories before him, and find his only revelation in the bright sky, and the green hills, and the blue billows, his only worship in the spontaneous adoration of a pure spirit, when it drinks in the simple loveliness of nature, his only temple the wide arch that bends over him, with its mountain pillars, its starry lamps, and its floor of earth and ocean, and his only music the outbreakings of joy in the notes of wild-birds, and the vernal cry of reptiles, the rush of winds through the forests, and the far-off roaring of uplifted waters; till his mind should return to its pristine health and delicacy, be alive to every tender emotion, and sensible to every moral blemish, and shrink from contamination, as from a deadly and destroying venom; till he should at last see, that if man would equably employ his various faculties, and keep the golden rule of moderation in all things, would never pervert the untaught feelings of nature, nor yield to the impulse of sense or selfishness, would be satisfied to be like his fellows, and believe the grandest rank is that of unblemished virtue, that he need not go away to imagined islands, or snow-clad mountains, or mansions beyond this sublunary world, for the Eden of his heart, and the heaven of his fancy.

Then, in the overpowering wish for the perfection he can picture, the wild longing for the freedom he aspires to, and the hope that these high aspirations are not all a chimera, he wanders forth amid the rudest and the grandest forms of nature, and feels his spirit harmonizing with their gloom and vastness; he looks abroad from the mountain peak, and rejoices that he is so far away from the dim abodes of wretchedness, and so far above the smoke of cities; he gladdens in the sun, as it rolls more brightly over him, and is braced and exhilarated by the pure wind that rushes around him; and he envies the eagle his wings, and thinks, if he could mount on as strong a pinion, he would not wheel around those rocks, and prowl on the farms below them, but would stretch away to some fairy island, at a returnless distance, and be happy in the company of ministering spirits and pure intelligences.

Then his mind takes a new energy, and his soul feels quickened to a new creation; there comes down to him a fire from the celestial altar, and he is rapt and beatified; his thoughts rush along like a mighty river, the well-spring of memory is broken up, and the images that he has been storing in years of solitary study come forth, and roll around him in all the wildness and magnificence of a stirred-up ocean; then he hurries over the sky, and sees it peopled with bright worlds passing away into the measureless distance of space, and he follows them in all their orbits, counts their number, and marshals the hosts of heaven; then he gazes on the clouds, as they gather around the high peaks, and sweep away over the valleys, and he traces their forms in all their folds and volumes, he sees them armed with lightnings, he hears the thunder bursting on the mountains, and listens with delight to the countless echoes that answer from rock and valley; and at once his fancy has crossed the wide sea, and is now among the islands of perpetual summer, and the night is still and bright around him, the black sky withdraws to a vaster distance, and all its lights are keen in brightness, and seem to hang as lamps from the ebon arch above them, the air is silent, the winds are in their caverns, the leaf hangs still in the forest, and the whole world seems at rest and quiet; then the mirrored sea begins to rise without a wind, and to roar far away with an awful warning, and a little cloud rises on the skirts of heaven, and moves, like a bird, over the waters, it spreads and spreads more wildly, till it sweeps the whole width of heaven, and it comes on, like the rapid march of a destroying army, with the rush of winds, the roar of thunders, and the bursting of billows; then the sea is tossed in mountains, the foam curls over its wild waves, and streams on the tempest, the dashing waters rush on the land with devouring fury, the broad lightnings launch from volume to volume of the black tornado, the earth is dark as death, and then brighter than tenfold noonday, the winds sweep the land in columned fierceness, and forests bow, rocks are shivered, and houses fall in ruins, the rain pours in a sheet of waters, and man shrinks to the earth, and feels himself a cipher amid the madness of the elements.

Then his eye catches a glimpse of the distant river, as it lies in the gilding of noonlight; and his fancy is like a fleet bird hovering around all the shores of classic and tropic loveliness; and he is now flitting up the valley of lovely Arno, and the bright spires, the lofty towers, and stately palaces of Florence are rising over the groves of elms and poplars, the meadows are full of blossoms, every shade is living with music, and every bower is loud with mirth and dancing, the plains are yellow with the loaded harvest, the hill-sides are hung with blue vineyards, and beyond them the snow of the Apennine rests on a sky of the softest and purest azure, the sun walks over this Eden in cloudless splendor, the earth and the heavens are beautifully magnificent, and he dreams not that vice and poverty and slavery are festering and crouching on a soil which should only be fruitful in virtue and glory.

And then he is away among the Paphian islands of the peaceful ocean; and he is sitting beneath the umbel of a palm-tree, watching the dancing of its long, spear-like leaves, and the waving of its nodding clusters, in the sea-breeze that plays around them; and the painted birds, in their gala of gold and crimson, come and go, wheel around, and settle on the branches, and they sip the liquid honey that drops from the opening blossoms, and snap the insects that revel in the sweets and glance in the sunbeams, and the air is full of their busy voices; again they rise in a cloud, and are floating off to a richer plunder, their wings glitter and glow in the clear light that rolls around them, and they seem like a curtain of gems, or the flow of a silken banner, their shrill music dies away on the wind, and the air is hushed in voluptuous stillness; then the green thrush comes from her bushy solitude, and sits on the palm-top, she sings her low, sweet song, and he thinks it is a flute, or a woman's voice complaining at a distance; then he is awhile at home, and the plaintive air of his native village is breathing around him, his heart swells, and the tears flow unbidden, he feels the pang of sorrow cramp his bosom, his soul is melted, and his whole spirit flows away like water. Then he looks out on the ocean, and sees its white waves breaking on the coral reef, and boiling over on the still lagoon, and the feathered flakes float away on the ripples, that come lessening and whispering to the shore; the light gulls hang in flocks over the water, they dip their bills, and carry off their prey in triumph, and their screaming rises along the coast like the confused shouting of an army; the tall crane stalks with measured step along the sand, and utters his voice like the deep bray of a trumpet; the flamingo stands, like a form of fire, on the wave-lashed rock, and the light glances richly over his scarlet plumage; and the white tropic-bird skims over the high green billow on his long black wings, or hangs, poised like a flitting cloud, far aloft in the horizon. Then he sees a fleet of canoes coming around a distant promontory, paddling over the smooth bay, and tossing the water around them, like wild-fowl in their gambols; the broad, matted sails swell out in the cool wind, that comes off from the ocean, and is flying to the hills and the woods, as if to rest in their dark recesses; they throw their long shadows before them, and the water is darkened around the prows, like a lake when a cloud flies over it; they come moving their oars to the sound of simple flutes and untaught voices; they touch the land, and then come forth with song and dancing, and march away to the woods in graceful order; their glossy mantles flow around their shoulders, their arms shine with rings of pearl, their heads are crowned with blue and scarlet feathers, and necklaces of the brightest and sweetest flowers are festooned around them, and spicy blossoms of snowy whiteness spangle their long, black locks; they walk erect in the dignity of nature, or dance to the sound of melodious music, and their cheeks of olive softness glow with the flush of health and motion, like the clear red that shines through the brown rind of the pomegranate. Then he follows them through the woods to a sacred enclosure, in the solitude of a retired valley, where the wooded hills are rising in an evergreen circle, and the palm waves in the wind, the bamboo nods on the rock, and the wild vines creep over the trees, and weave their arches of broad leaves and purple blossoms, where the cocoa, with its wide crown and columned trunk, and the bread-tree, with its fingered leaves and clustered cones, stand in ordered lines around them, and plantains, in their tufted bloom and fruitage, and reeds and canes, with their pointed blades and silken tassels, fence in the still retreat, and close it from the sight and entrance of profaner mortals. And there they move in circling choirs to a low and solemn measure, and their song is like the moaning of bereaved matrons, blended at times with the shriek of terror; and the priests come forth from their dark recess in a dress of fantastic wildness, they mutter over their fearful incantations, the music ceases, and the dancers are still and breathless; then a woman of a hostile nation is brought forward, she clasps an infant to her breast with the gripe of desperate fondness, they tear away the frighted babe from her clinging arms, and with a look of wild entreaty she sees it borne to a pile of fuel, and its little limbs bound in sacrifice; then her sight grows dark, and she falls with a faint shriek in a dead insensibility; and they consecrate the innocent to the demon of slaughter, to wait till the battle turn against them, and then to be slain and burned to the rattling of drums and the shouts of infuriate dancers. Then the warriors throw away their flowing robes, and rush forth in naked wildness, brandishing their clubs, and clashing their spears, and their shouts and their yells ring through the forest, like the outbreaking of a host of demons; their limbs writhe in the violence of their contortions, their eyes flash, and their features look unutterable fury; they hurl at once their arms toward the land of their foemen, and denounce against them insatiate vengeance; then they spring forward to the shore, and their war-canoes move swiftly over the waves, in ordered file and measured motion, and the oars chime to the song of battle; and midway on the sea the fleet of the enemy is advancing against them, and the waves foam before their hurried prows, and seem alive with their swarming numbers; then the fleets approach, a yell is heard, and the boats are mingled; and there is a rattling of arms, and a confused cry of wrath and agony; and in the heat of the battle, a tall sail and a white flag is seen moving to part them, it comes forward in the press of its canvas, and leaps over the waves with the pride and swiftness of a race-horse, it draws nigh, and passes between the contending furies, the canoes part, and shrink back in terror, the tumult is hushed, and a deathlike calm broods over the waters; then the ship comes to land, its sails are furled, its anchor moored, and the boat drops from its tackling, and heralds of peace, in white robes, with hymning voices, descend and glide slowly to the shore; then they move in majesty to the sound of sacred music, and the savage shrinks from before them, his voice is mute, his eye sunk, and his rage conquered; and they go to the Morai, and stop the rites of cruelty; the mother's heart gladdens, as they give back her infant, and the little innocent clings to her bosom, and twines its fingers in her scattered locks; and they proclaim aloud that war shall have an end, they cast down the bloody spear of battle, and raise aloft the white flag of redemption, and its wide folds play in the sweet winds, and glance in the sunbeams, like a banner of light in the land of the blessed.

Then he sees the sun rising over the mistress of nations, where she sits on her hills, in her mural crown, like the Berecynthian goddess on the summit of Ida; and he stands beneath the Doric dome of her protecting deity, and a pale and solemn light streams through the alabaster windows, and gives a faint hue to the fluted pillars, but leaves the niches in darkness, and, as it glances along the walls, tinges with a yellow ray the trophies of war, and the votive offerings of heroes, the Punic beaks, the Grecian palms, and the Gallic helmets; and half reveals, in the dim recess, the statue of her own peculiar Jove, whose right hand grasps the thunder, and whose left sustains a column, on which is inscribed, in brazen letters, "ROMA." And there he sees, arranged in silent order, the fathers of the republic, sitting on their curule chairs and benches, with staid and graceful dignity, in their long white robes and purple badges; and at their head, on a higher seat, the keen and sleepless consul, with his eye full of deep thought, and his thin and spiritual features alive with the workings of his mighty bosom; then a deathlike stillness pervades the high assembly, and there enters a tall, bony man, with a fierce and haggard look, and a hurried motion, and as he advances to take his seat, the senators retire before him, and shrink to the other side of the temple, as from the breath of a poisonous reptile; and at once the orator and the magistrate, reading him with the keen glance of indignation, rises from his curule chair, lifts his hand with commanding gesture, spreads the folds of his flowing toga, and bursts out in a voice of kindled wrath and insulted dignity; and as he pours forth his honest rage in unsparing and ceaseless invective, and launches around him the arrows of impassioned eloquence, the corrupted and corrupting worm writhes beneath his torture, and looks around for escape, but dares not fly from the fascination of that stern glance, which probes the deepest folds of his bosom: then, as the orator draws out, one by one, his foul purposes, and bares them to the light in their fullest blackness, and turns to the solemn statue in the act of invoking vengeance, he cowers to the earth, like a wretch when a storm has passed over him.

Such are his solitary musings, and so he could dream on for ever, taking in with delighted sense the sights and sounds that are moving and speaking around him, and linking them with all the stores of his memory, and all the creations of his fancy. But the sun is going down behind the mountains, and withdrawing the light that warmed and inspired him, and he turns a lingering eye, as the bright orb dips behind the far peak, and the yellow light streams up its last flash, and gives its last gilding to the rocks and forests; and he looks long and fondly on the amber circle that crowns the place of setting, and the gay clouds that burn in the clear flame of evening; then he sees a deep red stain hang around the western ridges, and it fades into a cold violet, and grows fainter and fainter, till the general blue closes over the darkened summits; then the stars come out on their night-watch, and the sky looks black and comfortless around them; the north-wind begins to whistle among the pines and stinted cedars, and his blood grows chill, his heart sinks, and the bright visions of his soul are darkened; then he hears the increasing call of hunger, his spirit becomes lifeless and barren, and opens to all the cold realities of life, and he would fain descend to the homeliest cot and the rudest shelter, and sit down by the fire of the coarsest woodman, to receive his cynic welcome, and partake of his hard fare, and his boisterous hospitality; and then he sees, that the finest and richest minds must at once bid adieu to life and all its pleasures, or be content to share in its toils, and buffet its billows.

II.

EXTRACT FROM THE PREFACE

WHICH ACCOMPANIED THE SECOND NUMBER OF "CLIO."

I LOOK upon Poetry as an art, whose charm lies in the exhibition of vivid imagery, new, varied, beautiful, and sublime; and in appeals to the simple affections of the heart. The poet, if we follow the etymology of the word, is a creator; one who fashions from the stores of his memory images of which earth furnishes no reality, and who combines them into groups which have an existence only in the imaginary world he has charmed into being. He gives to his conceptions a visible form of beauty or of power, and animates them with a fire from heaven, beaming forth in their eyes and features, like the sweet flow of light from a lamp in a vase of alabaster; or flashing abroad, in the kindlings of emotion, like the fount from which it was stolen. He takes you to the retirement of sensibility, and recalls to you all its nice and tender touches of character, and plays upon the springs which call forth those feelings of happy sorrow, which move us in our sympathies with others, which are always delightful, because they seem to us holy, and are always welcomed as the surest evidence that nature is concealed within us. Every tear that is shed then is to us a treasure; for it flows from a fountain in which we imagine angels might wash and be purer. Even when hé becomes the hierophant of nature, and leads us to contemplate the great principles of our being, when he is simply didactic, and his great object is the display of philosophic truth, he does not depart from his peculiar character. Every principle becomes with him a personification, and the great doctrines of science pass before him as so many beings endowed with life and majesty and beauty.

Nature is the charm of poetry, and not art. We ask for something in it which can stir and elevate, or melt and soothe us. The feeling of delight, when we meet with one of those effusions which genius sent forth, when the living spirit overshadowed it, when fancy put on its best attire, and the heart was tuned to its sweetest harmony, — this feeling, which defies the power of language to describe it, which is indeed a holy and inspired delirium, is the only test of true excellence in poetry. And it is this which invests poetry with its sacred character; for it is the feeling of infancy and childhood, — of those years on which we look as a dear, delightful dream, whose sunny spots we select as the very paradise of our being, which become the favorite contemplation of the mind that has seen all its early illusions vanish, and finds nothing but bare reality around it, and which it is ever sending forward to form the fairest and loveliest adornments of the unchanging abode to which it is advancing.

It is well to combine the perfections of art with the enchantments of nature; but I still think poetic beauty is loveliest when least adorned. You may study all the laws of versification, and all the rules of metaphor; you may write in lines of surpassing melody, and figures so exact that the nicest microscope of criticism could not find in them a flaw; yet without "the thoughts that breathe, and the words that burn," they are like those pieces of music which flow through the ear and leave no impression behind them, which are remembered only for a moment, as sounds that were soft and pleasant, but touched no chord in the bosom; while the poetry of nature, be it but a single conception, finds at once its home in the heart, is cherished there with a passionate devotion, and needs only the faintest tone of its music to awaken it in all the charms of its earliest loveliness. I do not mean to say anything against Pope and Campbell. But surely the sweetness of their versification, and the nice polish of their language, cannot be considered as giving them the high rank they hold in English poetry. They have taken their proud station there because they held a pen which could give life and vividness to their images, and call up at once their creations in all the distinctness of reality. Therefore it is that the dress they have so carefully wrought is so attractive, for it is the investment of an unaffected and living beauty. Whenever they depart from this, and Pope repeatedly does, all their melody and correctness do not conceal the deformity of thought that lurks behind them. Miserable indeed must be the mind that would weigh syllables against sentiment, and decide the fate of a truly pathetic effusion, because there was a want of exact harmony in its lines. The great desideratum of poetry is the inspiration, the *mens divinior*, which leads you away from the book you are reading, and carries you to some actual scene of sublimity or beauty; which sets before you, in colors that cannot be doubted, the dance and the battle; the valley winding away in the loveliness of its flowers and verdure, between banks of elms and maples; the lake reposing in the stillness of evening, and sheeted with the gilding of sunset; the volcano rising from among cities and vineyards, crowned with "its cloud by day and its pillar of fire by night"; or the mountain, invested with the purity of eternal snow, and ascending with the majesty of a monarch, till it gains a height where it no longer seems a portion of earth, but a cloud of glory suspended in the heavens. The works of a poet, who adds correctness to richness of fancy and tenderness of feeling, and who kindles up all with a glow of enthusiasm, are like an elegant figure of polished spar, bright with the irradiations of a fire within it. But if there be nothing but a faultless style and a smooth flow of sounds, we may read on, page after page, without a single emotion, lulled as effectually as we should be by the quiet lapse of whispering waters.

But while I stand forth as the advocate of bold and spirited poetry, and profess myself willing to set off against occasional negligences those redeeming flashes of pure and glowing thought whose excellence cannot be questioned, I would myself aim to avoid those extremes which have always led minds of more correctness than fire to settle down in the cold medium. We should neither adopt the licentious richness of Oriental imagery, nor those general expressions which represent no individuality. Every object should be described by a few of its strongest characters, but there should be a specific difference. We should not simply sketch the visible forms of objects, but we should animate them; for all things are living to the poetic eye. We should make every object the residence of a spirit, that can commune with us in our thoughts and feelings, and we should link it to the chain of our associations; but, at the same time, we should not allow this to be an excuse for a conceit, nor suffer it to degenerate into sickly sentimentalism. The Orientals have overloaded their pieces with a profusion of ornament, and an accumulation of minute details; while the Greeks sketched their pictures with a few bold strokes. The ancients presented the grand and simple outlines of nature, adorned indeed with their beautiful mythology; but they rarely connected external nature with their own emotions; while at this time every object calls up a sentiment, and the beings around us become only the cues of a reflection or a moral. There is, however, little danger of error, when the mind is deeply engaged, and alive to the importance of its subject; and after all, the best way to succeed is to think, not how, but what we would say.

In all nations in the infancy of literature, poetry is rude in structure, but full in inspiration. Men have then much of the feeling of childhood. Everything leaves a vivid impression, and kindles the mind of more than common susceptibility to an ecstasy of emotion. Objects strike so deeply as to rivet the attention solely upon them, and hence every image stands by itself distinct and individual. There is a quick perception of the stronger outlines, but there is no microscopic searching after concealed beauties. They see with an unprejudiced eye, and therefore they see and feel many things that escape our systematic investigation; and what they see is appropriated. But, vivid as their conceptions are, like all in the infancy of mind, they are wanting in powers of language. They are only beginners in the art of selecting and combining words. Hence a taste that has long been trained to delicacy and exactness will find much in them to shock it, — unwieldy expressions and rude epithets, discordant rhymes and broken measures; but the feeling and natural heart will find its attention riveted, its passions kindled, and its tears elicited, in spite of itself. These are the tributes of nature unfettered by art. They are the weapons by which taste, with all its refinement, is forced to confess the omnipotence of untaught feeling. In the early age of poetry, it is the quick burst of emotion that cannot be restrained; the gushings of a heart full to overflowing. Be it gayety or sorrow, delight or indignation, the tongue is eloquent, and the eye beaming with expression. Smiles are then unforced, and bright as the sun on curling waters. Tears are then pure, and flowing from the deepest fountain of the heart. They look then on all that is pleasant, with the delighted gaze of boyhood when his eye first catches a new and brilliant spectacle. They mingle with the loveliness of nature, and become a portion of its hills, its woods, and its waters. They kindle at the sight of baseness or cruelty, with the sparkling energy of a lion. They are ready to stand in the front ranks of danger, and to show forth, in fearless action, the spirit that is burning within them. Love, the great inspirer of all that is noble, the chief excitant to our highest and brightest efforts, is then passion, not art. Its language is that universal dialect of looks and actions, which is the same everywhere; not the artful leer, the counterfeited sigh, and the false tone of languishment. When the emotions are thus living, the incoherent language in which they are embodied has its charms. It can at least interest us, and is worth whole volumes of faultless insipidity. But there is an interval between the first dawnings and the full brightness of a national literature, when the freshness of early feeling still continues, but when art has begun its refinements. These first efforts of art are characterized too often by a childish playfulness, and all the tricks of figure and versification. Conceits, brilliant indeed, but far sought, puns and quibbles, delightful to minds that meet only to laugh and be merry, alliterations, acrostics, double and entangled rhymes, and every variety of jingling melody, are then cultivated and admired. These are loved and sought for a time, and then taste assumes her empire. Everything must then submit to the rigid laws of criticism. The long and patient application of the *labor limæ* is then the first precept inculcated on the youthful poet, and the laurel is conferred, not on him whose soaring is loftiest, but on him who is the most unwearied in his corrections. This is necessary to prune away juvenile luxuriances, and to give smoothness, compactness, and propriety to language. But when art has furnished its perfectest models, and poetic diction has been carried to its acme of improvement, then poets should return to nature, if they would aim to command the public mind. The refinements of poetry can be truly relished only by the cultivated; the happy expression of natural feeling finds a responding voice in all whose hearts have not been polluted by depravity. To the refined, natural tenderness and beauty can be no objection, but surely a high improvement. With those who judge only from their own emotions, polished language and versification, if not fully appreciated, will always be preferred to doggerel. The highest interest of a poet who aims at distinction is, then, to write only when he feels inspired, when his subject has gained full possession of him, and has wrought him up to that state of excitement where the visions of his fancy stand before him in living beauty. Then, if he be sufficiently prepared in the art, his language will flow abroad without effort, and the light of his soul will pervade every line and syllable. Such a poet, if he is endowed with the true spirit of genius, can hardly err.

END OF VOL. I.

www.ingramcontent.com/pod-product-compliance
Lightning Source LLC
LaVergne TN
LVHW020935110826
845150LV00004B/867

* 9 7 8 1 4 2 5 5 5 2 5 8 9 *